CHIN

CHIN

The Life and Crimes
of Mafia Boss Vincent Gigante

Larry McShane

KENSINGTON BOOKS
www.kensingtonbooks.com

KENSINGTON BOOKS are published by

Kensington Publishing Corp.
119 West 40th Street
New York, NY 10018

All Kensington titles, imprints, and distributed lines are available at special quantity discounts for bulk purchases for sales promotion, premiums, fund-raising, educational, or institutional use. Special book excerpts or customized printings can also be created to fit specific needs. For details, write or phone the office of the Kensington Special Sales Manager: Attn. Special Sales Department. Kensington Publishing Corp, 119 West 40th Street, New York, NY 10018. Phone: 1-800-221-2647.

Kensington and the K logo Reg. U.S. Pat. & TM Off.

Library of Congress Card Catalogue Number: 2015958944

ISBN-13: 978-1-61773-921-7
ISBN-10: 1-61773-921-9
First Kensington Hardcover Edition: June 2016

eISBN-13: 978-1-61773-922-4
eISBN-10: 1-61773-922-7
First Kensington Electronic Edition: June 2016

10 9 8 7 6 5 4 3 2 1

Printed in the United States of America

No man has a wholly undiseased mind; in one way
or another, all men are mad.

—Mark Twain

Isn't he a fucking nut?

—Genovese family member Joseph "Joe Glitz" Glitzia,
speaking to John Gotti about Vincent "Chin" Gigante

Prologue

Bringing It All Back Home

*T*HE OLD MAN, A BIT OF A BOUNCE STILL EVIDENT IN HIS STEP, moves easily along the sun-dappled sidewalks of his youth.

His neatly pressed white shirt matches the hair trimmed short atop his well-worn face. The spry senior citizen, semiretired and sharp as a stiletto at eighty-two, is clean-shaven. A pair of glasses marks his lone concession to age.

It's a warm spring morning, and Father Louis Gigante is headed to breakfast at Pasticceria Bruno in Greenwich Village, where he was born in the first half of the last century.

He's moved around across the decades, finally landing as a parish priest in the South Bronx. But the Roman Catholic priest—like an East Coast Tony Bennett—left his heart down here on Sullivan Street.

Father Gigante's résumé is impressive: congressional candidate, city council member, social activist, urban developer in the South Bronx. He's met presidential candidates and cardinals, mayors and multimillionaires. It's been an interesting run—at one point, he recalls, director Martin Scorsese expressed interest in making a movie about this life of his.

But today Gigante is here to discuss someone else: his older brother Vincent, dead since 2005. For years the Federal Bureau of Investigation had loudly insisted that Vincent, aka "The Chin," had ascended through the ranks of the Genovese crime family, from street soldier to hit man to capo to the most powerful and feared Mob boss in the United States of America.

For just as long—and just as loudly—Louis Gigante insisted that his brother was a sick man incapable of holding down even a menial job, much less running the nation's most lucrative and lethal Mafia family. The priest didn't stop there: he denied the very existence of Italian organized crime in the United States, even as he lived in its epicenter.

Through it all, the priest remained charismatic, quotable, indomitable. And he always looked good in a Roman collar.

When federal prosecutors accused Vincent of crimes ranging from racketeering to murder, Louis paid his brother's legal fees and served as his sibling's unwavering public defender. When Vincent wandered these same streets in his bathrobe, Louis was often seen on his arm. The priest insisted that his brother, rather than a dangerous Mafia don, was merely deranged.

"He's a mental case," the priest once said dismissively. "Why don't they leave him alone? Vincent is ill. Vincent is in need of psychiatric treatment."

Gigante orders a cup of espresso, an egg on toast and *sfogliatelle* (a sweet Italian pastry). He's a regular at Bruno's; the cannoli, he confides, is the best in the five boroughs, and people come from far and wide to carry a boxful back home. It's right around the corner from the tenement where he grew up with Vincent, their brothers and their immigrant parents.

"Father G.," as he is known to friends, is the last of the Gigantes left in the old neighborhood. He lives across La Guardia Place in an apartment that once belonged to his brother Pasquale, and where Vincent eventually moved in with their mother. Father G. still stops in during the week at the offices of the South Bronx development company that he founded back when the borough was famously burning. Weekends are spent upstate on bucolic property purchased from a close friend, the infamous music business executive Morris Levy, one of Vincent's business associates.

Sometimes during his rural getaways, he'll light a cigar and relax, the fragrant smoke wafting silently toward the ceiling.

The priest's eyes narrow when he's making a point, and they dance when he's making a joke. He reaches across the table to touch an arm gently for emphasis during a ninety-minute stroll down his personal memory lane.

"I was always at Vincent's side, and he had the greatest regard for me," he says in a raspy voice. "He was the proudest guy in the family about me becoming a priest. My whole family loved it, but he cherished it because he was a religious man."

He tells a few old tales of life in the neighborhood, about his hardworking parents and his childhood on Sullivan Street, about growing up with Vincent. He talks about the bonds of loyalty and devotion shared with his departed brother: "I certainly knew, and he knew, that he could always depend on me and trust me. And he was very proud of me."

And then, out of the blue, Father Gigante has a confession to make.

"Was my brother the boss of the Genovese family?" he asks aloud. "Yes. He rose to that, picked purposely by Vito Genovese."

CHAPTER 1

ANOTHER SIDE OF VINCENT GIGANTE

ONE "CHIN." TWO FACES.

Over two decades atop the Genovese crime family, Vincent "the Chin" Gigante was a man perpetually divided.

He was a ruthless Mob boss. He was a helpless mental patient.

He controlled a far-reaching business that earned tens of millions of dollars. He rarely ventured more than a one-hour car ride from his Greenwich Village roots.

He was a made man in the Genovese crime family. He was a baptized member of the Holy Name Society at Our Lady of Pompeii Church.

He callously ordered the deaths of other mobsters—including Gambino family boss John Gotti. He was raised a devout Roman Catholic, attending Sunday Mass until his death.

He was widely considered among the brightest in the Mafia underworld, with a vision beyond that of his contemporaries. He was a high-school dropout, with a recorded IQ just north of 100 –a slightly above average score.

He had a wife and five kids in a house in suburban New Jersey. He kept a mistress and three more children in a town house on the Upper East Side.

He recognized the threat of electronic surveillance from investigators, and forbade his underlings—under penalty of death—from uttering his name. He eventually wound up on prison tapes speaking openly with family members, including a panicked call on 9/11.

Most incredibly and indelibly, the ultimate stand-up mobster played a broken-down man in a stunningly successful ruse to dodge and vex prosecutors. It was a piece of improvisational street theater that ran longer than anything on or off Broadway during his eight decades on earth.

There were hints, whispers from informants, and finally a long-awaited admission that the whole thing was a brilliant scam. But for three decades authorities were powerless to prove Gigante's sanity and convict him, as they would any other criminal.

"Mr. Gigante's case is truly fascinating," marveled one prison psychiatrist. "His ability to sustain his 'crazy act' over many years and to have deceived at least three prominent forensic evaluators into believing that he was mentally ill and incompetent places Mr. Gigante into the ranks of the most cunning of criminals."

A full decade before launching his long-running psychiatric charade, a prison evaluation cited Gigante's natural skills in leading such a "Jekyll and Hyde" existence. First tipped by a Mob insider in June 1970 that Gigante's mental-patient act was a scam, the FBI needed another twenty-seven years to prove the truth of his claim.

It took another six years before the Chin finally confessed to the ruse in 2003, after federal prosecutors seemed poised to charge Gigante family members with abetting his psychiatric subterfuge.

His bizarre behavior continued even behind bars: Gigante toyed with prison psychiatrists while desperately holding out hope for a successful appeal, which ultimately was rejected by the U.S. Supreme Court.

Despite his national reputation, Gigante devoted his entire life to keeping his efforts carefully hidden from the eyes of the public or the hidden recorders of federal investigators.

During the 1980s his operation was as successful as any Fortune 500 business: The Genovese family raked in more than $100 million a year in profit, law enforcement said. The same authorities who chased the Chin grudgingly hailed his family as "the Ivy League of organized crime" and the "Rolls-Royce" of criminal enterprise.

The Chin controlled all numbers operations in Lower Manhattan, as well as the annual St. Anthony's Feast in his neighborhood, where he turned piety into profit. By 1985, when Gigante was surreptitiously running the Genovese family, and Anthony "Fat Tony" Salerno took the law enforcement heat as its straw boss, the family's assorted illegal enterprises included gambling, extortion, loan-sharking and bid rigging. The Genovese influence extended to the garbage, concrete, construction and music industries; they held an iron grip on the labor that allowed them to dominate the New Jersey waterfront, the Javits Convention Center and the Fulton Fish Market. The family was stealing money on every window installed at the city's vast housing projects and skimming cash from New York's enormous concrete industry.

Gigante boasted a workforce of more than four hundred dedicated men at his twenty-four-hour beck and call. In the Mafia galaxy, no Mob star burned brighter than the famously nocturnal Gigante.

"The alleged status of Vincent Gigante as boss of the Genovese organized crime family makes him the sun around which all the planetary criminal activities revolve," observed U.S. District Court judge I. Leo Glasser.

Yet, this titan of illegal industry was most notorious for his "Oddfather" routine, where he played a serial psychiatric-hospital patient who wandered the city streets clad only in his ratty bathrobe, well-worn pajamas and decrepit pair of slippers. Gigante occasionally added a floppy cap to complete the carefully mismatched ensemble.

Gigante, on close to thirty occasions, admitted himself to a suburban mental hospital for treatment of his self-diagnosed mental illness. Among his Mafia pals, the visits were genially known as "tune-ups." Each one added to his wacky aura of invincibility, sparing him prosecution while insuring his continued reign atop the world of organized crime.

The brutal gangster and his doddering alter ego lived side by side within the Chin, and helped him become the most successful Mob boss of the last half-century. He surpassed headline-making next-generation Mafiosi like Gotti, old-time leaders like Frank Costello and even the namesake of his crime family (and his Mob mentor), Vito Genovese.

"You know, every time a Mob boss gets indicted, he becomes 'the most powerful boss,'" said former federal prosecutor Greg O'Connell. "John Gotti captured a lot of attention. But we knew Gigante was the guy. The Chin was the *capo di tutti capi*—'the boss of bosses.'"

His long and successful reign was inexorably linked to his strange persona, captured in scores of FBI surveillance photos and witnessed by countless passersby on the streets of Greenwich Village. Gigante couldn't do it alone; it took a village of cooperating relatives, neighbors and mobsters to support the performance and spare him from the clutches of law enforcement.

But the Chin was the unquestioned star of this production, which improbably mingled Mob hits with method acting: Marlon Brando in a dingy bathrobe.

His was an extraordinary run atop one of New York's five Mafia families, from the early 1980s into the new millennium, when the constantly pursuing feds and trigger-happy fellow mobsters insured a steady turnover of leadership in New York's other four families. The Chin and the Genoveses always rose above the fray.

To provide proper perspective, Gigante spent more time in "office" than four-term President Franklin Delano Roosevelt did in the White House—and FDR didn't spent his time dodging death threats, ordering executions and avoiding federal bugs.

But the Chin was more than a gangster whose life paralleled the explosive growth of the Mafia in the twentieth-century United States, along with its decline in the twenty-first. He became a part of pop culture; his ceaseless head games with prosecutors and the FBI eventually inspired a memorable episode of *Law & Order,* the tale of dodgy Uncle Junior on *The Sopranos* and a satiric novel, *I Don't Want to Go to Jail,* by New York newspaper columnist Jimmy Breslin.

Gigante became a headline writer's dream at the New York tabloids, where his exploits were chronicled in big, bold, black type (THE ODDFATHER!) with tales that only seemed to confirm his legendary lunacy.

Breslin's novel referenced the Chin's real-life devotion to two women, both named Olympia, on either side of the Hudson River. It was a maneuver consistent with the mores of 1960s Greenwich Village, the Chin's longtime home and base of operations, but hardly acceptable among the hard-line, old-school men of the Mob.

Yet no one dared challenge the Chin about his dual domestic lives—or anything else.

From inside his headquarters, the dank Triangle Civic Improvement Association, and from behind bars, Gigante oversaw an era of relative peace and prosperity for his family in a business where homicide marks a management change and treachery remains a marketable skill.

In contrast, Gotti's run atop the Gambino family lasted barely seven years before he went away to die in the same Missouri prison where Gigante eventually followed.

The Chin proved far more adaptable. As the Mob's founding "Mustache Petes" made way for the next generation, he rose through the ranks in the 1950s and 1960s as a protégé of Genovese. His ascension continued through the turbulent 1970s, and Gigante assumed his seat as boss in 1981. When other bosses, including Gotti, went to jail in the '80s and '90s, the Chin dodged prosecution and stayed on top of the Genovese family into the new millennium—even after the feds finally put him in prison.

Even his installation as Genovese boss, the culmination of his Mafia career, was swathed in secrecy. Gigante demoted predecessor Salerno, but arranged for Fat Tony to serve as a figurehead. The cigar-chomping, fedora-wearing old-timer took a one-hundred-year prison term after his conviction as a member of the Mob's "ruling commission," leaving the Chin free and in charge.

Salerno died behind bars rather than rat out the real boss. Gigante stayed on the streets and at the top of the family.

Gigante invested more than three decades of his life in pretending he was certifiably insane, a performance that included small touches (not shaving or combing his hair) and grand ones (greeting FBI agents as he stood naked in the shower, holding an umbrella). By one count he duped a half-dozen psychiatrists into thirty-four separate diagnoses of schizophrenia as he operated with impunity atop the Genovese family.

His efforts rivaled the Oscar-winning work of Jack Nicholson in *One Flew Over the Cuckoo's Nest,* with one difference: If Randle P. McMurphy wanted out of the mental hospital, Gigante returned there again and again. The dedication to his craft earned Gigante his memorable tabloid sobriquet, the Oddfather, along with the respect of his underlings.

"His family revered him," said George Stamboulidis, the federal prosecutor who led the team that finally convicted Gigante.

Forces on both sides of the law were equally impressed by a show that at times resembled something conjured up by director Scorsese and "the LSD king," Owsley Stanley. Imagine *GoodFellas* on a bad acid trip. John Pritchard Jr. ran the FBI's Genovese Squad in the mid-1980s as the agency tried desperately to convict the elusive Chin. He came away with a reluctant respect for the Mob boss.

"Chin was probably the most feared gangster in New York," said Pritchard. "He was so clever. . . . He was a quiet, calculating, behind-the-scenes guy. Chin didn't want people to know he was the boss. It was enough that the people in the neighborhood knew. He was known among the people as a guy who could get things done, a la *The Godfather.*"

Pritchard was among the first to use the phrase most often used to describe the Chin's dependence on the insanity defense: "Crazy like a fox."

Philip Leonetti, an Atlantic City mobster with a vast knowledge of Mafia lore, put Gigante in a class by himself.

"Within our family, we viewed the Chin as a very, very smart man, a very secretive man, very cunning and very ruthless," Leonetti recalled. "He was old-school Cosa Nostra—stay low-key, follow the rules and make money. He wasn't flashy. I mean, Christ, he spent his whole day in a bathrobe.

"He wasn't trying to be a celebrity. He was a gangster and he knew this thing, La Cosa Nostra, this thing, better than anyone in the country."

Leonetti's was a dead-on assessment: Gigante did not keep a standing reservation at the Copacabana, or pose for photos with an arm wrapped around Frank Sinatra, or chase showgirls around the Las Vegas Strip. His primary interests were the Genovese family, the prestige, the power. He was comfortable in the confines of Sullivan Street.

There was money, too, but it mattered less to Gigante than his peers atop the other families. Part of his crew's loyalty was based on the Chin's generosity when it came to kicking up cash (a standard Mob practice where the family head receives a percentage of every illegal dollar pocketed). Gigante routinely allowed his capos to keep money that would routinely go to his contemporaries astride New York's four other crime families.

He became the last acolyte of a fading tradition, a true believer in a disappearing world, a man of old values surrounded by thugs and turncoats. He never abandoned his roots—geographic or otherwise.

Gigante seized control of the Genovese family during the Ronald Reagan presidency; by the time he pleaded guilty in April 2003 on federal charges of lying to doctors about his mental health, it was Reagan who was suffering from Alzheimer's.

The Chin's reign became a constant in an ever-changing world. Three post-Reagan presidents filled the Oval Office during his time as boss, and the Soviet Union collapsed as his crime family thrived. The World Trade Center was twice targeted by terrorists. There was a bombing in Atlanta at the Olympics; and the New York Rangers won their first Stanley Cup since 1940, when Gigante, living a couple miles south of Madison Square Garden, had celebrated his twelfth birthday.

Gigante endured, firmly entrenched as the Howard Hughes of organized crime. Long after he didn't need the money or the aggravation, the Chin remained the biggest boss in the nation's biggest city—and the "craziest" gangster since the hotheaded Benjamin "Bugsy" Siegel, who was the real thing.

At the end, after spending the last eight years of his life behind bars, Gigante returned to the Village for his funeral Mass, a small and exclusive gathering of family and friends. There was none of the pomp associated with many Mob farewells, the endless floral arrangements or lengthy funeral cortege.

His life had come full circle: a final farewell in the old neighborhood, just the way the Chin would have wanted it.

"He didn't move far," said Henry Hill, the former Lucchese family operator who turned federal informant in the early 1980s. "All that money, that so-called power—the power to assassinate and kill—and he hasn't left a four-block area in forty years."

CHAPTER 2

POSITIVELY SULLIVAN STREET

V INCENT LOUIS GIGANTE, THE FOURTH OF SALVATORE AND YOLANDA
Gigante's six boys, arrived in a home still shrouded in loss and
grief.

The parents were Italian immigrants, married in their native
Naples on October 20, 1920, before setting off for New York City in
the era's tidal wave of new arrivals from their homeland. Records
from Ellis Island show Salvatore and Yolanda (her name misspelled
as "Iolanda") arrived three days after New Year's in 1921, crossing
the Atlantic Ocean aboard an Italian ship, the *Pesaro*.

He was twenty-five, and his pretty bride just eighteen.

At five-four, with black hair and brown eyes, Salvatore listed
his occupation as "workman," while Yolanda described herself as
"housewife." Handwritten beneath a question about their intended length of stay was the notation "perm"—permanently.
The newlyweds would find a home in Manhattan, joining relatives already living in Greenwich Village.

As they did for all new arrivals, the ship's captain and surgeon
signed off on documents attesting to the Gigantes' mental and
physical well-being. Both Gigantes checked the "yes" box when
asked if they could read.

The couple settled into a tenement at 181 Thompson Street,
sharing the space with Salvatore's brother Louie and his wife. Salvatore and Yolanda would spend their whole lives in the neighborhood, never moving beyond a radius of a few blocks, relocating

only to find space for their expanding family or to stay ahead of the wrecking ball in the constantly evolving area.

The Gigantes soon welcomed three boys: Pasquale, Mario and Vincent. Salvatore, a jeweler by trade, hustled to support the family; and like many of the local women, Yolanda picked up work as a seamstress, specializing in piecework for ladies' coats. It was during a rare vacation that the hardworking young couple endured a heartbreaking blow.

During a 1925 trip home to see family in Naples, eighteen-month-old Vincent suffered horrific burns from an accidental spill of a large pot of water boiling for pasta. The child spent two agonizing weeks in the hospital before dying. The devastated Gigantes returned to the Village, where they welcomed their fourth child on March 29, 1928. There was little debate; the new arrival, another boy, would be named for his late brother. An unbreakable bond between mother and son was forged, one that would last two lifetimes.

Vincent's doting mom provided her boy with the nickname that followed him through life. Although the name would one day echo with menace, it sprang from her love.

"My mother, as a Neapolitan woman, would call him 'Chenzino.' It's the diminutive of *Vincenzino,* 'little Vincent,'" explained Louis Gigante. "That's how he got the name, 'cause Mama would call him 'Chenzino.' She never spoke English to him. *Vincenzino.* So the kids called him 'Chin.'"

The Village was already heavily Italian by the time the Gigantes arrived. More than fifty thousand Italians settled in the neighborhood between the 1880s and 1920s; the vast majority were young, single men. By 1920 the area was about 30 percent Italian and supported a pair of churches catering to the new arrivals: Our Lady of Pompeii, on Carmine Street, and the nation's oldest Italian-American parish, St. Anthony of Padua, incorporated in 1859 and located on Sullivan Street.

The city's first Italian-American mayor, Fiorello La Guardia, was born in 1882 on the same street as both Vincents.

The Village had also earned a reputation as a haven for artists and eccentrics. Mark Twain once walked the local streets, as did bohemian/social activist/journalist John Reed. The insular neighborhood was also home to a long tradition of taking care of its own and minding its own business, particularly among its Italian immigrant community. The Village's padrone was a local fixer, able to provide an assortment of services for his constituents. It could be anything from a job opportunity to notarizing documents to arranging steamship tickets for a trip back to Italy.

Among the first padrones was Louis Fugazy, who immigrated to the Village in 1869 from his hometown of Liguria. Fugazy was still living on Bleecker Street when Louis Gigante arrived; the old man died in 1930. A Neapolitan immigrant named Vito Genovese would fill his shoes.

With the arrival of Ralph and their last son, Louis, the Gigante family was complete. The five sons were raised as devout Roman Catholics, with Sunday Mass a regular part of their routine. Yolanda always favored Our Lady of Pompeii on Carmine Street.

The Bureau of Prisons, in a 1960 evaluation, characterized Chin's childhood as "normal . . . and healthy." Louis Gigante said the brothers, though born years apart, remained a tight-knit group despite the difference in ages. The connection to one another and to the Village streets remained, and it endured unbroken as they grew into adulthood.

During a sit-down years later with prison officials, the Chin recalled the number one household rule: "Respect your parents." Each boy was assigned regular household chores, and Gigante's only bad memories of childhood were dealing with a speech impediment and a minor heart condition. Gigante, who described Salvatore and Yolanda as a loving couple, could not recall a single instance where he watched his parents fight.

Salvatore was only occasionally moved to spank one of the misbehaving boys. Mom Yolanda's method of discipline involved a paralyzing stare, which young Vincent inherited, using it to great effect in later life. "A happy childhood" was Gigante's recollection decades later. By all accounts, the future Mob boss with a penchant for bathrobes dressed quite normally, too.

The Chin specifically mentioned that he was always quite close with his mother. There were, he added, no family secrets, although there was one sad chapter in their history. Gigante's maternal grandfather committed suicide at age thirty-seven. The circumstances were strange. He swallowed poison to avoid testifying against "the Black Hand," a Mafia-esque group operating in Naples. Fearful his family would be targeted if he took the stand, Pasquale Scotto took his own life.

Though living in the nation's largest city, the boys were raised as if they remained in their late grandfather's homeland.

"My mother and father were not American," said Louis Gigante. "They were Neapolitans. Their culture and everything [was] completely imposed on us, the way they knew life."

The Gigante kids learned English on the streets and at school as their parents spoke strictly Neapolitan at home.

"Never spoke English until I was in school," recalled Louis Gigante. "Being the youngest, the other four [brothers] spoke English to me. I just never heard it from my mother."

Salvatore landed a job on Canal Street with a jewelry business started by another immigrant: William Kelly.

"He hung out with the Irish jewelers. . . . You know how he made his money?" asked Louis Gigante. "He worked there with them, and then he would be their representative in the Italian neighborhood. Every woman who was getting married would go to him, and he would display the rings in the house."

With the onset of the Great Depression and hard times in the jewelry business, Salvatore took other work, including one stint with the New Deal-sponsored Works Progress Administration (WPA).

"I was very proud of him," recalled Louis. "My father worked all his life. He made a living, and supported us very well."

Yolanda chipped in, too, bringing sewing work home to the cramped apartment—much to Salvatore's dismay. A good Neapolitan wife was supposed to raise the children and cook the meals. Salvatore, his pride stung, took his wife's sewing machine and sold it.

"I was angry a little," she recalled decades later. "But don't you worry. I bought a secondhand machine for ten dollars. I worked day and night."

The Gigante family's economic fortunes improved once Salvatore landed a better job in the jewelry trade, but it required a long commute.

"Newark. Poor guy had to go to Newark all his life," said Louis Gigante. "And he was an engraver in a big jewelry company. That was what he did. He didn't just engrave initials. He's cutting the stones."

Each night the entire family would gather at the dinner table to discuss the day's events in two languages. It was an essential part of their life, with each of the boys expected to contribute to the ongoing conversation. The sons addressed each other in English, while the parents spoke only in their native tongue.

As young Vincent was finding his footing in the world, the nascent American version of La Cosa Nostra was starting its bloody evolution into the powerful institution that became an integral part of New York City for the next eight decades.

Gigante's Mob mentor, Vito Genovese, was smack in the middle of the Mob wars that gave birth to the five Mafia families of New York. The crime family that would carry the Genovese name emerged from a period of unprecedented bloodshed and betrayal.

Genovese arrived in the New World in 1913, a teenage boy whose family left their own village in Naples to settle south of the Gigantes on the Lower East Side. The young man quickly gravitated toward a life of crime and easy money, falling in with a group of like-minded and ambitious Italian immigrants.

A Sicilian youth named Giuseppe Bonanno—rechristened "Joe" in his new country—followed the same path. Bonanno eventually became the right-hand man of Salvatore Maranzano, known respectfully as "Don Turrido." Maranzano was a barrel-chested bull capable of breaking a man's neck by using only his thumbs, a very useful skill in their new enterprise.

The boss carried himself with an air of class and legitimacy despite his illegitimate business. Maranzano boasted of speaking Latin and Greek, and proclaimed himself well-versed in classical literature. He attended the seminary, studying to become a priest, before opting for a more secular career. A handsome and under-stated man, the only jewelry he wore was a watch and his wedding ring.

"He looked just like a banker," said Joe Valachi, a street hustler later inducted into the Maranzano ranks. "You'd never guess in a million years that he was a racketeer."

Maranzano established an import/export company in Little Italy as a cover for his booze business during Prohibition. Decades later, in his novel, author Mario Puzo's fictional Corleone family did much the same with their "olive oil" operation.

But the dominant family belonged to Giuseppe "Joe the Boss" Masseria, who rose to prominence during the bootlegging days of the Roaring Twenties. His group was rife with young, hungry talent, which included a quartet of future bosses: Charles "Lucky" Luciano, Gaetano Lucchese, Vito Genovese and Francesco Castiglia, who later was reinvented with an Irish-sounding first name and surname, "Frank Costello."

Barely five feet tall, Masseria would casually demolish a five-course meal—complete with wine—with the gusto of a dog tear-ing through a bucket of steaks. He did so with about the same amount of grace.

The two factions were soon at odds, with a demand by the im-perious Masseria setting off a bloodletting later dubbed "the Castellammarese War"—a nod to a small Sicilian coastal town once called home by many of Maranzano's troops. The boss de-manded $10,000 in tribute from his underlings, asserting it was his right as the *capo di tutti capi*. Conflict inevitably followed.

Maranzano presented himself as the populist choice, the antithesis of the greedy Masseria in the bloody battle that ran roughly across eighteen savage months in 1930 through 1931. The fighting became so fierce that Bonanno delayed his wedding to work full-time for the Maranzano forces. Dozens of men on both sides were killed in the struggle.

The need for soldiers led to Maranzano's induction of Valachi in a secret Mafia ceremony. The East Harlem resident's life of crime began as an eighteen-year-old getaway driver for a burglary ring, and ended decades down the road with his decision to become the first Mafiosi to turn informant.

An act of pure treachery would end the war, with Luciano—an up-and-comer growing increasingly frustrated by Masseria's intransigence in the ways of making money—finally selling out his boss. It was anything but lucky when Luciano invited Masseria to lunch in Coney Island on April 15, 1931.

Before meeting with Joe the Boss, Luciano—reportedly accompanied by Genovese—arranged a quiet meeting with Maranzano and concocted the plot that would end the hostilities. They met at a private home in Brooklyn, where the conversation, fraught with importance, was nonetheless clipped and quick.

"Do you know why you are here?" Maranzano asked in Sicilian.

"Yes," Luciano replied.

"Then I don't need to tell you what has to be done?" Maranzano inquired.

"No."

The lunch date was set for the Nuova Villa Tammaro restaurant on West Fifteenth Street, near the renowned Luna Park and a relatively new attraction, a roller coaster known as the Cyclone. The typically wary Masseria arrived in a steel-armored sedan with inch-thick windows. Luciano later recounted Masseria's last meal: a three-hour orgy of food and drink consumed in a veritable feeding frenzy.

The meal was followed by a card game, with Luciano excusing himself to use the men's room. The sounds of gunfire soon rang out inside the quiet Italian restaurant. According to Luciano, the shooters included Genovese, Siegel and Albert Anastasia. Masseria's body was riddled by a half-dozen bullets, and his body was found still holding the ace of spades in one hand.

The killing, rather than assuring peace, brought only more death. Luciano expected the murder to grease his ascension as a boss equal to Maranzano—only to find the new boss was just like the old boss. Maranzano declared himself king of the New York underworld and the number one boss in the nation. Luciano's anger festered and his impatience grew.

His feelings were shared by colleagues who felt Maranzano was just another Mustache Pete, their derisive term for mobsters past their expiration date. Another plot was hatched. On September 10, 1931, four men appeared waving badges at Maranzano's tony offices atop the landmark Grand Central Terminal. The boss's unarmed security force, surprised by their arrival and cowed by the badges, let them inside.

Maranzano was stabbed and shot repeatedly, his blood pooling on the office floor as the life ebbed from his body. The Castellammarese War was over, with both its chief combatants claimed as Mob fatalities.

The survivors sorted things out, agreeing the day of a single boss claiming infallibility while lining his pockets was done. There would instead be five bosses, each with a vote on business and a seat on what became the Mafia's ruling commission. The head of the family that would become known as the Genoveses was headed by Luciano himself. Genovese became his right-hand man, and Frank Costello among his top lieutenants.

The Mob's boom years were about to arrive. And so was Vincent Gigante, just three years old when the war ended.

The Chin was an undistinguished schoolboy, posting average grades before dropping out of school in his sophomore year of high school. He later enrolled in a trade school, where he played on the football team and—by his own recollections—became "socially active. . . . School was fun."

Years later, he recounted a suspension from that time, although he could not remember the details. The first hints of his future career soon appeared, although the details are lost to history: Gigante's initial arrest came when he was age fourteen, with the juvenile record sealed. Even federal prosecutors decades later knew nothing of the case.

When he was sixteen years old, the Chin was finished with his formal education and eager to learn the lessons of the crowded neighborhood streets. Gigante was never bothered by his lack of schooling, and later in life he turned it into a punch line.

Asked decades down the road to spell "world" backward, he informed an inquiring psychiatrist, "We'll be here all day."

Vincent's posteducation interests were simple: the boxing ring and the street corners of the Village.

"Vincent was what he was—a kid from the block," said Louis Gigante. "What did he do as a kid, sixteen years old? He was running crap games. A sin? Maybe, in the eyes of some jerks back then. Las Vegas—the whole world was gambling. This whole neighborhood was full of gamblers."

The priest recalled a Sunday afternoon when he stumbled across his brother's busy dice game, where Vincent was likely the youngest of the ten men looking to roll a natural.

"I must have been about ten years old," he recounted. "He had a big game . . . and I'm walking on the street. I live around the block here, on the corner. He says, 'Louie, Louie, c'mere.' So, anyway, that's first time I ever shot dice. He says, 'Take the dice. Throw them.' I did it to satisfy him. 'Maybe we'll get lucky with the kid.'"

On another night their mother dispatched the family's baby to deliver a message to his big brother. Young Louis initially had no idea where to look, but then decided to check in a spot unknown to the local police. He walked into a nearby tenement, up the dark stairs and into a hallway on one of the upper floors. There was Vincent, running his floating crap game.

"The building's still there!" the priest recalled. "And that was his game, and he made money. He knew what the rules were, but everybody did it. So that was his life. He was a street kid all the time."

One of the rules was that Chin kicked up some of his cash to the neighborhood's bigger fish. By then, Vito Genovese was back in town after his extradition from Italy, where he fled for eight years to dodge a murder rap. He was quickly accepted as the new padrone of Greenwich Village, and took young Vincent under his wing.

"Vito Genovese was the most honored man in this neighborhood," recalled Louis. "Took care of everybody's needs. On Christmas, on holidays, he sponsored programs for the poor. That's how they operated."

The Chin took his first adult pinch in 1945 for receiving stolen goods, the first of seven arrests before his twenty-fifth birthday. He recalled those years as a time when he ran with local street gangs and took no lip. If somebody somehow irked the young Chin, he responded with his fists.

The teenager moved from corner to corner back then: first on Sullivan Street, then in the renowned Stillman's Gym at 919 Eighth Avenue in Midtown Manhattan. The dank boxing hangout between Fifty-Fourth and Fifty-Fifth Streets featured two rings and a permanent funk conjured from years of perspiration and minimal attention to cleanliness.

It was home to some of the fight game's big names: Rocky Graziano, Jack Dempsey, Georges Carpentier, Primo Carnera, Fred Apostoli, Joe Louis and Rocky Marciano. All the fighters, champs and chumps, paid the same fifteen-cent entry fee to enter a school of boxing higher education: "Eighth Avenue University," as it was known.

Vincent Gigante, like his brother Ralph, and a strong, silent Village kid named Dominick Cirillo became students of the fight game, hanging at Stillman's in an era where the city gyms served as petri dishes for Mafia moneymaking schemes.

Jake La Motta was another Italian-American kid who turned

to the ring for salvation, only to find a cesspool of corruption. He was forced to take a dive on November 14, 1947, against an otherwise overmatched fighter named Billy Fox, who was managed by the mobbed-up Frank "Blinky" Palermo, a Philadelphia gangster later jailed for extortion.

LaMotta famously received a title shot after throwing the fight, and he captured the middleweight title. He told the whole sordid tale thirteen years later to a U.S. Senate subcommittee investigating the fight game. Later, Robert De Niro won an Oscar for his portrayal of LaMotta in *Raging Bull*.

The same year as the fixed LaMotta fight, middleweight champion Rocky Graziano rejected a $100,000 bribe to dump a bout, which was later canceled.

Managers were, by and large, a collection of thieves and almost to a man tied in with the mob, LaMotta wrote in Raging Bull, his pull-no-punches autobiography. *And I also noticed that around the gym all the time there were the mob guys, for the very simple reason that there's always betting on fights, and betting means money, and wherever there's money there's the mob.*

So it was no surprise that when Gigante stepped into the ring for his first bout, his manager was Thomas "Tommy Ryan" Eboli, a future head of the Genovese family. Or that his sparring partner Cirillo would become a longtime friend and confidant as the two drifted into organized crime. Or that his brother Ralph would also move from the ring into the same illegal arena.

Chin apparently used the birth certificate of his brother and namesake, dead nineteen years, to land a professional boxing license. The fighter was just sixteen when he stepped into the ring against Vic Chambers in Union City, New Jersey, on July 18, 1944. It was an even pairing, with Chambers fighting for only the third time. The Chin lost on points, but returned to the ring eleven days later.

The precocious boxer, standing six feet tall and fighting in the 175-pound light-heavyweight division, reeled off ten straight victories by decision, and twice fought on the undercard at Madison Square Garden. He scored the only knockout of his career in a two-round defeat of undistinguished Frankie Petrel on February 2, 1945. The loss put the beaten fighter's career mark at 4-6-1.

He returned to the mecca of boxing four months later to lose a four-rounder against a fellow fighter with the same 10-1 record, Vic Chambers, whose only defeat had come in a rematch with Gigante. The Chin took their third fight in a four-round decision.

Kid brother Louis recalled attending one of Vincent's fights at the Ridgewood Grove in Brooklyn—the closest thing the Chin had to a home base. Gigante fought there a half-dozen times, winning five. His last bout came there on May 17, 1947, when Jimmy Slade scored a seventh-round TKO against the Chin.

"He was a very good, very good boxer," his brother Louis recalled. "He fought a lot, and then he gave it up."

Vincent Gigante stepped out of the ring with a career mark of 21-4, despite his lack of a power punch—a problem the Chin would rectify in the years ahead. Gigante underwent surgery on his nose in 1950, a remnant from his brief time as a fighter.

Brother Ralph followed Chin into the ring in 1948, the start of a truncated career that lasted just ten months and fourteen fights. While compiling a mark of nine wins, three losses and two draws, the 152-pounder made the pages of the *New York Times* after an October 8, 1948, six-round decision over Chino Prado of Mexico.

The headliner that night was middleweight Rocky Castellani, another Italian kid, this one an import from Luzerne, Pennsylvania. He scored a seventh-round knockout over hometown favorite Walter Cartier of the Bronx before a crowd of 2,465 at the St. Nicholas Arena, knocking the local kid on the floor three times in rapid succession—the last with a right to the jaw that put him down for good.

Castellani was an up-and-comer managed by none other than the ubiquitous Eboli, whose connection to the city's fight game ended with his arrest in Madison Square Garden. After Castellani lost a January 11, 1952, fight to Ernie Durando, the manager ignited a brawl by punching referee Ray Miller in the ring.

The mobbed-up Eboli, apparently expecting a different result, flew into a rage when Miller stopped the fight in the seventh round after Castellani—a marine who fought at Iwo Jima—was knocked down twice. Two of Castellani's other cornermen could do nothing to halt the rampaging Eboli, possessor of an Irish temper reflecting his mob nickname: Tommy Ryan.

Eboli and his brother Patsy continued the rampage in the locker room, where they delivered a beatdown with fists and feet to "matchmaker" Al Weill. They knocked him to the floor and broke his glasses. Eboli was convinced the dicey Weill was somehow behind the defeat.

The assault, in addition to landing Eboli in court, was featured in *Life* magazine with a picture of the enraged manager on the ring apron as he advanced with menace toward Weill. The magazine recounted the bizarre scene in a long exposé of boxing corruption just months after the beating. According to the report, there were rumors that Weill had "double-crossed" Eboli—raising the specter of a fixed fight. In a rematch two years later, Castellani won easily.

Eboli's license was immediately suspended for life, and he spent sixty days in jail after pleading to a reduced charge—not that it mattered much. By then, Eboli and Gigante were ready to move up in class.

CHAPTER 3

CHANGING OF THE GUARDS

GIGANTE TURNED EIGHTEEN IN 1946, BETWEEN WORLD WAR II and the Korean War. Not that the service was ever in the cards for him: Vincent was qualified 4F, unfit for duty due to "antisocial behavior" apparently linked to his teen arrest.

His new career with the Genovese family got off to a rocky start. There was a 1947 arrest for grand larceny and auto arson. He settled with a plea to the reduced charge of malicious mischief and probation.

The Chin did his first bit behind bars in 1950 after District Attorney Miles McDonald of Brooklyn started cracking down on local bookmakers and corrupt cops, who took cash to look the other way. Gigante, along with a Sullivan Street pal named Peter Lombardi, was popped for distributing gambling cards to Brooklyn College students and other young bettors: "Even down to elementary school," charged prosecutor Julius Helfand. "This was the eastern arm of a national betting syndicate" that extended to St. Louis and Minneapolis, he said.

Gigante told the arresting officers that he was a "jobless tailor" living in the Village.

Brooklyn college hoops star Michael DiTomasso, twenty-one, identified Gigante as the guy who provided the gambling cards, where bettors had to pick the winners of four games from a slate of contests across the country to collect a $10 payout. Anyone who could nail fifteen of fifteen would win $500.

DiTomasso said his take for peddling the cards on Gigante's behalf in December 1949 and January 1950 was $12 a week—on a good week.

A second Chin codefendant was cleared of his part in the plot when he admitted printing the betting cards—but only, he insisted to authorities, because Gigante scared the hell out of him. Gigante was sentenced to sixty days in the Rikers Island workhouse by an avuncular judge, who passed along his advice for the Chin to wise up about the wiseguys.

"We don't think you're totally bad," declared the sentencing judge. "We would just like to pull you up by the bootstraps."

The year 1950 was big for Gigante on the home front, too. Once he came out of jail, he married a neighborhood girl, Olympia Grippi, in a traditional Catholic ceremony at Our Lady of Pompeii. The pair had known each other for years, with the Chin first falling for her when they were both kids. She, too, came from a big Italian clan, with six sisters and a brother.

Gigante popped the question to his first love during Sunday Mass in the Village. They moved in with his parents and then had four children in rapid succession: Yolanda, Rosanne, Salvatore and Andrew.

The growing clan moved several times as the family expanded, although they never went beyond a two-block radius of Thompson and Bleecker Streets. Newlywed Gigante was arrested once more in September 1951 after cops found him carrying two blackjacks.

And he was put in cuffs three times in 1953: He paid a $1 fine for shooting dice, a throwback to his days as a Village teen. A disorderly conduct charge was resolved without prosecution. A bookmaking arrest resulted in a $75 fine.

FBI documents indicate he was involved, but never arrested, for working with a car theft ring operating out of the Village in 1955. The Chin and pal Dominick "Fat Dom" Alongi were suspected of stealing late-model Cadillacs and selling the hot luxury cars out of state.

And then the Chin disappeared from the police blotter as he

moved off the streets and up the Mob ladder. With the powerful Vito Genovese as his guru, Vincent was soon working as a gofer, a bodyguard, and then the future don's driver. The latter was a position of importance, trusted with guarding the gangster's life.

By now, Vito Genovese had beaten his long-ago murder rap. The ambitious Mafioso was accused of killing one of his "business" partners during a 1934 dispute over cutting up the proceeds of a rip-off. After learning there was a witness ready to implicate him, Genovese bolted for his homeland in 1937. After years of wrangling, he was finally brought home to face the consequences.

However, the guy expected to sing was suddenly silenced for good.

Cigar salesman Peter LaTempa never reached the witness stand. While in police protective custody at a Brooklyn jail, the damning witness fell ill and was given prescription pain pills to combat a balky gallbladder. Instead, he wound up popping enough poison to kill eight horses, according to an autopsy.

It was hardly Genovese's first murder to serve his own ends. Authorities had long suspected the widower had ordered the husband of his second wife strangled in 1931 to clear the way for their own marriage.

The young Vincent Gigante was never accused of any killings, Mob or otherwise, but an FBI memo from the era flatly stated that he was up to the task. The Chin "obtained his status and position" via his "reputation as an efficient hit man," the FBI document said, "as well as through his close association with [top Genovese associate] Frank Tieri."

Vincent landed a no-show job through the Mob as a Village building superintendent, where his lackadaisical approach to work nearly killed him. On the evening of May 12, 1956, Gigante arrived at St. Vincent's Hospital with a stab wound to the right side of his chest.

A report in the long-defunct *World-Telegraph* provided the de-

tails: The Chin wound up brawling with a black underling infuriated because he was left to handle most of the work in Gigante's
frequent absence. When some of Gigante's Mob associates arrived
to put a beating on the black man, a full-scale melee erupted as
the victim's friends flew to his aid.

Other problems were less complicated. The Chin collected—
and ignored—a number of traffic tickets.

At this point Genovese was openly feuding with family head
Frank Costello. A bootlegger once financed by legendary gambler Arthur Rothstein, Costello assumed the mantle as head of
the nation's richest borgata (family) following Luciano's conviction on a prostitution rap.

Costello was regarded as the nation's most powerful Mob
boss, and was widely referred to as "the Prime Minister of the
Underworld." He arrived in New York from his native Italy in
1895 as a four-year-old boy, and he never looked back.

He did a ten-month stretch in 1915 after his arrest for carrying a pistol before moving into organized crime. The dapper
and savvy Costello worked his way quickly toward the top of the
Mob hierarchy, and was credited with calling a "peace conference" in the wake of the 1929 St. Valentine's Day Massacre in
Chicago.

By the time Costello succeeded the deported Luciano as head
of the family in 1946, he wielded considerable political power as
well. Costello's close ties with the Manhattan Democratic Party
organization, aka Tammany Hall, gave him access to appoint
judges and party leaders.

Corruption-busting ex–New York governor Thomas Dewey
once ripped Costello as the "gangster boss of Tammany Hall."
Costello, always tight-lipped about his business, once denied his
role as a kingmaker by declaring he couldn't even fix a parking
ticket.

During a 1951 appearance before the Kefauver Committee,
the Genovese family boss deflected questions about his vast influence.

"What was your ability to persuade politicians?" one senator asked in the nationally televised hearing.

"I can't explain it," replied a raspy-voiced Costello.

The California Commission of Organized Crime offered a more cogent explanation: Costello's illegal businesses maintained a $400 million fund for bribing public officials. The West Coast agency also estimated that Costello's slot machines alone pulled in $2 billion a year.

Despite his time on the lam, Genovese believed himself the rightful heir to the Mob family throne. He was Luciano's underboss before bolting to Italy, and intended to right the wrong of Costello's rise. Bitterness festered in the capo—and he fomented the same ill will among the family rank and file.

He would wait for more than a decade before making his long-planned move. Taking down such a formidable target required precise planning and a small, silent group of participants. It was eventually conceived as a two-man job: One shooter, one getaway driver. The gunman was reportedly handpicked by Anthony "Tony Bender" Strollo, a Genovese capo from the Village.

On the evening of May 2, 1957, Costello went out for dinner and drinks on the East Side of Manhattan, a few blocks from his palatial apartment on Central Park West. He was joined by Philip Kennedy, a onetime semipro baseball player now reinvented as an actor and modeling agency manager. The two dined in Chandler's Restaurant at 49 West Forty-Ninth Street before heading to meet Costello's wife and *National Enquirer* publisher Generoso Pope at L'Aiglon on East Fifty-Fifth Street.

The urbane underworld figure, who believed his problems with Genovese were a thing of the past, traveled the city without a worry or a bodyguard.

Costello and Kennedy made one more stop, grabbing a drink at Monsignore down the block from L'Aiglon. When Kennedy suggested a final nightcap, he was overruled by the boss. Costello wanted to get home and field a phone call from powerhouse Washington lawyer Edward Bennett Williams, the future owner of the Redskins.

The two hailed a cab outside Monsignore around 10:40 P.M. and headed uptown to Costello's residence at the Majestic, just across the street from both Central Park and the equally upscale Dakota.

Another car made the same trip earlier in the evening, carrying two men. The large black car, with fins on its rear, was driven by Tommy Eboli. Riding alongside him, armed with a revolver, was his old boxing charge, Vincent Gigante.

The Chin had prepared for this night for weeks in advance, eating and shooting and shooting and eating. The formerly fit Gigante had intentionally bulked up to three hundred pounds, a hedge against future identification by any eyewitnesses. And he invested a considerable amount of time taking target practice in the week before the two men double-parked in the darkness on Central Park West, near Seventy-Second Street, and waited patiently.

The cab with Costello stopped outside the thirty-story building with its spectacular views, and the boss walked inside as Kennedy paid the driver. Before the taxi could pull away from the curb, Kennedy recalled, he heard a blast "like a large firecracker."

Costello was inside the Art Deco building's stately foyer when the hulking Chin blew past the building's doorman in hot pursuit, a revolver in his right hand pointed directly at the shocked boss. As he approached Costello, Gigante delivered a menacing five-word line that proved more bark than actual bite: "This one's for you, Frank."

Sufficiently warned, Costello spun, threw up his hand and instinctively flinched. The bumbling Gigante squeezed the trigger of a .38-caliber revolver from point-blank range—firing a single shot, which reverberated through the marble lobby like someone had just fired a cannon—and missed his target. The kill shot was a near miss. Costello suffered a gory-looking scalp wound, but nothing more.

As the blood poured from Costello's head, the rotund Gigante—more than one hundred pounds above his fighting weight—waddled from the scene without firing another bullet or checking to make sure the job was done. With the roar of its revving engine, the black car zipped away beneath the sparkling skyline.

A stunned Kennedy paid the cabbie and ran inside to see what had happened. Costello was hunched over, holding a handkerchief now crimson with blood to the side of his bleeding head. Two terrified building employees stood frozen nearby in disbelief.

With his night on the town having come to an abrupt finish, Kennedy ran back outside to hail another cab. He led the bleeding Costello to the street, loaded him into a cab and ordered the hack to hightail it toward Roosevelt Hospital on Tenth Avenue.

Word of the attempted assassination tore across the city so quickly that cops and reporters were already there when Costello's cab arrived at 11:08 P.M. The Mob boss later told his attorney that one thought ran through his mind during the ride downtown: he was going to die.

He did not. The magic bullet had entered through the front of Costello's fedora and exited through the back, traveling along his skull from left to right and tearing off a chunk of flesh above his right ear. The bullet slammed into the lobby wall, with cops later recovering two bullet fragments.

Costello was quickly patched up and sent on his way, exiting the hospital with his hat—bullet holes in its front and rear—pulled tight over a head wrap. Bloodstains marred his pricey double-breasted brown suit as Costello waded into the waiting crowd. It became immediately evident that he had no intention of violating the Mob oath of omerta, and would keep his mouth shut tight about the entire near-death experience.

"I didn't see anything," he told the disappointed homicide detectives at Roosevelt. On his way to a car parked outside, Costello was accompanied by his wife, who was decked out in a dress and a fur stole. Costello even flashed a smile for the horde of photographers. The *New York Times* ran a photo of Costello on its front page, while the tabloid *Daily News* went with large type only: FRANK COSTELLO IS SHOT.

In smaller print below: *Ambushed at Apartment Door.*

Below that came the news that red-baiting Senator Joe Mc-Carthy had died.

The building doorman, a gentleman named Norval Keith, got a pretty good look at the well-dressed and well-nourished shooter, who wore a dark suit with a matching hat.

Cabdriver Samuel Miseveth, who rushed the bleeding boss to the hospital, gave a first-person account to the *News* about his famous fare.

"It hits me like a flash, Frank Costello!" the cabbie recounted. Kennedy ordered Miseveth to mind his own business and drive before returning his attention to the bloodied Mob chieftain.

"Don't worry, Frank," Kennedy had said. "Say a black Cadillac hit you."

Miseveth deduced there was more to the story: "There's something crazy here, I figured. You don't get hit by a black Cadillac in an apartment building lobby."

A pale and nervous Costello said little as they sped through Manhattan. Once at Roosevelt, Costello gave the cabbie $5 for a forty-five-cent fare.

The audacious attempt on Costello's life was a sensation from coast to coast, and the shooter was in the wind. The New York Police Department (NYPD) launched a full-court press to track down the would-be killer, with more than sixty detectives assigned to the investigation. They rousted more than two hundred people, including a who's who of Mob bigwigs, and grilled them all.

Concerned the assassin could return and finish the job, the cops assigned a pair of detectives to the lobby where the bullet flew. The initial police description of the as-yet-unidentified suspect was "between thirty and thirty-five years old, six feet tall, heavy thighs, potbelly, wears a size-50 suit and waddles while he walks."

The city's tabloid seized on the details, and the fugitive gunman became "the Waddler" or "the Fat Man." Whatever you called him, the shooter with the flabby physique was the most wanted man in the country, with the combined forces of the FBI, the Coast

Guard and—somewhat bizarrely—the Motor Vehicle Bureau all called into the pursuit. Even Western Union was alerted to keep an eye out for any kind of suspicious activity, particularly a money transfer.

As the hunt for the shooter heightened, the architect of the hit—Vito Genovese—hunkered down in his Atlantic Highlands, New Jersey, compound. Bodyguards surrounded him in case the failed murder sparked a war within the family.

The first break in the probe offered another clue to the amateurish effort: The black getaway car had an outstanding recent parking ticket that raised alarms. The cops ran the plates and discovered that Gigante purchased the car two weeks before the botched hit.

By May 16, the cops had the Chin's name. What they didn't have was the Chin, or any idea how to find him, given the silence on the streets about the failed hit. A "49" notice was sent to every detective squad in the city, with a picture of Gigante and word that he was wanted for questioning in the Costello shooting.

Word leaked to the papers in early June with the suspect's identity, setting off another media feeding frenzy. Chief of Detectives James B. Leggett was uncomfortably fielding questions about the previously unknown Gigante, who had suddenly made the leap from Mob obscurity to fugitive celebrity.

"I only wanted him for questioning because he answers the physical description of the man who did the shooting," said Leggett, downplaying the news. He was blunter when asked about the Chin's odds of survival now that his name was known: "If anything happens to him, it won't be on my conscience."

Newspaper reports linked Gigante with Strollo, who had reportedly met with Costello earlier on the day of the shooting to get a handle on the boss's evening itinerary. The Chin had served as an occasional bodyguard for his Village compadre Tony Bender.

An ancient FBI document offered testament to Strollo's loyalty to Don Vito and his résumé, which had just expanded to include attempted murder. The FBI summary stated: *Strollo has a reputation of being a racketeer of the notorious hoodlum Vito Genovese and is considered the hoodlum who controls all the illegal activities in the Greenwich Village area. [Informant] advised that Strollo was the top man in shylocking, bookmaking and gambling activities in the Greenwich Village area.*

The *Daily News* expressed its dismay that the suspect wanted as the nation's most notorious non-marksman was nothing more than "a fat ex-pug and underworld hanger-on." Further media disappointment came when Gigante's no-show handyman job became public knowledge. This nondescript schlub was the daring and elusive Mob killer who tried to take down Frank Costello?

In the next few days, all law enforcement and court personnel in the city received a "Stop Card" calling for the Chin's immediate detention. And the NYPD began to put the squeeze on the Gigante family, particularly Vincent's pretty young wife and his two reputedly mobbed-up brothers, Mario and Ralph. Civilian sibling Pasquale was also questioned; kid brother Louis, two years away from his ordainment as a priest, received a pass for good behavior.

Olympia Gigante, alone at their 134 Bleecker Street apartment, was visited anywhere from fifteen to twenty times by the NYPD. Dubbed a "sultry brunette" by the city tabloids, the young wife kept her mouth shut and stood by her missing man—a pattern that continued for the rest of her life.

"He's not around," she told the *New York Herald Tribune*. "I don't know where he is. He's disappeared."

The loyal spouse gave police the same line. Their response was to put the Gigantes' cramped Greenwich Village home under round-the-clock surveillance.

Mario and Ralph took a more confrontational approach. Mario, thirty-three, was driving a car with a dead headlight when cops pulled him over on August 12, 1957, at the corner of Sullivan and Prince Streets. Riding shotgun was brother Ralph, twenty-seven, as things escalated from bad to worse.

When a detective moved in to frisk the brothers, Mario,

nabbed for driving without a license, uncorked a roundhouse punch at the unsuspecting cop. Both brothers were immediately arrested; Mario was charged with felonious assault and Ralph with vagrancy. Each carried a wad of cash, with $717 recovered from Ralphie and $671 from Mario. Cops found a hatchet and a baseball bat inside the car. Neither would be much help in changing a flat.

Nine days later, when tempers on both sides cooled, Mario paid a $30 fine ($25 for a reduced charge of disorderly conduct and $5 for the headlight). However, three months after the Costello hit attempt, the cops were no closer to putting their cuffs on the portly prey. It was the Chin himself who finally ended the coast-to-coast manhunt.

Vincent Gigante looked quite a bit different when he walked into the West Fifty-Fourth Street police precinct on August 17 than he did departing the Majestic in haste three months earlier. The Chin's expansive gut had noticeably receded over the summer, and Gigante had swapped his thick tangle of black hair for a crew cut. His new high-and-tight look was recorded for posterity in front and side views via his mug shot. His attorney, David M. Markowitz, accompanied him as he casually arrived around noon.

Gigante was as terse in the precinct as he had been in the lobby of the Majestic: "Do you want me in the Costello case?" Then he stopped talking.

Cops wasted no time in tracking down Costello, hopeful the slick boss's memory could be jogged by the sight of the thuggish gangster in the much-thinner flesh. Costello was at the precinct by 4:45 P.M., arriving in an unmarked NYPD vehicle and accompanied by three city detectives.

Fifteen minutes later, with a smile on his face and a cigarette in his hand, Costello strutted confidently from the precinct. He offered no comment to the reporters outside—or, as it turned out, to the investigators inside.

Deputy Inspector Frederick Lusen nevertheless characterized

the taciturn Costello as "very cooperative." The feared mobster was later brought back for a second round of questioning, with the exact same results—nothing.

Leggett described the suspect as "a small-time gambler," while the *Times* expressed surprise that Gigante was still breathing after his monumental miss. In a rather un-*Times*-like passage, the paper raised the possibility that Gigante "had been feared the possible victim of a gangland ride."

Costello's pal Kennedy seized the surrender as an opportunity to reiterate 100 percent that he absolutely, positively had no idea who pulled the trigger that spring night. He definitely had not identified the man who turned himself in: "It's a closed incident, as far as I'm concerned."

Markowitz insisted his client, who had rarely, if ever, ventured beyond the Village, was living "about five hundred miles" from the city during the manhunt. North? South? West? The lawyer never offered any details.

He additionally insisted that Gigante had an alibi: He was down in the Village when the shot was fired, and he had learned about the Costello hit from the radio. There were, no doubt, friends and family willing to swear to his whereabouts.

Gigante's sudden return thrust the case back into the national spotlight. After the Chin's surrender, national gossip columnist Dorothy Kilgallen—right beneath an item on the debutante daughter of deep-pocketed philanthropist Cornelius Vanderbilt Whitney—weighed in with the scuttlebutt on the suspect.

On August 28, 1957, Kilgallen wrote: *A surprising number of chaps in the underworld guffaw at the idea of Vincent (the Chin) Gigante being the one who shot Frank Costello. They admit he's a rough type, but they don't believe he's the one who creased "Uncle Frank's" skull.*

Prosecutors didn't bother to call Kilgallen as a witness.

The legendary office of District Attorney Frank Hogan quickly asked for $150,000 bail on Gigante. That was a staggering sum for the times, and especially for a case that wasn't murder. An outraged Markowitz dismissed it as a "sum which is entirely out of line."

Manhattan judge George Tilzer cut the defense lawyer short: "Gigante has shown an open defiance of law and order. This is a serious matter."

The assembled grand jury needed just one hour to return an indictment: Attempted murder one. Those summoned to testify included four witnesses, several detectives and Costello, who would only confirm that yes, indeed, somebody had shot him in the head on the night of May 2, 1957. He did not know who, and he did not know why.

According to the charge, Gigante "willfully and feloniously with a deliberate and premeditated desire" had "attempted to kill [Frank Costello] with a pistol." The penalty for conviction was steep: the street thug who once did two months in jail was now facing 12½ to twenty-five years.

Gigante, casual in a suit with a gray polo shirt, sat impassively while chewing gum throughout the grand jury process. He was even mellower at his arraignment one day later, smiling at reporters and waving at the crowd of family members in court.

"There is nothing more here than an assault—an attempted [assault]," claimed Markowitz, quickly correcting himself. "Just because a person is in the public eye doesn't make it an attempted murder. They must convince Your Honor that this was an attempted murder."

The ensuing bail hearings became a contentious tale all their own. The $150,000 was initially granted, with the prosecution arguing their call to throw the suspect behind bars was solely motivated by their concern for Gigante.

"There is a good possibility that his life night be in danger," said prosecutor Vincent Dermody. "The safest place for him is in jail. Those who might have sent him to do the job on Costello would be the ones he would have to fear."

Markowitz battled successfully for a reduction to $100,000, still an exceptionally high figure. Meanwhile—in a move foreshadowing the future—Gigante checked into a hospital, albeit with a legitimate gallbladder issue. Five days later, the Chin walked out of jail.

His parents, his brother Pasquale and five friends pooled their "bankbooks and stocks" totaling $117,000 to cover the bail. Mom Yolanda personally provided the bondsman's fee of $3,030 as the Chin's new lawyer attacked those who regarded his client—a married man, father of four, neighborhood main-stay—as a nefarious Mob hit man.

The bail money was "an answer to the accusation that sinister forces are behind the defendant," snapped attorney Maurice Edelbaum, who was now representing Gigante.

A somewhat stunned spokesman for DA Hogan put a positive spin on the development. Making such a high bail was indeed "rare," he acknowledged, but it had occurred "a few times be-fore."

Maurice Edelbaum was a city kid himself, born in Brooklyn and a graduate of Fordham Law School. By the time of the Gi-gante case, he had almost twenty-five years in private practice. The Gigante case boosted the lawyer's profile. Edelbaum would become one of the most prominent lawyers in the city over the next decade, handling the cases of notorious Colombo crime family member John "Sonny" Franzese and New Jersey Teamster boss Anthony "Tony Pro" Provenzano—a reputed Genovese cap-tain later implicated by the FBI in the never-solved murder of Jimmy Hoffa.

Edelbaum went on to achieve notoriety in a pair of high-profile cases: Edelbaum managed to clear Isidore Zimmerman, who did twenty-four years in prison for a 1937 murder committed by some-body else, and the attorney won an insanity acquittal for a for-mer medical student accused of stabbing his mother-in-law while tripping on LSD.

Zimmerman had worked as a city doorman, a job that would loom large as the case against the Chin moved forward.

*　*　*

The trial was set for April 1958, with the first juror—a city public-relations executive named John F. Byrne—quickly seated. Edelbaum received a two-week delay to finish a federal case before jury selection resumed. The all-male panel was chosen in short order, with Gigante ordered back behind bars for the trial's duration.

When opening day arrived in May, the pro-Gigante contingent was out in force, filling several rows in the Manhattan courtroom. Wife Olympia became a constant presence, along with her in-laws. The Chin's mom, Yolanda, sat mutely in the back of the courtroom, silently praying the rosary throughout. Assorted other relatives and neighbors filled out a group that swelled at times to forty people.

Testimony started slowly, with NYPD detective Nathan Udry recounting the repeated police visits to the tight-lipped Olympia Gigante. Dinner companion Philip Kennedy took the stand to recount the pleasant evening that preceded the failed assassination.

Kennedy once again said he saw nothing—and only heard the gunshot from a distance. "It sounded like a large firecracker," he recounted yet again, under questioning by prosecutors. "In the lobby I saw 'Mr. C,' and he was bent and holding his head."

The two paralyzed building workers "stood in utter panic to one side," he recalled.

"Was there blood?" asked Judge John A. Mullen.

"Yes, there was," he replied.

Edelbaum rose from the defense table for his cross-examination. But the lawyer was hardly confrontational as he faced down the witness. Instead, he turned to the defense table and asked Vincent Gigante to rise from his seat and stand.

Had Kennedy, inquired Edelbaum, seen this man on the night in question?

"No, sir."

The trial tedium disappeared with the explosive appearance of the government's star witness: the doorman Norval Keith, who had worked at the Majestic for twenty-two years. The fifty-five-year-old employee took the subway in from Queens each night to his job at the posh building.

Keith seemingly appeared in the courtroom from nowhere. In fact, he came directly from a hotel across town, where the prosecution had kept him hidden for the past nine months. He had one major problem for an eyewitness: One of his eyes didn't work so well. His damaged left orb allowed Keith to discern nothing more than light and shadow.

The prosecution addressed the problem head-on. Keith was asked to read the clock on the courtroom wall about sixty feet away. He nailed his reply: 12:05 P.M., and time seemed to be running out on Gigante.

The prosecution had Keith step down from the witness stand, walk toward the defense table and take a long look at the defendant. Keith didn't flinch in the presence of the accused shooter.

"I heard this man say, 'This is for you, Frank,'" he announced before the rapt courtroom. "The next thing I witnessed, he raised his right hand and fired a shot. I saw Mr. Costello pacing up and down in the lobby, holding a handkerchief to the right side of his head."

Gigante then ran right past Keith to the waiting getaway car. The doorman wasn't done; he testified that Gigante had walked right past him on the way inside, too.

"I saw a big, dark car double-parked near Seventy-Second Street," he recounted. "A big man got out of it, brushed past me and went into the lobby. I looked inside after him."

The bombshell testimony, laid out in short order by the prosecution, seemed devastating for the defense.

Edelbaum stepped up for his shot at Keith, looking to score a few points against the very confident witness. The lawyer suggested the doorman maybe had a few drinks before Costello's arrival: "Did anyone bring you black coffee that night in question?"

"No, sir," the genial Keith replied.

The attorney then focused on the physically transformed defendant. Keith said it was still the man with the gun, only forty pounds lighter.

"What about his hips?" Edelbaum inquired.

"They were much larger on May second, much broader," the doorman said.

Edelbaum brought Keith down from the witness stand for another look at the Chin. From close range, the witness estimated Gigante had lost a full nine inches from his waistline in the last year. The *Daily News* turned the exchange into a classic headline: WITNESS STILL HIP TO CHIN THOUGH THERE'S LESS OF HIM.

Norval Keith stepped down from the stand, his testimony finished.

The doorman was followed by NYPD detective Edward Lehane to bolster Keith's claim regarding the Chin's post–attempted hit weight-loss regime. Lehane, who had the mobster on his radar for about five years, duly noted Gigante's decision to go with a new haircut before returning to the city.

One more riveting piece of courtroom theater awaited. On May 20, 1958, just a few weeks past the first anniversary of his near-death experience, the prosecution summoned Frank Costello. The reluctant witness, by turns, was pleasant, polite and perturbed. He was not at all helpful to prosecutors, who were intent on convicting the man who fired a bullet at his head.

The mob boss began by describing himself as a retired real estate executive and New Orleans casino operator. The lone mention of his criminal past had nothing to do with his lofty position as head of the Genovese family for twenty years. Instead, he acknowledged working as a bookie shortly after becoming a naturalized citizen in 1924.

And then, for the first time in public, the godfather gave his version of the night when he literally dodged a bullet.

"I walked through the front door," Costello recounted. "I heard a shot—it sounded like a large firecracker to me at the time. I paid little attention to it at the moment. Then I felt something wet on the side of my face. It was blood, and I realized I was shot."

Costello acknowledged that he spun toward the sound, but he swore that "nobody was in sight." His three-hundred-pound assailant had dashed from the lobby with the speed of Olympic gold medalist Jesse Owens. Costello never caught even a glimpse of the would-be killer. In fact, he couldn't imagine why anybody would want to see him dead.

"I know no human being who would have a motive," he told the jury. Costello made an excellent point, for no witness or prosecutor had provided a motive for the daring murder attempt. The prosecutor sat down, and it was now Edelbaum's turn.

The first rule for defense attorneys is simple: Never ask even the simplest question unless you know the answer. Maurice Edelbaum launched his contentious cross-examination 100 percent certain that Costello wouldn't implicate his client under any circumstances. He started slowly by reviewing all of Costello's testimony before the Kefauver Committee.

The Mob boss at one point snarled at Edelbaum over his line of questioning: "Please don't raise your voice."

"I'll give the orders in this courtroom," interrupted Judge Mullen.

Edelbaum asked Gigante to rise yet again at the defense table. Costello carefully donned his glasses, a showy gesture that meant nothing. He peered at the Chin without a glimmer of recognition.

"Do you know any reason why this man should seek to take your life?" Edelbaum asked.

"No reason whatsoever," Costello replied evenly.

"Is the reason you won't say you saw the man because you'll be indicted for perjury?" the lawyer pressed.

"Absolutely not," said Costello.

Edelbaum wrapped up his interrogation with one final question, delivered for the jury in a booming voice: "You know who shot you that night. You know who pulled the trigger that night. Why don't you tell the jury who it was?"

Costello, cool as ice, turned the query around: "Well, I'll ask you, 'Who shot me?' I don't know."

After the trial, Edelbaum told a friend, "I would have dropped dead if he answered." The lawyer, still breathing, turned and sat down alongside Gigante. The gangster stepped down from the stand and strolled back into the courtroom. "Thanks a lot, Frank," Gigante declared in a voice loud enough for the press to hear.

There was one scary moment for Costello before his silent exit. A self-proclaimed "well-wisher," sporting a black eye and a leather jacket, approached the Mob boss with a brown paper bag. Inside, as it turned out, was a gift of cigarettes and candy for Costello's wife, Bobbie.

Both sides rested their cases, with the prosecution calling sixteen witnesses across the eleven-day trial. Despite the pretrial claims of an alibi, neither Gigante nor anybody else ever took the stand to explain where he was on May 2 or for the next three months. Edelbaum called just a single witness: a probationary cop named John DePalo who bore a slight resemblance to the Chin and was called to stand in a lineup.

The defense lawyer, in his final address to the jury, harped on the doorman's bad eyesight and alleged boozing. Norval Keith "had D.T.'s right here in this courtroom on the stand," he declared.

Assistant District Attorney Alexander Herman urged the panel to ignore Costello's testimony, dismissing his much-hyped appearance as a sideshow.

"I put him on in the nature of an exhibit—a corpus delicti, as it were, the man who was shot, the guy who got it in the head," the ADA said. "No one in the police department or the district attorney's office or the defense table gives a hoot in hell about Costello. But he's a threat to the community. And when he's shot, it's important."

After getting instructions from Judge Mullen, the jury began its deliberations at 3:30 P.M. on May 27. They took a two-hour dinner break before resuming at 8:30 P.M. The courtroom remained packed, with the tension rising as the clock ticked toward midnight.

Then word came through the otherwise-empty courthouse: There was a verdict. At 11:45 P.M., after just over six hours of deliberations, jury foreman Hayward T. Carter rose to deliver the verdict: Vincent Gigante was not guilty of the attempted murder of Frank Costello.

It was a unanimous decision for the ex-boxer.

The courtroom was bedlam, a combination of Times Square on New Year's Eve and a winning Super Bowl locker room as three dozen Gigante supporters burst into wild applause. Mom Yolanda, still clutching her rosary, credited divine intervention for the jury's decision.

"It was the beads! It was the beads!" she told anyone within listening distance. Her husband, Salvatore, stoic throughout the trial, burst into tears at the foreman's declaration. He was joined by the Chin's weepy wife.

Sitting at the defense table, Gigante watched impassively as the wild scene unfolded. When the foreman was done, he slumped slowly into his chair with relief. The acquitted shooter then signaled for his supporters to bring the celebration down a notch.

"I knew it had to be this way because I was innocent," the subdued Gigante said outside the courtroom.

The Chin wore a dark suit, dress shirt and perfectly knotted tie when he posed for a postverdict picture. An exulted Olympia planted a kiss on her husband's cheek, and he wrapped his right hand around her shoulder. His left arm pulled Edelbaum close. Gigante stared straight into the camera, his face betraying no sign of excitement or surprise.

Prosecutor Herman was less than graceful in defeat. Gigante remained "a young punk on the way up in the underworld who was chosen to kill Costello to earn his spurs," he sneered.

Jury foreman Carter said the panel was unimpressed by the

evidence against Gigante, dismissing the state's overall case as weak. And, he added, the jurors were unconvinced by Keith's confident courtroom identification of the defendant.

THE CHIN'S NOT GUILTY OF CREASING COSTELLO, trumpeted the *Daily News*.

The trial was over, but speculation about Gigante's role in the shooting and his whereabouts immediately afterward would endure for decades. The *News* reported at one point that Gigante was shipped to Florida for an immediate weight reduction program, while other reports claimed the Chin fled upstate to a Mob-run "fat farm" to slenderize.

Joe Valachi confirmed the latter was the case: "The Chin was taken somewhere up in the country to lose some weight. I'd say he was around three hundred pounds, and you couldn't miss him. They found out the doorman at Frank's place was half blind and they wanted to slim the Chin down, so he, the doorman, wouldn't recognize him."

The turncoat soldier also took a shot at Gigante's poor aim: "The Chin wasted a whole month practicing."

In one of the trial's more bizarre postscripts, the only person to do time for the shooting of Frank Costello was . . . Frank Costello. On the night he was wounded, cops searched his pockets and found a piece of paper with a mix of words and numbers that added up to a short stretch in jail: *Gross casino win as of 4-27-57—$651,284.* Police discovered the figures matched the exact figures from the new Tropicana casino in Las Vegas, where the Mob boss was a very silent partner—much as he had been a silent witness.

When Costello refused to address the note or identify Gigante before the grand jury, Hogan hit the Mob boss with a thirty-day contempt sentence. He served half the time. Costello was also carrying $3,200 in cash that night. When police returned the money, he was $2,400 short. The mobster considered his loss the cost of doing business.

Facing a choice of retirement or bloody internal family war-fare, Costello made up his mind for good after another gang-land hit where the shooters did not miss—six times.

Fellow boss Albert Anastasia was known as the Mob's "Lord High Executioner" for his work with Murder Inc., the Mafia's preferred contract killers. He was reportedly one of the shooters in the Masseria hit, and was regarded with considerable trepida-tion as a ruthless and remorseless killer.

There was no questioning his belief in murder as the solution to life's many problems: Annoyed when a random Brooklyn citi-zen turned fugitive bank robber Willie Sutton in to the NYPD in 1952, Anastasia reportedly ordered the man's execution. Arnold Schuster was gunned down outside his Borough Park home sev-enteen days later as payback, and the case was never solved. Anastasia's rise to running his own family came after the 1951 murders of boss Vincent Mangano and his brother, Philip.

Anastasia arrived, as was his custom, for a shave at 10:20 A.M. in the lobby barbershop of the Park Sheraton Hotel, Chair No. 4. His face was swathed in hot towels when two men marched through the hotel's front door and into the barbershop on Oc-tober 25, 1957.

The duo wore suits and sunglasses, and they meant business. They opened fire on Anastasia from close range, and a half-dozen bullets found their mark, including one that tore through the back of his head and stopped in the left side of his brain.

The hunter was now the game, and Albert Anastasia was dis-patched in the same brutal fashion as his many victims. The postmortem photo of his bloody body ranks among the most in-famous in Mafia history, with Anastasia flat on his back, his arms splayed to either side, the towels still obscuring his face. Two city workers later lugged him out inside a body bag.

The image lingered with Costello.

Five barbers, a manicurist and several customers in the hotel were all in agreement once the shooting stopped: they didn't see a thing. Vito Genovese and Carlo Gambino, the slain mob-

48 LARRY McSHANE

ster's treacherous underboss, were assumed responsible for the daring hit.

Life went on for Costello, who retired from the business and kept his thoughts about Gigante to himself. Business was business, and boys will be boys. Gigante moved up in the family that was soon identified by the surname of its new boss, Don Vito.

Years later, George Wolf, Costello's lawyer, recalled arriving for a dinner party at his client's tony apartment. Breaking bread with Costello was none other than Vincent Gigante, the man who once tried to kill him.

After the trial the newly acquitted Chin left the courthouse for the familiar streets of the Village and his Bleecker Street home. But freedom was fleeting for Gigante as the wheels set in motion by the botched Costello hit made him a target for a subtle bit of revenge.

The Chin, back on the streets of the Village, enjoyed a mere forty-one days of freedom before Costello and his friends in the Mob exacted their payback on Gigante and his boss—delivered in the form of a stunning and unexpected new federal indictment.

It was 6 P.M. on July 7, 1958, when Gigante was arrested at the Lexington Social Club, conveniently located at the corner of Sullivan and Spring Streets. News reports noted the suspect was dressed rather slovenly, and prosecutors called him a prime mover in an international drug ring.

The main target of the federal probe was arrested two hours later near the Jersey Shore: Vito Genovese. It was the latest in a run of incessantly bad news that beset the new family boss in the months after the Costello shooting.

Vito Genovese was already known as one of the high-level mobsters involved in the foiled national Mob summit meeting in the tiny upstate hamlet of Apalachin in November 1957, an event that forced Director J. Edgar Hoover of the FBI to pull his head ostrich-like from the ground and acknowledge the existence of an organized crime syndicate run by Italian immigrants and Italian Americans.

Just one week before the drug bust, Genovese was summoned to appear before a U.S. Senate subcommittee investigating what was then known as "the rackets." The senators' interest in Genovese was piqued by prior testimony putting his reported net worth at $30 million. This was in an era when virtually all professional athletes worked off-season jobs to make ends meet.

The estimate of his cash reserves was provided in part by his bitter ex-wife, Anna, who dumped the don and exposed his revenue streams from gambling, nightclubs and Mob-controlled unions in property settlement papers. The widow whose first husband was reportedly executed on Genovese's say-so was now killing him, much more slowly and publicly.

Genovese took the stand and refused to say a word. He invoked the Fifth Amendment more than 150 times before quietly stepping down. Asked if he was a member of the secret society that emigrated from Italy, the Mafia boss declined to answer. He did the same when asked directly if he had ever "killed a man."

Gigante, likewise, was drawing unwanted attention during his scant few weeks of freedom after the acquittal. Hoover, in a national FBI dispatch, promoted Chin to the agency's "top hoodlum" list. Oddly enough, Hoover noted the gangster went by the alias "Billy Chin," an obscure nom de guerre from his days in the ring.

Gigante was merely a supporting player in the heroin bust, with most of the newspaper ink dedicated to Don Vito. JAIL GENOVESE ON DRUG RAP, trumpeted page one of the *Daily News* above a smaller statement, *T-Men Arrest Rackets King*.

The headlines sat above a picture of Genovese as he arrived in Manhattan for court. The accompanying photo captured the boss, his eyes hidden by dark glasses, riding shotgun alongside one of the arresting agents who invaded his Atlantic Highlands home. A half smile played across the godfather's face, as if he knew this day was somehow inevitable.

The case was brought by U.S. Attorney Paul Williams, who would run for governor later that year based in part on his crime-busting three-year run as a federal prosecutor. He lost to Nelson Rockefeller, a defeat that did little to eclipse his stellar work at putting crooks behind bars.

Williams moved up after obliterating crimes from prostitution to corruption in a pair of upstate counties, and was among those who prosecuted powerful Teamster boss Jimmy Hoffa.

He stood front and center in announcing the arrests, with authorities charging the multimillion-dollar ring's tentacles extended to drug sources in Europe, Mexico and Puerto Rico. Williams personally greeted the suspects when they were brought into court.

"Genovese was the hub around which this entire conspiracy revolved, and Gigante was one of his protégés and a rising star in the underworld," said Williams. "The arrest of Genovese is one of the most important arrests ever made in this field."

Reveling in the takedown, Williams predicted this latest offensive "could easily drive the Mafia out of the narcotics business." Or not, as it turned out. Codefendants Genovese and Gigante exited the courthouse side by side, neither saying a word.

In perhaps the most stunning development in the case, this takedown of a powerful and previously untouchable Mob boss was based primarily on the testimony of a low-level drug dealer named Nelson Cantellops.

The prosecution's star witness, unlike the defendants, hung around the lowest rungs of the criminal ladder. The man known as "the Melon" had three minor busts, including attempted forgery and marijuana possession, before his 1958 arrest for peddling heroin. His criminal past made Cantellops a poor fit for business partner with a Mob boss: a junk dealer reaching into the highest level of the well-insulated Mafia hierarchy.

The official version of his participation was that a street informant tipped a federal drug agent about Cantellops's dealings with Genovese, and the inmate, who was doing five years on his heroin bust, agreed to testify against the Mob boss and his cohorts. Cantellops improbably swore the boss had met with him personally, a tale that still rings false in the new millennium.

Tommy Eboli, the Chin's old manager and by now a Genovese mainstay, ordered a hit on the witness before the indictment even became public, according to Valachi.

"There's some Spanish guy testifying against the old man, and we got to find him," Eboli told him. "His name is Canteloupes, you know, like the melon."

Gigante was specifically accused of delivering narcotics from the city to a Cleveland mobster, driving to Ohio with a second man. Cantellops also claimed the Chin provided his introduction to Genovese, arranging a September 1956 meeting at an emergency turnoff on the West Side Highway.

It took several months for the case to come to trial, and fourteen weeks for prosecutors to lay out all the evidence. It took the jury just twelve hours to convict Genovese, Gigante and thirteen codefendants. It was the first criminal conviction for the elusive Don Vito since a 1917 bust for carrying a pistol, when he did sixty days.

The sentence this time was fifteen years for the sixty-one-year-old Genovese, who would never walk again as a free man. The dapper, bespectacled boss offered only a wry grin when the verdict was returned shortly after 10 P.M. on April 3, 1959.

A resigned Genovese accepted his fate with a single, terse comment to the judge. "All I can say, Your Honor, is that I am innocent," he said before leaving for the federal lockup.

The Chin received just seven years at his April 17 sentencing after the judge was flooded with letters attesting to his character from neighbors in Greenwich Village.

The conviction irked Gigante for the rest of his life, lingering long after he entered into his "crazy" Mob boss era. During a June 1997 "forensic social assessment" done upon his arrival at the federal prison in Butner, North Carolina, Gigante made a point of declaring he had "always been against drugs."

Asked specifically about the drug-dealing conviction, the Chin, with the haze of his purported mental illness suddenly lifted, offered a one-word answer: "Framed." And maybe he was right.

In *The Last Testament of Lucky Luciano,* the original boss of the family claimed that Cantellops was paid $100,000 to testify. The payment came half from Luciano and half from fellow boss Carlo Gambino, as retribution for the Apalachin debacle. Costello and Meyer Lansky, the notorious financial wizard for the Mob, were also in on the fix. Costello kicked in half of Luciano's payment for a guarantee that Gigante would go down with Genovese.

"As far as I know, Cantellops never set eyes on Vito until they got in the courtroom," Luciano supposedly said. "I don't know if the [federal] narcotics bureau knew that Genovese was a gift, and I don't give a shit."

Cantellops, once sprung from jail, didn't last long. The ex-con informant was killed in a 1965 bar fight, and his murderer was never found. Genovese remained behind bars; the Mafia don, betrayed by his bride and by the lowly Cantellops, would die on Valentine's Day, 1969.

Gigante fought his case, and managed to avoid prison until running out of appeals in February 1960. His criminal efforts continued unabated during the legal fight, with an FBI memo sent just days before his incarceration identifying him as "the person who 'kept order' in the Greenwich Village area."

Before heading off to prison, the Chin took care of one last bit of business. New York University bought up the tenements on Bleecker Street, leaving the Gigantes—his parents, his brother Ralph and his own family—looking for a place to live. He approached one of the building owners at 225 Sullivan Street about finding a new home for the clan. Two apartments opened up—no waiting list, not a lot of questions. His family moved into one, with his mom and pop taking the other.

CHAPTER 4

COLD IRONS BOUND

*T*HE CHIN ARRIVED AT THE FEDERAL PENITENTIARY IN LEWISBURG, Pennsylvania, on February 18, 1960, leaving his family behind in their new homes. His admission paperwork listed his codefendants from the trial, with the name Vito Genovese right at the top.

As would become de rigueur for the gangster later in his life, he sat down for an initial assessment by the prison staff. Their analysis: Gigante was vain, dangerous and—most tellingly— quite at ease in acting the part of somebody else.

A March 18 summary read: *He takes pride in the praise showered upon him by the clergy and to be recognized as a henchman with racketeers, giving him the role of a Dr. Jekyll and Mr. Hyde personality. It is anticipated that prior patterns will prevail following discharge . . . in view of past history, therefore, prognosis in this case for community adjustment must be guarded.*

His IQ tested at 101, putting Gigante in the average range. However, his intake evaluation noted he had an "inferior intelligence and depends primarily on his brawn for existence." His reading and writing skills were those of a ninth-grade student.

A report by a prison committee recounted: *He was reared in a high delinquency area of New York City and has associated with big time gangsters most of his adult life. He was a light-heavyweight prize fighter prior to an injury.*

If the Chin was a lousy candidate for rehabilitation, he became a model prisoner during his time in the federal lockup. His weight had ballooned back up to 288 pounds. While he turned down a spot in the educational program, Gigante became a hard worker who caused few problems during his time in the federal lockup.

But he did make the announcement more than once that the prison was holding an innocent man: *Gigante denies all allegations. He claims that because he was acquitted (in the Costello hit), he would be charged or sentenced eventually. He claims that he "never saw, spoke or handled narcotics in my life." He claims to "hate" narcotics.*

At a 1962 meeting with the parole board, Gigante vented his rage at a prison official. "You know I was framed!" he roared loudly enough for other inmates to hear.

His postprison plans, the Chin said, were to move back with his wife and kids in the Village, while resuming his career as a truck driver. Two of his children, he confided, were already attending parochial school. Gigante also said he intended to "participate in all phases of our Catholic program" offered to Lewisburg inmates.

In a detailed March 2 "Report of Medical History," Gigante confirmed that he had never suffered from depression, amnesia, nightmares or excessive worry. No, the Chin confirmed, he had never checked into a mental hospital for any reason.

In her own sit-down with prison doctors, his mother described her beloved son as a healthy and happy kid. She never mentioned any boxing injuries or any psychiatric issues.

Authorities noted that Gigante, while under the employ of Genovese, was also a presence at Village clubs and church groups preaching an antidrug message. The Chin, in neat penmanship, signed off on a document attesting that he had never used drugs.

Gigante's Lewisburg file was clean, except for medical reports detailing a pair of workplace injuries. He suffered a fractured left big toe in a boiler room mishap, and hurt his wrist a year later while working in the prison icehouse.

His boss at the prison power plant weighed in with a glowing June 1961 review of his charge: Gigante was a "very good maintenance man." He could be "depended on to complete assigned duties without supervision and to the best of his abilities."

The Chin endured one devastating blow behind bars: His father, Salvatore, passed away on May 9, 1961, succumbing to lung cancer forty years after coming to America. After his diagnosis the dying Gigante patriarch moved into Chin's two-bedroom apartment with his daughter-in-law and four grandkids.

The death hit Gigante hard, and years later he recalled how moody it left him behind bars. His father was dead; his widowed mother was alone in her apartment; his wife was at home with their kids.

Prison paperwork indicates the Chin was almost assigned to the federal penitentiary in Atlanta, where Genovese and family soldier Valachi were doing their time. It was there that one of the most earthshaking developments in Mafia history was playing out.

Genovese, who once stood as Valachi's best man, now decided his old pal was an informant and needed to die. A fellow Mafioso charged that Valachi was working for the FBI, and that was enough for Don Vito. Valachi dodged several murder tries before finally killing another inmate in a case of mistaken identity: Valachi thought the innocent man was sent by Genovese. Valachi famously became the first member of the crime family to flip in 1962.

The next wouldn't follow for another twenty-four years.

Gigante finished his Lewisburg time as a pleasant and compliant inmate. A February 7, 1964, a progress report noted his hard work, his "neat and orderly" grooming habits and his role as a "well-known leader of the young, more aggressive Italian-American inmates."

Prison doctors "found no special abnormalities" and "considered that he is experiencing good health at this time," the report concluded.

The Chin was released on October 16, 1964, and ordered to remain on parole through August 21, 1966. When he returned to the streets of Greenwich Village, the neighborhood had changed dramatically—on the face of things, anyway.

A Jewish kid could land from Minnesota with little more than the clothes on his back and an acoustic guitar to reinvent himself as Bob Dylan, voice of a generation. Comics Joan Rivers and Bill Cosby were headlining at local clubs. A guitarist named Jimi Hendrix was plugging in at the Café Wha? New music for a new generation echoed through Washington Square Park, and the sweet smell of marijuana wafted down Sullivan Street.

There was one change that directly affected him—the FBI had cultivated informants inside organized crime. Unlike Valachi, they spoke only on the condition of anonymity, and each was clearly terrified of the Chin. One flatly told his FBI handler that "if the word got out about him, he would 'clam up' and provide no further information."

Chin showed little interest in the social evolution or the FBI's attention, preferring to go back in time and revisit the illegal businesses of his past: running numbers, loan-sharking, skimming from local bars. Gigante quickly reestablished himself as head of all the Genovese operations in the old neighborhood, according to a snitch's May 1965 report.

Heavily redacted FBI documents from the time identified Chin as a Genovese soldier, even as his status continued to climb. Details were scarce, but in a January 1966 rocket to his New York office, Hoover issued orders to put Chin on their Mafia to-do list.

Hoover instructed his Big Apple charges: *Inasmuch as Gigante has been reported to be a "button guy" in the Vito Genovese "family," you should reopen this case, conduct an appropriate inquiry and bring the investigation up to date.*

Chin went on about his criminal business. In his downtime, Gigante joined the Holy Name Society at Our Lady of Pompeii and became a fixture in the pews at Sunday Mass. The mobster did take one notable step that October, the first in what became a lifelong journey: To avoid his parole officer, Gigante had his lawyer call authorities to report the mobster was "in a markedly nervous state" and would need several months of rest. It worked, beyond the Chin's wildest expectations.

Free of his minder's attention, the Chin was spotted strutting through the Village with a menacing German shepherd at the end of a leash in the summer of 1967. He reportedly owned a number of Village bars, including Goody's, a notoriously dank dive that was home to poetry readings in the 1950s. It was now home to a hard-drinking crowd comprised of bohemians from the Village past, down on their luck and content to booze the day away.

The FBI's attempts to catch the Chin in a crime of any kind in this era turned up nothing more than a $15 traffic ticket in 1968. Gigante's time behind bars had fostered both a healthy paranoia about law enforcement and a serious aversion to jail cells.

Vincent's brother Mario, by now a fellow Genovese associate, took a sweeter approach to legitimate business: Mario operated out of the B&G candy store on West Fifty-Fifth Street. FBI surveillance had spied Mario conferring with Eboli while his brother was locked up in Lewisburg.

Ralph Gigante, like Mario, was also involved in Genovese family business. Mario showed promise as an earner, bringing in money for the family and eventually working his way into position as a trusted Genovese capo. Ralphie's rise was more of a fall.

His ancient, yellowing clip filed in the *Daily News* newspaper morgue is marked with a single derisive word: *Hoodlum*. Ralph became involved in the gambling side of things, reportedly doubling up as a loan shark, providing cash at a usurious rate to bettors who fell behind in their payments.

Ralph was a bit player in one of the era's college basketball point-shaving scandals. He was busted on October 5, 1962, for offering North Carolina State player Donald Gallagher a $1,000 payoff two years earlier to shave points in a game against Duke. The players in the scam didn't necessarily throw the games; instead, they insured that the favorite won, but failed to cover the point spread.

If NC State was favored by six, and instead won by five, the gamblers collected and the Wolfpack had a victory. It was win-win—until everybody lost. Ralph Gigante was scooped up with fourteen players and a dozen co-conspirators.

The biggest loser was Jack Molinas, once a national college-hoops star at Columbia University. As a sophomore he led the Lions to a 22-0 regular season mark and a berth in the 1951 NCAA tournament. The Ivy League center with a deft scoring touch became a first round NBA draft pick—the fourth player taken overall by the Fort Wayne Pistons in 1953.

His career ended just months later when the six-six forward was suspended indefinitely after admitting to making bets on the Pistons. His defense: "I only made wagers on my team—and always that we'd win. I did not know there was anything wrong with that."

NBA officials disagreed. Molinas was never reinstated, his once-promising career cut short.

There were rumors and reports that the ex-hoopster developed a relationship with Tommy Eboli and the Chin, but neither was implicated in the scandal that ran from 1957–1961.

The investigation took down twenty-seven college programs—powerhouses St. John's, Seton Hall, NYU and Connecticut among them. The thirty-seven fixers on the teams were cited for tanking a staggering sixty-seven games. Trial testimony indicated Ralph Gigante was also involved with games played by Columbia and two Philly schools, St. Joseph's and LaSalle.

But Molinas was charged and convicted as the ringleader, with a sentence of ten to fifteen years behind bars. He did five, mostly in the draconian Attica Correctional Facility in upstate New York. His postprison career included dealing in pornography and furs imported from Taiwan.

His tale was later cited as the inspiration for *The Longest Yard,* the box office smash where a point-shaving quarterback ends up behind bars. Star Burt Reynolds walked away a hero at the end of the Hollywood version. Molinas didn't share the happy ending.

The aging hoops star was standing in the backyard of his Hollywood Hills home when a bullet tore into the back of his head. No one was ever arrested, despite police suspicions of a gangland hit—perhaps in an insurance fraud.

Ralphie Gigante's second bust came with a comic, rather than tragic, twist.

A gambling investigation by city cops focused on action at Googie's, a saloon at (where else?) 237 Sullivan Street. A pretty undercover officer named Ann King came by the bar, ostensibly looking for her degenerate gambler husband.

Ralphie provided a shoulder to cry on, along with the odds at local racetracks. After he took a few bets from King, the female officer returned the favor by putting Ralph in handcuffs.

"I can't believe it," he moaned after his arrest. "You're too sweet to be a copper."

Within eighteen months of the Chin's release, his brother Pasquale—identified by the FBI as "probably a suspected member of the Genovese family"—was also spied hanging out with his sibling at the mobbed-up Vicarl Social Club on Sullivan Street. The space was the forerunner to the infamous Triangle Civic Improvement Association, the social club on the same block and the Chin's future base.

With Genovese locked up, the acting boss of the family was the Chin's longtime associate Tommy Eboli, the erstwhile fight manager and getaway driver installed immediately after Vito went to jail. Shortly before assuming the mantle, Eboli filed a tax return stating that his gross earnings for 1959 were $18,742.

He was about to get a big raise.

One of Tommy Eboli's first duties as the stand-in don was the murder of Anthony "Tony Bender" Strollo, done on direct orders from the imprisoned Genovese, according to FBI documents. The once-trusted capo and co-conspirator in the Costello hit had

left his home in Fort Lee, New Jersey, on April 8, 1962. He was
never seen again, and his body never recovered.

A July 1963 FBI memo stated: *Strollo was allegedly killed . . . for
disobedience of orders, namely his failure to cease narcotics operation.*

The guy with the Irish alias was no stranger to homicide.
While Tommy Ryan was running a crap game on the East Side
with a fellow mobster in 1956, a pair of dim-bulb stickup men
held up the players and made off with the cash.

James Rocoreto and Michael Langone were next seen in the
trunk of a parked car on the Lower East Side, their bodies repeatedly hacked with an axe.

Eboli assembled his Mob cabinet: underboss Jerry Catena, who
was a moneymaking Genovese veteran, consigliere Mike Miranda
and top capos Phil "Benny Squint" Lombardo, a future boss,
along with brother Patsy Eboli.

It was this regime that instituted the oft-discussed and oft-
disputed Mafia ban on drug dealing, most likely as fallout from
the convictions of Genovese and Gigante—along with the increasingly stiff sentences for drug dealing.

A 1963 FBI memo declared: *Thomas Eboli had recently instructed
all of his associates that absolutely no one in his organization would be
permitted to handle or participate in any dealings involving narcotics.
Informant learned that any violation of Eboli's instruction would result
in "a visit with Tony Bender."* (That was the Genovese equivalent
of "sleeping with the fishes.")

Another FBI memo said the Mob was getting out of the drug
business for another reason. The dope trade was giving them a
bad reputation, and they wanted to avoid "the unfavorable publicity" that would result from a "narcotics conviction."

Vincent Gigante went a step further: he brought a personal
"Just Say No" policy to the streets of the Village during the
1960s.

"I'll give you a story, one little story," said his brother Louis.
"That was an era of drugs, kids getting into drugs, okay? Vincent
has a self-importance. This is *our* neighborhood. One of the
kids—a great athlete, I taught him to play basketball—wandered

into drugs. Vincent would not allow him to come home and live
with his mother on the block. The kid could not come on the
block, 'cause he was infected by drugs. And that's a true story."

If the Genovese family was getting away from the drug trade,
there was still always sex (prostitution) and rock and roll. Oddly
enough, the Mafia clan—made men whose tastes generally ran
to Frank Sinatra and Jerry Vale—was in the music business courtesy of an old pal of the Chin: Morris Levy.

Levy was a tough guy from a tough neighborhood and an
even tougher childhood. His father and his older brother died
of pneumonia when he was just four months old, leaving the infant alone with his widowed mother in a Bronx tenement. Like
his friend Vincent Gigante, Levy's formal education ended
early: a thirteen-year-old Morris left school for good after assaulting his seventy-five-year-old homeroom teacher.

"I could get an A in any class," he once boasted. "But I had this
one teacher, she had no business teaching school. Miss Clare . . .
never got fucked in her life, probably. And she hated me."

Levy lashed out after a classroom argument over a math test.

"And I got up—I was a big kid—took her wig off her head,
poured an inkwell on her bald head and put her wig back on her
fucking head. Walked out of school and said, 'Fuck school.'"

The rough-and-tumble teen first met Eboli a year later. The
unlikely pair became fast and lasting friends.

"I hit Broadway when I was twelve," Levy once said. "I started
working in the checkrooms at the nightclubs. [The Mob] owned
all the clubs and had all the liquor licenses."

He scuffled for a while, working as a dishwasher, a cook and a
coat checker. He spent a year in the navy at the tail end of World
War II, launched a failed business in Atlantic City and returned
to the city of his birth. Gigante and Levy first met as bouncers at
a Village nightclub, one of many operated by the Mob in those
days. The Chin never strayed far from the neighborhood. Levy
moved north on Broadway, where he launched Roulette Records
and the legendary jazz club Birdland (previously owned by a

mobster with the decidedly nonmusical name of Joe "the Wop" Cataldo).

It was in the latter nightspot where a Mob loan shark collector stabbed Levy's brother Irving, who made the fatal mistake of ordering the gangster's wife—a known prostitute—to leave the establishment. Instead, it was Irving who departed. Permanently.

Roulette, which opened in 1956, was an independent label based on the eighteenth floor at 1790 Broadway, with rumors that Eboli provided the seed money. A sign hung on the wall of Levy's office: O LORD, GIVE ME A BASTARD WITH TALENT. His lament was answered, as some of his label's early signees included Count Basie, Frankie Lymon and the Chantels.

Levy was among the first in the industry to realize the value of owning a song's copyright. Among his biggest earners: "Lullaby of Birdland," which he commissioned, and "The Yellow Rose of Texas," which he bought up. He routinely took cowriting credits on the work of legitimate songwriters, collecting a piece—or maybe all—of their royalties.

His son Adam, then a kindergarten student, also received cowriting credits on some songs. Nobody complained.

Levy was a multimillionaire businessman with the mouth and attitude of a straight-up gangster. The mogul, a street-smart philosopher prone to profanity, did not believe in redemption: "If a guy's a cocksucker in his life, when he dies he don't become a saint." His raspy voice reeked of intimidation, a complement to his imposing physical presence.

While known throughout the music business, Levy lacked the name recognition (and varnished public relations) of future generations of industry executives: David Geffen, Berry Gordy, Herb Alpert. And that was fine with Levy, who didn't really give a shit and never denied his Mob connections.

"I know Cardinal Spellman, too," the hard case once declared. "That don't make me a Catholic."

Backed by the Genovese muscle, Levy was known for playing nothing but hardball when it came to making money. He feared no one: Levy once went toe-to-toe with Beatle John Lennon and never blinked. His menacing reputation extended across the Atlantic, where a young Graham Nash was singing in the Hollies.

When the chart-topping British band first came to New York, Levy wooed them with dinner at his club the Roundtable (complete with a visit from a curvaceous belly dancer) and some free time in a Manhattan recording studio.

I suspected it wasn't out of the goodness of his heart (a muscle insiders claimed had been left out of Morris' body), and that something else was going on, Nash wrote in his autobiography. *But having dinner with Morris Levy was one thing; getting into bed with him was another altogether. We heard stories . . . how he put his name as a writer on all the records that Roulette released . . . and held the mortgage on Alan Freed's house, how . . . Nah, better not go there.*

The elusive Levy had skated from the 1960 payola scandal, which destroyed Freed, the renowned Cleveland DJ and a close pal.

It was unclear when the Genovese family became Levy's silent partners, but it preceded Gigante's release on the drug charges. *Since before 1963, Morris Levy has been a lucrative source of cash and property for leaders of the Genovese LCN family,* one FBI report declared.

Levy eventually put Eboli on the payroll for $1,000 a week after the two launched Promo Records in 1969. And he also struck up a friendship with the Chin's brother, Father G., who remains a fan to this day. "Morris Levy . . . genius," he declared. "He never knew one note from another note, but he knew how to make money."

The upper echelon of the Genovese family certainly agreed. And so did the chart-topping leader of the Shondells, legendary rocker Tommy James.

"I honestly never would have had my success without Morris Levy," said James. "I would have been lucky to be a one-hit wonder with a fluky song called 'Hanky Panky.'"

By the time the voice behind "Mony Mony" and "I Think We're Alone Now" was done with Levy, the cost of doing business with the mobbed-up record exec reached into the high eight figures—

and James had a genuine fear of becoming number one with a bullet.

Or a revolver filled with them.

The 1960s

"What did I know about the Mob?" Tommy James asked from his home in the Jersey suburbs. "From watching the TV show *The Untouchables,* that's it."

Once he signed a recording contract with Levy, that changed quickly. By the time James extricated himself from the tentacles of Roulette Records and the Genovese family, he was out somewhere close to $40 million in stolen royalties.

The naïve Niles, Michigan, native, with a song called "Hanky Panky," was still named Tommy Jackson when he arrived in Manhattan for the first time in mid-1966. His name had already changed before young Mr. Jackson walked through Levy's imposing mahogany door—he was now Tommy James.

He was just nineteen, and the owner of what everyone agreed was a no-doubt-about-it hit single already filling dance floors in Pittsburgh. The newly christened James was shopping his record to the big labels in the big city, hoping to break out nationally. In one heady day he sat with executives falling over each other to bid on their shot at making him a star.

"Columbia said yes," he recalled. "Epic, yes. RCA, yes. Atlantic and even Kama Sutra—yes. The last place we talked to was Roulette, and Morris Levy wasn't even there. I didn't go along. I was beat after a long day. They just dropped the record off. So I went to bed feeling great. We were going to sign with CBS or one of the corporate labels."

Around nine-thirty the next morning, the phone began ringing in his hotel room. And ringing. And ringing.

"One by one, all the record companies that said yes the day before called and said, 'Tom, we gotta pass,'" he recounted. "I'm wondering what's going on, and finally Jerry Wexler at Atlantic leveled with me. Morris had called all the other labels."

The man known as "the Godfather" of the music business delivered the same message to each one: "This is my fucking record. Back off."

They did. Tommy James and the Shondells were officially signed to Roulette. "First offer I couldn't refuse, I guess," he said with a wry chuckle.

Within weeks "Hanky Panky" was sitting at number one on the music charts—ahead of the Beatles' "Paperback Writer."

Levy was open about his affiliation with Eboli, Gigante and the rest of the Genovese family. And he was just as open about the financial arrangements that would be shared by Morris and the Mob.

"They made it very clear up front. You go for your royalties . . . it wasn't gonna happen," James recalled. "I couldn't get paid. It was like taking a bone from a Doberman."

An armed Doberman, with a very bad disposition and some equally ill-tempered and well-armed friends.

James later heard the story of Jimmie Rodgers, a hit-making Roulette artist from the 1950s, who broke out with the smash single "Honeycomb." Five more gold records followed, without any money coming the performer's way.

Rodgers walked away with two years left on his contract, opting to stop recording rather than make money for Morris Levy. And then one night he was driving through the San Fernando Valley to his California home when a car appeared behind him, flashing the high beams. When Rodgers pulled over, he was yanked from the car and beaten within an inch of his life. Rodgers suffered a fractured skull, broken arm and all the skin on his legs peeled off as the attacker dragged him across the asphalt. The battered singer was left lying in the road.

James's second visit to the Roulette offices coincided with the arrival of two goons, who pulled Levy aside to recount their baseball bat attack on a New Jersey entrepreneur who ran afoul of Morris. Levy, himself, was an imposing figure who stood a scary six-three and weighed 230 pounds.

One of the two thugs was Nate McCalla, an even more imposing figure who stood an even scarier six-four and weighed a hulking 240 pounds. Nate's pals included John "Sonny" Franzese, a Colombo family associate of great repute who would one day become the oldest prisoner in the federal penal system. McCalla, a decorated Korean War hero, ran his own record label for Levy while handling all kinds of other business for the boss.

Around Roulette, McCalla's hands were valued as highly as his ears.

Eboli was a fairly constant presence around the offices, as were the Chin, Fat Tony Salerno and the truly terrifying enforcer Gaetano "Corky" Vastola, a Levy friend and confidant for three decades. James recalled the first time he was introduced to Gigante, who was dressed casually in black slacks and a white shirt with the collar open.

There was little friendly about their hello. Even the bombastic Levy was chastened by the presence of the Chin, a big man with a well-kept mane of black hair.

"Morris had a hold of me, he walked me over," James recounted. "He said, 'Tommy, this is Mr. Gigante.' He didn't call anybody 'mister'—nobody. Morris was a big guy, right out of central casting. And when Morris says, 'This is Mr. Gigante,' [Chin] looks right at me."

"Hi. How ya doing?" offered the taciturn Gigante, a fan of Elvis Presley from the 1950s. Four words were enough to send a clear message to the long-haired rocker.

"I shook his hand, and I knew it was serious business," James recalled decades later. "Listen, I didn't feel that he was menacing as much as serious. The funny part is these guys used Roulette almost as a social club. They'd hang out in Morris's office, come in, listen to the music.

"But, of course, Roulette was used for everything from laundering money to God knows what. We couldn't talk about any of this. My whole life became walking on eggshells. If I hadn't been so young and stupid, I would have been more afraid."

James remembered how he'd flip on the television to see people he'd met just days earlier at Roulette coming out of a New Jersey warehouse in handcuffs. The Internal Revenue Service was constantly poking through the office, trying to find something—anything—on Levy.

"That," he said, "is the kind of shit that kept happening."

Levy's secretary, who spent a lot of time steering mobsters to her boss's office, finally explained the whole thing to the stunned young rocker.

James and the Shondells accompanied Democratic presidential hopeful Hubert Humphrey on campaign stops around the country in 1968. The band became a huge live attraction, playing dates alongside the likes of the Beach Boys, the Animals and the Monkees.

James came home for the Roulette Christmas party, hosted by Levy at one of his clubs, the Roundtable, where the music business partied with their Mob partners.

And then, two months into the new year, Vito Genovese died on February 14, 1969. When James stopped by the offices in the ensuing days, the entire leadership of the family was assembled, filling the chairs and the L-shaped couch in Levy's inner sanctum.

"I remember three of the guys ended up becoming heads of the family—Chin, 'Quiet Dom' Cirillo and Tony Salerno," said James, who was also quite friendly with a fourth: Tommy Eboli. His alias of Tommy Ryan only confused the Midwestern kid, until it was explained the mobster was born in Italy and a member of La Cosa Nostra with the rest.

James spent weekends with the gangsters in the mountains, where they all had weekend retreats on property owned by Levy in Ghent, New York. (An informant later revealed Levy put up the cash for Fat Tony's place.) It was totally surreal: teen idol meeting Mob stars. James remembered watching Salerno playing outside with his son on a cold winter's day. "I got pictures of Tony with a cigar hanging out of his mouth," he said.

Levy's place was dubbed Sunnyview Farm, and a plaque on the front door neatly explained the reason for its very existence: A SUNNY PLACE FOR SHADY CHARACTERS.

In 1971, during an outbreak of Mob violence, Levy bolted Manhattan. James was advised by his lawyer that it might be a good idea to do the same, as gangsters unable to find Levy might take aim at his top moneymaking artist.

"He seemed to know everything that was going on up there, and I was told that it might be a smart thing if I left town for a few weeks," he recalled. "I thought, 'This is freaking great. You mean I have to go on the lam?'"

The chart-topping James racked up twenty-three hit singles and 100 million records sold, without receiving a penny in royalties. The only gold records that James ever collected were the ones he stole from the walls of the Roulette offices. It wasn't until 1972 that he finally mustered the courage to bolt from Roulette.

"I had it out with Morris and told him, 'I'm leaving,'" James recalled. "And he said, 'You ain't fucking going nowhere.' We really had a blowout. I didn't know if I was gonna get out of there."

James looked back on his days at Roulette with a mixture of admiration, amusement and horror: "Morris had a lot of good qualities—qualities that I respected. But he just had this dark thing about him. You know, in many ways he was a stand-up guy." (James exhibited a temporary slip into Mob speak.)

"But there was always this—he'd rather steal five grand from you than make it honestly."

CHAPTER 5

RAINY DAY WOMEN #12 & 35

*A*S THE TURBULENT 1960S "ROCK AND ROLLED" ON, THE FREE LOVE generation found an unlikely ally in their call to tune in, turn on and drop out: the devout, Roman Catholic Chin. With his marriage now well into its second decade, Gigante was smitten by a woman in the old neighborhood shortly after his return to the city from prison.

Olympia Esposito was a Greenwich Village girl, too: Olympia from the block, straight out of Mott Street. She soon became pregnant with their oldest girl, Lucia, followed by son Vincent and daughter Carmella. But Gigante didn't abandon his spouse of fifteen years: at one point in 1967, unbelievably, the Olympias on each side of the Hudson were simultaneously with child.

Rita Gigante arrived on January 24, 1967. In keeping with the family tradition, her name was chosen by Chin's mother, who decided to honor her new grandchild by invoking a nineteenth-century nun eventually known as the "saint of the impossible." Family members noted the first initials of the mom and her brood of five spelled out *R-O-S-A-R-Y.*

Vincent Esposito, Gigante's second child with his mistress, was welcomed six months later. Speaking years down the road, Gigante told prison officials he couldn't explain what sparked his extramarital affair and secret second family.

The summary of a 1997 psychiatric exam stated: *He denied any marital discord between him and his wife. Mr. Gigante explained that he*

*was blessed in having met two beautiful women and producing two lov-
ing families. He stated that he continued to love his wife and his para-
mour. He reported that he was an active and loving father to the children
of both families.*

Olympia Gigante seemed equally confused by her husband's
behavior. She would say there was no marital rift prior to her
husband's philandering—although she also pleaded ignorance
about Gigante's mistress and their offspring.

Regardless of the Chin's dual devotions, the situation couldn't
stand. Armed with a $5,000 gift from his mother for the down
payment, Vincent bought a suburban home on the Jersey side of
the George Washington Bridge for a reported $50,000 in 1967.
The place even came with a swimming pool, even if its new owner
preferred to avoid the sun.

Mom, Dad and the kids officially became residents of Old
Tappan, New Jersey, a leafy and sleepy town in Bergen County.
The Chin wasted little time in ingratiating himself with the local
authorities. He made the acquaintance of Detective Lieutenant
Herbert Allmers of the Bergen County Prosecutor's Office, who
introduced Chin to local police chief Charles Schuh.

That December, the new family in town presented the chief
with a Christmas card stuffed with a $100 bill. It was signed, *The
Gigantes.* He also invited the entire department to stop by the
two-story Colonial house for a little housewarming party.

Olympia Gigante handled the Christmas card duties the next
year, when the local cops received cash gifts as well, and there
was another holiday bonus awarded in 1969—a regular Christmas tradition, like the star atop the family tree. There was no attempt to hide the payments, regarded by the Chin as nothing
more than a suburban good-neighbor policy.

The alleged bribing of an entire suburban police force would
become an integral part of the Chin's legend, generating huge
headlines on both sides of the Hudson—and providing the impetus for a defense that made no sense. What happened next
was both incomprehensible and brilliant: a twisted mix of des-
peration and flat-out genius.

Facing another possible jail term, Vincent Louis Gigante went crazy. Or, at least, it seemed that way, and would until somebody could prove different.

The Chin was already operating out of the Triangle in the Village, even as he did his *Green Acres* time in the suburbs. He and his driver/bodyguard Fat Dom Alongi had landed jobs at the end of 1969 "selling cars" for a Dodge dealership in Smithtown, Long Island—not that either man had ever ventured to far-off Suffolk County, or ever intended to make the trip.

The two busy beavers were previously "employed" as salesmen for the Scott Novelty Co. in Newark, New Jersey, producer of a popular line of women's hats. The Chin was also on the books for a legitimate income at P&G Motor Freight in the Bronx, earning $300 a week as a "troubleshooter settling union disputes." If nothing else, it seemed more suited to his skill set than haberdashery.

The FBI took note of his embrace of suburbia in a June 1969 memo, and the agency was in New Jersey Federal Court three days later looking to subpoena all telephone records from the home. The Gigantes lived anonymously among the commuters and suburban families, just another Italian-American clan fleeing the city for a little more room and a bit more quiet.

Word of the alleged bribes broke in February 1970, splashed across papers in both the city and the suburbs. Olympia was identified as delivering the cash to Schuh, who allegedly spread the money around the four-man department. A *Daily News* story reported quite accurately that Gigante was the target of law enforcement surveillance for some time before the scandal became public.

The Old Tappan town council, which outnumbered the local police, voted 6–0 to put Schuh and his $10,000-a-year salary on the shelf as the probe unfolded. The FBI quickly reached out to the Bergen County prosecutor for details. On St. Patrick's Day, 1970, a grand jury indicted both Gigantes, the chief and his four cops.

The allegation sounded far more ominous than it was: No

"quid pro quo" was alleged, and the officers were accused of a misdemeanor charge of accepting cash payments for doing their job. Some of the cops collected a paltry $15.

The charges against the Chin were more serious: Gigante and another Village expatriate, Michael Zupa, allegedly paid Schuh for information about law enforcement keeping eyes on his New Jersey home. Oddly enough, Schuh was not charged with providing even a single detail to his purported benefactor.

It was a huge splash for the county's new Confidential Squad, and one Bergen County prosecutor—in a staggering touch of overstatement—described the indictment as a "historic document." Detective Lieutenant Allmers would later insist that he had no idea that Gigante, the Costello shooter and one of the secret society's most recognizable names, was a figure in organized crime.

Longtime Old Tappan resident Douglas Bissett, who became the town historian, said the claim was quite possibly true, even though absurd on its face. "You didn't even know he was here," said Bissett. "If somebody mentioned the name Gigante, you wouldn't even know about it, anyway. Who knew the name at that point?"

The Chin posted $25,000 bail; his wife put up $10,000; they both walked out of the Hackensack Courthouse. Vincent left without speaking to reporters—a duty left to his brother's keeper, Father Louis. In the first of many appearances on the silent Vincent's behalf, the priest came west from the South Bronx to hold a news conference and answer the charges.

The money was a "Christmas gift to policemen," said Louis Gigante. He denied that his older brother was part of the Mafia, and he accused (with some justification) the local authorities of trying to "railroad" the Gigantes.

More unexpected trouble lurked. With a bit of the Chin's blood in the water, he was arrested again on March 31, 1970, for failure to register as a convicted narcotics violator. It was annoying on both a professional and a personal level for Gigante, who was once again labeled a drug dealer for a crime he relentlessly denied committing.

Arrested with five other Bergen County men, Gigante posted $500 bond after one of the defense lawyers (again with some justification) denounced the charge as a "harassing type of complaint." The Chin now faced a pair of criminal cases; he was unaware of an Internal Revenue Service probe launched two years earlier, an attempt to nail him on the same kind of IRS charges that landed Al Capone behind bars in Chicago during the 1930s.

He was due back in court on May 12. John Carridi, his lawyer, appeared at the courthouse one day earlier to announce his client was undergoing psychiatric treatment at St. Vincent's Hospital in bucolic Harrison, New York.

Blindsided prosecutors, flummoxed by the lawyer's out-of-left-field assertion, responded only that they needed to confirm the unexpected claim. It would take them more than a year to get a psychiatrist in the room with Chin.

Gigante had first checked himself in for care at the Westchester County facility on April 27, 1970. "I feel like sleeping forever," he told a staffer. He also signed, in neat penmanship, a document that explicitly said his treatment would last only as long as Gigante felt like staying.

I may give the director written notice at any time of my desire to leave the hospital, the admission form read.

He headed home after a short stay, only to return on the eve of the May court date. Olympia Gigante signed off on this admission: *My husband needs care and he does not realize it.*

At the same time, authorities said, Gigante was running a successful numbers operation in the Village—and keeping other crime families from horning in on his action.

There was a third self-admission on September 28, when Gigante said he was "feeling very apprehensive." He made no mention of voices, hallucinations or conversations with God. All that would come later.

An FBI mole surfaced almost immediately to declare the whole thing was a scam.

Informant advised this may be a rouse [sic] *to avoid prosecution of bribery . . . from a recent arrest in Old Tappan, N.J.,* read an FBI memo filed less than a month after the Chin's May admission. Another memo later that month noted drily that Gigante was "diagnosed as a schizophrenic."

There was another crucial development in the sanity scam: Gigante's mom and his wife began providing a revised medical history on the Chin. They told the psychiatrists that Gigante was a bad kid, contradicting earlier tales of his idyllic Village upbringing. The new version would eventually claim he needed psychiatric care as a child, threw massive temper tantrums, was afraid of the dark and skipped out of school.

There was no mention of Gigante's role as paterfamilias for his two sets of kids with the Olympias on each side of the river.

The genesis of the infamous act remains unexplained to this day. Some suggested it was lifted from another Mafioso who pulled a similar stunt, but there's no proof to that claim. Jerry Capeci, dean of the city's Mob reporters, can't recall anyone ever recounting the inspiration for the rational Chin's sudden embrace of the loony life.

Howard Abadinsky, a Mob historian and St. John's University professor, acknowledged he'd never heard a believable backstory for Gigante's mental metamorphosis.

"Good question for which I do not have an answer," said Abadinsky.

Fellow mobsters suggested Gigante's deep devotion to the Mafia and its traditions convinced Chin to figuratively flip his lid. And maybe, said one, Gigante was just having a few laughs at the expense of his government tormentors.

"Maybe our life was the only life he knew," suggested Gambino family underboss Sammy "the Bull" Gravano. "Maybe he enjoyed driving the feds nuts—which he was."

Atlantic City gangster Philip Leonetti agreed: "That was his world, and he did whatever he wanted—and that's what he wanted. Everybody's different. That's not what I wanted."

Then the mobster paused, reflected for a second and laughed. "But then again, he was nuts."

Self-preservation was undoubtedly the main motivator, no matter how the concept was conjured in the Chin's fervid brain. But one informant gave the FBI another explanation for the ruse: the macho, married-with-a-mistress father of eight feared that another prison stretch might turn him into a rat . . . or a homosexual.

A heavily redacted report from an anonymous informant laid out the scenario: Gigante feigns mental illness to avoid incarceration as he would "crack" and become an informant or "fag" if incarcerated for any length of time.

Whatever the source, two things became evident: The Jersey prosecutors and judges lacked any concept about how to dispute, much less disprove, the Chin's crazy behavior. And playing crazy was like hitting the legal jackpot, sparing Gigante from appearances before the Waterfront Commission and a Queens grand jury probing Mob influence in legitimate business.

Eboli was subpoenaed in the same batch of Waterfront Commission invites that Gigante dodged. The aging godfather was served after stepping off a cruise ship from France, the last stop on a European tour, which included a visit to his ancestral homeland.

The vacation, Eboli claimed, was anything but relaxing: He quickly checked into Holy Name Hospital in Teaneck, New Jersey, citing a heart ailment. The FBI noted at the time that Tommy Ryan was the boss of the nation's largest and most powerful crime family, with more than eight hundred criminal-minded employees.

Eboli's medical dodge only pointed up the brilliance of the Chin's new approach: there was no EKG for crazy.

A confused FBI suspended its investigation of the Chin in November 1971, citing "the apparent hospitalization of subject." During that same year the Genovese capo resolved a festering business dispute between his family and the Colombos.

The unresolved Jersey case lingered on, too, with no end in sight as the months went by and the Chin became capo of the Greenwich Village crew. He was spotted near the Triangle within days of his October 9 release, following his third admission to St. Vincent's. He was strolling the streets in one instance, and riding inside a chauffeured car in another.

The Chin and Fat Dom were still taking bets on horse racing and sports, while running the local numbers game and doing a little loan-sharking. Pete's Novelty Shop, a small Village store purportedly kept in the name of Chin's mom, Yolanda, was put under federal attention. Alongi was seen inside, counting large stacks of cash, but not a single customer was ever seen buying anything.

Frustrated FBI agents, in a somewhat comical move, began collecting the trash from outside 225 Sullivan Street. They turned up nothing. Attempts to set up a permanent surveillance spot were routinely disrupted by the hostile Village residents, looking out for one of their own.

Gigante became more brazen, chatting quite rationally with underlings on the street as the FBI watched helplessly. The IRS case continued, with one internal memo stating Chin and Fat Dom were about to get fitted for handcuffs once the Department of Justice in Washington signed off on the case.

Fourteen months after Carridi's shocking announcement, a prosecution psychiatrist finally had a chance to sit down and evaluate Gigante. The incredible session took place in Yolanda Gigante's Sullivan Street digs, where Dr. Henry Davidson found the Chin lying asleep in bed, "unkempt and unshaved."

Those same three words would endlessly appear in future psychiatric evaluations, FBI reports and newspaper stories as a sort-of shorthand for the "crazy act," as the piece of performance art eventually became known.

Davidson recounted the sit-down in great detail after spending two head-spinning hours with Gigante: *[The Chin] sat in a chair with a passive but sleepy look on his face. Most of the time, he remained completely mute. Occasionally, he would give a kind of echo to my questions—for instance, when I asked him about medicines, he said sleepily "medicines, medicines." Or when I asked him if he was afraid of anything, he replied "war, war."*

Whatever Gigante said was delivered in a flat, emotionless monotone. At one point during the doctor's questioning, the Chin stood up and walked quickly out of the dining room. Minutes later, without explanation, he returned.

The doctor was told of Chin's vampirish schedule: up until 5 A.M., asleep most of the day—the same business hours that later marked his run as family boss. Gigante's strange schedule was fostered by his belief that the FBI didn't work the midnight shift.

At one point Gigante ventured a little too far afield with the doctor. He popped a Thorazine "as if he were eating a potato chip." Asked why, Gigante's response was simple: "Needed it."

"This kind of dramatic gesture," Davidson wrote, *"is sometimes seen in malingerers."*

The psychiatrist also raised the possibility of Ganser's syndrome, strange behavior brought on by arrest or imprisonment. Law enforcement generally dismissed the psychobabble and "considered it faking," the doctor said.

Five days later the authorities popped into the Triangle to make a gambling arrest. The Chin was not among those taken away by city cops.

Gigante finally arrived in court—he almost never missed a date—to hear his doctor Michael J. Scolaro testify that the Chin's April 1970 admission followed an overdose of prescription medicine, which was possibly a suicide try. The Chin was also suffering from hallucinations, the doctor revealed.

Gigante's FBI file for the first time made mention of Father G.'s presence in the courtroom. Newspaper clippings on the priest were soon a regular feature of the growing file.

Dr. Henry Davidson took the stand on June 4. The Chin's performance made an impression, and the doctor acknowledged the veteran mobster appeared schizophrenic, but he added a caveat.

"Generally, schizophrenia begins in late adolescence," he testified. "It is characteristically a disease which begins maybe at eighteen, nineteen, twenty years of age. It is quite rare to have it begin in the fifth decade of life, which is the forties. This is quite rare."

Davidson didn't stop there. Rather than a two-week hospital stop on his own terms, the doctor maintained, the Chin needed "intensive treatment." He suggested electroshock therapy, a conclusion that the defense fought mightily to circumvent.

The sanity struggle came to a bit of a crossroads at a June 11, 1971, hearing. Judge Morris Malech noted that the defense wanted Gigante declared crazy, but not *too* crazy.

"It seems to me somewhat anomalous to say this defendant is insane insofar as his ability to stand trial, his competency to stand trial, so that he's too insane to be tried and yet he's not insane enough to be treated properly," the judge told attorneys for both sides. "You understand? It is a problem."

As the hearing was winding down, a voice came from the audience in the Hackensack courtroom.

"Your Honor, may I approach the court?" the man asked.

"No," shot back Malech. "It is improper to do so."

The man in the crowd was undeterred: "Why is it improper?"

"I've said it was improper," the judge volleyed back.

"It's impossible that a citizen cannot address the court?" the man asked theatrically.

"When I say that, for all I know, you may be about to award me a commendation," said Malech, who later put off a decision on Gigante's mental state. "Frankly, I don't know what you have to say. It's improper to have a citizen at any time just get up in this courtroom and speak because he's wearing the robe of a priest. It is improper."

Father Louis Gigante was quick to respond.

"It's not impossible," the priest responded, "if you wish to speak."

And Father G. was a man prone to speaking his mind.

CHAPTER 6

WITH GOD ON OUR SIDE

*L*OUIS GIGANTE'S METAPHORICAL ROAD TO DAMASCUS BEGAN ON the streets of the Village, detoured south through Georgetown University, and led him into the South Bronx.

From the start the youngest of the Gigante boys was a smart and athletic kid who developed into a basketball prodigy. He attended the local Catholic school, Our Lady of Pompeii, where the religious youth developed a close rapport with one of the nuns. She wound up steering him toward the priesthood—not that it took a lot of nudging.

"I always remember wanting to be a priest," recalled Father Gigante, who kept a correspondence with his mentor-in-a-habit for decades.

He recalled fond memories of his youth on Thompson Street and the surrounding environs.

"I grew up on that block," he reflected decades later. "I became a great basketball player from that Boys' Club. They took the immigrant kids, and we went into that club. I learned there, became a basketball player, went to Georgetown."

Young Louis became an all-city basketball star at Cardinal Hayes High School in the Bronx. His game had been honed on the courts of the West Side, where the Village's West Fourth Street court remains one of the game's legendary outposts. At five-ten, Gigante was a scorer, a lightning-quick scrapper and a demon on defense.

His hoop dreams came true when Louis Gigante earned a basketball scholarship to the Catholic university, moving to Washington and joining the Hoyas. Though later to become an NCAA powerhouse, Georgetown was a middling program at the time: they earned just one postseason bid between 1943–1970.

They had Gigante to thank for that single trip.

In the 1952 through 1953 season, with junior guard Louis Gigante running the show, the Hoyas—led by the future priest's seventeen points—knocked off NCAA-bound Navy and nearly upset eventual NCAA champion LaSalle and its star, Tom Gola.

Father Gigante giddily recalled an upset victory over Maryland when he shut down future NBA star Gene Shue, who managed just eight points against his stifling defense.

Georgetown received an NIT bid, with Louis Gigante returning to play in the old Madison Square Garden on Eighth Avenue before a hometown crowd of fifteen thousand (Louisville beat the Hoyas, 92–79, despite his thirteen points).

The senior cocaptain, known to teammates simply as Lou, returned to the Garden for the twelfth game of the next season against mighty NYU, its campus just a jump shot from his old haunts. It was the last contest of his college career: Lou suffered a season-ending broken foot.

The charismatic Lou became a leader around campus, too, as he struggled with doubts about following his vocation. There was a girlfriend, and a decision to be made. Lou's mom dealt with the issue in the way that she knew best.

"I prayed a lot for her," she said. "Now she's married, and has four children."

Father G. went to St. Joseph's Seminary in Yonkers, and was ordained in 1959. Vincent was thrilled by his kid brother's vocation.

The neophyte priest spent two years in Puerto Rico, becoming fluent in Spanish, before returning to St. James Church on the Lower East Side of Manhattan. The young priest earned a small measure of notoriety by halting a "rumble" between two local youth gangs and earning a reputation as a guy who could get things done.

"I was never one to push myself on the public," Father G. recalled. "People were pushing me. If you look up my life—I mean, the *News,* the *Post,* the *Times,* they liked the story. They liked the priest who was out in the street. They liked that stuff."

He landed in the South Bronx at St. Athanasius in 1962 and never left the beleaguered parish. His brother Vincent was about halfway through his stretch in Lewisburg by then. The young priest harbored no illusions about the Chin's position in the old neighborhood.

"He controlled it. He controlled all the crime," said Father G. "Made sure nobody was getting hurt. Men [or] women with problems went to him. And he had his little bundle of friends. What did they do? Play cards. I cannot tell you. I didn't get involved in the intricacies of it. But I certainly knew. My brother was a good man. And he had to abide by the rules and regulations he accepted to be what he wanted to be.

"And he did. And he knew that he could depend on me and trust me. And he was very proud of me."

If the working-class Bronx neighborhood around the church was devolving into a nightmare of arson, drugs and poverty, the parish had a good reputation: Cardinal Terence Cooke once served as its pastor. Those days, as the priest would learn, were well in the past. The parish's eight thousand members, who once filled the church for a dozen Masses each Sunday, dwindled to about two thousand within a decade of Father G.'s arrival.

"It can only be compared to war, what happened here," he once observed. "And we lost the war. We've lost the war, but that doesn't mean our hopes are lost."

Father G. was one of five parish priests who became a band of South Bronx brothers.

"My best friend was one of the priests," Father Gigante said decades later. "We loved it. It was tough work, but we loved it. The only place we ever recreated was in the room, around eleven o'clock at night, having a few drinks, 'cause we lived together. That was great."

The neighborhood's steady, incessant decline lit a fire in the priest, who was known to walk the area while wielding a baseball bat. Yet even as he became the South Bronx's most vocal advocate, he stayed in touch with his Village roots and the family.

"I came home sporadically to see my mother on Sullivan Street, around the block," he recalled. "Get to see my brother Vincent all the time, but life went on."

So did Louis Gigante. He earned a master's degree in psychological counseling at Iona College. When the archdiocese tried to move him to another parish, Father Gigante politely refused to leave St. Athanasius.

"I really believe a priest should move to a place, and live and die there," he said in 1981. "Otherwise, if it's three years here and three years there, it's just like pumping gas. You never really get to know the people."

Father G.'s ministry was all-inclusive. He served as chaplain for the Italian-American Civil Rights League, which was Mob boss Joe Colombo's brazen attempt to deny the very existence of the Mafia. When Colombo was gunned down during a 1971 rally, the priest heard the news on his car radio. He immediately drove to the hospital to perform the last rites on the wounded don – who was paralyzed, but lingered for another seven years

Father Gigante was introduced to the group's lawyer, a formidable young attorney named Barry Slotnick. The lawyer's legal role models included brother Vincent's old defense attorney, Maurice Edelbaum. Interestingly, Father G. also baptized the children of a future Bronx prosecutor, Philip Foglia. The powerful priest had the ear and the support of his bosses: Cardinals Cooke and John O'Connor.

Up in the increasingly lawless Bronx precinct known as "Fort Apache," the priest improbably went into the construction business. The South East Bronx Community Organization, also known as SEBCO, was formed in the fall of 1968, with thirteen organizations banding together in an effort to rebuild the area.

When his secular efforts ruffled some feathers in the church's Fifth Avenue chancery, Gigante invited Cooke for a tour of the neighborhood to set a few things straight.

"He may not have understood what I was doing, because nobody around him tells the truth," the priest said bluntly. "They all have their axes to grind."

His political career launched in April 1970, when the cigar-smoking priest—with an abandoned car and a vacant, trash-covered South Bronx property as a backdrop—announced a bid for the U.S. Congress. He became the archdiocese's first political candidate, finishing third in a six-man field.

A year later, Father G. founded the Bruckner Democratic Club to build a constituency beyond the pulpit. In 1973 the priest was elected to the city council. When redistricting forced him to run again one year later, he was returned to office.

Although he opted not to run again in 1977, Louis Gigante was a guy with more than a little political sizzle when he left the business. He considered running for city council president, but his ambitions were trumped by unspecified "family reasons." By now, his brother Vincent, who was solidly into the insanity act, was living on Sullivan Street with their mom.

There was, at one point, a conversation about Father Gigante following in La Guardia's footsteps, from Greenwich Village to City Hall.

"Look at me," Father G. now says self-deprecatingly. "I was asked to run for mayor one time. I said, 'You're out of your mind! I'll get killed.' I was hot."

SEBCO, with a staff of three, opened its own offices in January 1978, and was formally incorporated as a not-for-profit a few months later. Father Gigante served as its president, and collected a salary for his efforts. He told the *New York Times* that the money allowed him to support his widowed mom.

Unmentioned: the priest also footed the bills for Vincent's legal bills.

"I didn't take a vow of poverty," Father G. said of his SEBCO income. "People think that I don't get paid and that I'm a saint for doing it. That's their problem."

Louis Gigante, in the nascent days of the post–Stonewall Riot gay rights movement, became one of the most vocal supporters of legislation to bar housing and workplace discrimination against homosexuals. He specifically blasted the church hierarchy; this was a typically ballsy move for a priest whose bosses would fight against gay marriage well into the next century.

"The chancery is presuming that all homosexuals are perverts who want to grab kids and hunt them, which is a horrible accusation," he said in 1974. "I am troubled as a Catholic. They have encouraged bigotry and irrational fear. The real threats to family life are poverty, ignorance, hopelessness, blind fear and lack of loving communication between human beings. The values which sustain family life are trust, compassion, dignity and love." (The sexual orientation of the Gigantes' gay brother, Pasquale, remained a family secret.)

When not saying Mass or saving his slice of the South Bronx, the priest was soon palling around with one of Vincent's friends: Morris Levy of Roulette Records.

"He became very close to me, and loved me, and we just hung out together," the priest recalled. "And so he went upstate and bought some eight hundred acres and built a mansion. And so when I was fatigued from everything I was doing, I'd run up there on a Friday and come back Sunday morning at six o'clock to do Mass. Two or three Masses. I loved it. When I got up there, I just slept."

The two socialized in the city, too, with the so-called "slum priest" sometimes coming down to Manhattan to hit the clubs. On the night of February 26, 1975, the two men were joined at the Blue Angel nightclub by Nate McCalla and an attractive young woman. Father Louis was wearing a three-quarter-length leather coat, with his Roman collar tucked into a pocket.

As they left the club on East Fifty-Fourth Street, they encountered a city police lieutenant, another cop and a third man heading out from dinner at a restaurant named Jimmy Weston's.

Lieutenant Charles Heinz noticed the good-looking lady as the two groups passed.

"You're a beautiful young woman," witnesses recounted Heinz as saying.

Not a word was spoken as McCalla grabbed the cop and pinned his arms down while Levy rained punches on the helpless lieutenant's face. The beating was so fierce that the outnumbered cop, a fourteen-year NYPD veteran, lost an eye.

The priest broke up the fight—blessed are the peacemakers—and the trio climbed into a waiting limo and left, police later said. The injured officer noted the license plate on the fleeing vehicle, and the car was traced to its owner. When questioned, the man recalled that one of the people in the limo was a priest.

As the investigation heated up, Father Gigante walked into a Bronx police precinct and asked if the cops were interested in speaking with him. Tips had already led the cops to Levy and McCalla after the injured cop, with his one good eye, picked the pair out of a lineup.

The story exploded once the *Daily News* reported the priest, along with his religious vows, had taken an oath of omerta and refused to testify before a grand jury. His two pals were nevertheless indicted for assault.

The priest insisted his decision not to take the stand was done on the advice of his lawyer after prosecutors asked him to sign a waiver of his immunity. Gigante claimed that he offered four times to testify without the waiver, but prosecutors refused. Father G. insisted he was walking toward his own car when the brawl broke out behind him.

"I heard shouting and screaming," he told the *Daily News*. "I turned around and saw three men fighting with Levy. The report said the men weren't intoxicated, but believe me—they were drunk and assaulting people."

The priest's leather coat was torn before things subsided.

The case mysteriously disappeared before McCalla and Levy went to trial, although Heinz brought a civil suit that was settled out of court. The priest's ties to the well-connected Levy fueled speculation of a connection with his brother's life of organized crime; the talk proved nothing, although rumors resurfaced across the years.

But Father G. was always treated with deference by Vincent's Genovese associates. FBI agent Charlie Beaudoin, who worked the Gigante case in the 1980s, said the priest carried himself with a touch of gangster swagger.

"People are still afraid of him," said Agent Beaudoin. "He was treated like a capo when his brother was alive. He was like a PR guy for Vincent."

Father G. was back in the headlines in October 1979, when the priest spent seven days behind bars after refusing to testify about conversations he had with city prison officials on behalf of mobster James Napoli. The chats, where Gigante urged authorities to cut Napoli some slack from the rigors of life behind bars, were secretly taped.

The priest was unrepentant about his efforts. Napoli was an "old and dear friend," and Father G. argued that he was entitled to keep their conversations private because of his vocation. He appealed a contempt citation all the way to the U.S. Supreme Court, only to lose.

Supporters turned out in Lower Manhattan to give him a hero's farewell when the priest went off to do his ten days of time, trimmed by seventy-two hours for good behavior.

CHAPTER 7

A PAWN IN THEIR GAME

W HILE BROTHER LOUIE WAS MAKING HIS WAY THROUGH THE PO-
litical jungle in the Bronx, the Chin was stuck fighting the
charges in New Jersey—and the former boxer was winning on
points in a battle that promised to go the full distance.

His lawyer continued to oppose any form of long-term treatment, and Father G. maintained his public defense of Vincent
Gigante. "Is there any proof that he is connected with the
Mafia?" the priest asked reporters at one point. "Where does
that information come from?"

By now, charges of Vincent Gigante's Mob links were supported by reams of FBI documents culled from anonymous informants and frequent surveillance of the Genovese veteran.
Yet, the Chin continued to walk the tightrope between street
boss and psychotic, checking himself back into the hospital
again between September 20 and October 19, 1971. His explanation: "This was ordered for me by my lawyer."

Another hospital visit came right before Christmas: "I feel
nervous all the time."

So did anyone who was doing business with the Chin, who was
now in full control of the Village streets. His wife would come to
visit on weekends, bringing along their youngest child, Rita, to
Yolanda's apartment. During a 1972 trip, the five-year-old girl
was sitting beneath the dining-room table in her grandmother's
apartment, out of her father's view.

A man was brought in for a business discussion with Vincent. Voices were raised, drowning out the sound of the Italian music playing in the background. The Chin finally spoke.

"Don't ever fuckin' disrespect me," he said before bashing the man in the head.

The stunned victim fell to the floor; blood now ran like a red river toward the terrified child. The beating continued, first with pinky-ringed punches and finally with a shoe stomping the man's head.

"I'm done with him," Gigante declared. "Get him out of here."

The FBI agents who came looking for Gigante after the April 7, 1972, mob murder of "Crazy Joe" Gallo encountered a far less menacing version of the Chin. Gallo was gunned down during an early-morning forty-third birthday celebration at Umbertos Clam House in Little Italy. Earlier in the night Gallo was partying with actor Jerry Orbach, who later played NYPD detective Lennie Briscoe on *Law & Order.*

The curtain came down on Gallo in a hail of bullets around 5 A.M. His new bride and stepdaughter watched in horror as the mortally wounded mobster staggered into the street and collapsed in an execution that was as stunning as it was dramatic. The killing happened just south of Gigante's kingdom, and two agents were dispatched to find the Chin and squeeze him for details.

The pair started at the Chelsea apartment door of Chin's brother Pasquale, who graciously invited the feds inside and answered a few questions. His brother Vincent, according to Pat, was suffering brain damage from old fight injuries. When the agents mentioned the Gallo hit, Pasquale replied that "it would be useless" to interview the Chin because "he did not appear to understand any of the recent publicity surrounding the killings."

And then, as if dropped from the sky, the Chin appeared, walking around the apartment in an apparent daze and ignoring the bewildered agents. The dumbfounded feds finished up with Pasquale and headed for the door, without even speaking a word to their intended target.

The agents noted in a subsequent report: *[Gigante] was obviously quite disturbed. No attempt was made to interview him under these conditions.*

Advantage, Chin—and Vincent Gigante held the upper hand in other ways. The feds were still staking out his home in the suburbs, long after he had relocated to the Village. An April 1972 report indicated that even in Chin's absence, floodlights on the property kept the house lit up like a "Christmas tree." While the FBI remained focused on New Jersey, the Genovese family was in turmoil on the other side of the river.

In the early-morning hours of July 16, 1972, there was a turnover in leadership for the family. The demotion of its boss was announced on a Brooklyn street in a hail of bullets.

It was around 1 A.M. when Genovese boss Tommy Eboli exited the Crown Heights apartment of his mistress. Driver Joseph Sternfeld held the car door open for his boss, but Eboli never made it inside.

A lone assassin was waiting inside the cab of a red-and-yellow truck, and he sprang into action at the sight of the mobster. His aim was true: Eboli took five bullets in the head. Blood poured from his wounds, red covering the gold crucifix hanging from his neck.

Sternfeld told cops that he dove for cover after the first shot, and never laid eyes on the killer—although later reports indicated he gave up the names of some possible suspects. The hotheaded Eboli was gone. The murder was never solved, with Genovese bigwig Frank "Funzi" Tieri and boss Carlo Gambino—reportedly irate over an unpaid debt—cited as the possible forces behind the hit.

In a telling sign, the upper echelon of the city's mobsters steered clear of his funeral.

Tommy James recalled getting the news at the Roulette offices. The place was in total chaos as Levy tried to figure out what this meant for business, and James tried to figure out exactly how his career had led to this bizarre moment.

"It happened six blocks from where I was playing in the Brooklyn Paramount Theater," said James. "They shot him all over the place. The night before he was killed, he had his arm around me, telling me how proud they were. This was not a guy prone to fits of sentimentality. It kind of put an exclamation point on things when he was hit the next night."

Long-retired Frank Costello enjoyed a bit of a last laugh when the FBI visited him two days after the shooting. He was back in his Central Park West apartment after a weekend at his Long Island summer home when agents came knocking to ask about Tommy Ryan's murder.

The perpetually cool Costello said he had only met Eboli twice, both times while out for dinner. The pair's paths hadn't crossed in about six years, he added. One agent asked about Eboli's role as the getaway driver and backup shooter for Gigante in the murder attempt of fifteen years earlier.

Costello advised that Gigante was acquitted of this charge and he never heard that Tommy Ryan had anything to do with the shooting, read an FBI summary of the conversation. *Costello advised that he does not know anything concerning the murder of Eboli and does not expect to hear anything.*

Eboli's removal seemed sudden, but it was actually a long time coming. His headstrong ways in the years after Vito Genovese's incarceration alienated many in the family. Eboli had once advocated removing many older Genovese members from the books in a cost-cutting move, sounding more like a bloodless CEO than the boss of a family. His position was regarded by many as disrespectful toward the old guard. Though he was the acting boss, Eboli was informed the incarcerated Genovese would have the final say-so on his ultimately rejected plan.

Father G. presided over the final send-off for his old Greenwich Village neighbor. A police surveillance attempt failed when their red station wagon broke down, leaving NYPD photographers stranded as mourners headed from a Queens funeral home to a cemetery in Paramus, New Jersey.

Eboli's bronze coffin was festooned with an arrangement of purple orchids and yellow roses. His widow, dressed in black, denounced the media coverage of her husband's execution.

"He was a very good man," she said through tears. "The newspapers filled him up with trash, and he didn't deserve it."

The death of his old manager accelerated the highly regarded Vincent Gigante's climb up the Genovese ladder. The *New York Times* even cited Chin and his brother Ralph as candidates to succeed Eboli, although Tieri was designated the likely front-runner.

With a typical touch of Genovese misdirection, the position actually went to Benny "Squint" Lombardo, who was content to let Tieri serve as the titular don and represent the family at meetings of the Mob's ruling commission. It was a lesson not lost on Vincent Gigante, who benefited from more than his boss' leadership lesson: the Chin was given control of the late Eboli's lucrative gambling interests on the West Side and in Lower Manhattan.

Lombardo pulled the family strings as Tieri, Carmine "Little Eli" Zeccardi and Tieri held the boss's seat before finally the old man turned things over to Fat Tony Salerno. Lombardo retired to Florida, where he died in April 1987.

While Gigante's role grew in prominence, the back-and-forth continued in the Jersey case—hanging over the Chin's head like the sword of Damocles. An informant, in a possible bit of disinformation, advised the FBI that Gigante "is going psycho and is undergoing treatment."

Another Mob insider said, "Chin's medical problems during recent months are all pretended, and he is putting on this act for reasons of his own." Yet, even the informant was perplexed by the scam, admitting he could envision "no logical reason for Chin putting on an act."

But it was Bergen County prosecutors who were losing their

minds as the case stretched into a third year. Assistant Prosecutor Charles Buckley finally offered Gigante a deal: plead guilty to a lesser count, with a sentence of no jail time and outpatient psychiatric treatment.

Gigante pondered his options while, among other legal and illegal pursuits, hobnobbing with guests attending a "large wedding followed by a magnificent reception," according to FBI surveillance.

The prosecution finally managed to get a second psychiatric sit-down with Vincent Gigante in August 1972, when Dr. Joseph Zigarelli of Paterson shared a typically twisted session with the mobster. Their meeting featured all the physical and mental hallmarks of the still-nascent act: Gigante appeared unshaven and with his hair a mess. He squinted at the doctor "with a perplexed facial expression."

With Vincent's mother sitting in the waiting room, Zigarelli began his questioning. Gigante's left leg shook, and his muttered answers came only after much hesitation.

"I ain't sick," he offered at one point.

"I came to see my doctor," Gigante announced later.

On several occasions the Chin stood up and tried to join his mother outside the office. Zigarelli was convinced that Gigante was the real deal. *The patient is not mentally competent and cannot adequately consult with his attorney in his own defense,* the psychiatrist wrote in a letter to prosecutors.

Gigante's new treating psychiatrist examined him yet again for the defense. The news, unsurprisingly, was even worse for prosecutors.

He was in no position to stand any trial, and it is doubtful he would ever be advanced enough mentally to do anything but lead the narrowed life he is leading at the present time, wrote Dr. Hugh McHugh, who remained blissfully unaware of the Chin's expansive exploits outside his office.

By August 1972 the case was crumbling. Defense attorney Joseph Greaney was angling for a dismissal; by now, one of the "bribed" cops was actually appointed the new police chief of Old Tappan in a very pointed rebuke of the prosecution.

Informants were almost simultaneously reporting Gigante had shown "no indication of emotional instability." Nevertheless, the FBI declared another hiatus in its investigation of the Chin; it would remain shut down until February 1973.

The legal wrangling ratcheted up that same month, when Greaney's motion to dismiss was shot down by the trial judge—but not before the defense lawyer doubled down on the insanity claim.

Gigante was "suffering from catatonic regression resulting in a return to infantile feelings and behavior," the attorney insisted. "He will never be well again. The last time I saw him, he didn't even know who I was. He will never get any better."

The defense lawyer noted the relatively minor case had dragged on for three years, with no end in sight. "If three years is not reasonable, what is?" he asked. "Is it five years? Or three years and three months?"

Accused co-conspirator Zupa's case had just finally gone to trial, with ex-chief Schuh brought in as the prosecution's star witness. His testimony was far more beneficial to the defense.

Yes, Gigante gave him Christmas cards with cash, but that was a common practice among local residents and businesspeople, the chief testified. No, he never considered the gifts to be a bribe, Schuh added under oath.

Zupa was acquitted of bribery on March 13 when a judge blasted the prosecution's moldering case as weak at best.

"The state has failed to prove a prima facie case against Mr. Zupa," announced superior court judge Thomas S. Dalton. As for Schuh, the judge was even more dismissive: "His testimony was so replete with contradictions, as not to be worthy of belief. It was not worthy of credibility."

Among those in the courtroom, hanging on every word, was attorney Greaney. An unidentified Genovese associate sat down with his FBI handler that same month to give his professional assessment of the Chin's mental health. It was detailed and damning, and left no doubt that Gigante was running a one-of-a-kind game.

According to the note summary: *[The informant] advised that he has made numerous observations of Vincent Gigante. . . . During these observations, [he] saw Gigante regularly acting in a normal manner. [He] stated that due to Gigante's normal behavior, he believes that Gigante's "mental problems" are largely inflated.*

[He] stated that he has observed Gigante carrying on conversations with other individuals, playing cards in a social club and conducting his normal routine unassisted. . . . As a result of his observations, he thinks that Gigante is in complete control of his faculties.

The memo never reached prosecutors or the judge. In early October the case against the Chin was dismissed because his mental condition was "deteriorating instead of improving." Charges against Olympia Gigante were dropped as well.

By now, all the cops were cleared as well by a judge, who proclaimed the cash was "something of a customary action at the time. I am satisfied there is nothing to indicate criminal involvement." A full 750 of the small town's 3,800 residents had signed a petition urging their reinstatement.

The "history-making" indictment ended with a thud, rather than the expected law enforcement triumph. Historian Bissett, years later, dismissed the whole thing as a bit of a fiasco.

"It really wasn't much when it all turned out," he said. "They shut down the whole police force, checked it all out, and it was nothing. It was a big thing for a very small town. But in the larger scheme of things, it was nothing. We still joke about it."

The FBI summed up Gigante's winning first act with an air of resignation: *Local prosecution against Gigante dropped due to ruling that subject mentally incapable of standing trial. Gigante continues to run his illegal activities from Greenwich Village.*

The Chin's lawyer and psychiatrists were already using the insanity ruling as a battering ram to drive off other inquiring prosecutors. In a January 4, 1973, missive to the Queens district attorney, McHugh said the Chin was in no shape to appear before an investigative grand jury: *[Gigante's] entire world [was] confined to the block where he lives and the church he attends regularly with his mother.*

Other investigators, despite determined efforts, had little to show for their Chin-chasing labors. A grand jury hearing allegations of a gambling operation run by Gigante and Alongi came up empty despite initial optimism. A probe into the fatal stabbings of two Village club owners produced nothing. The IRS probe was dying a slow, lingering death; it was finally scuttled in August 1974.

Chin and brother Mario were cited in a newspaper story as the moneymen behind a ring smuggling illegal cigarettes and fireworks into the city, but neither was ever charged. And a federal prosecutor asked for portions of testimony related to Chin's mental-health claim in Bergen County, mounting an unspecified case.

Still, nothing—other than a brief FBI memo that Gigante dodged the federal case "by using insanity as a defense."

There was also evidence that officials were underrating the kooky criminal. The NYPD, three months before the IRS case was dropped, ranked the powerful Genovese capo as a paltry number forty-four on its list of top "100 Public Morals Violators."

Weeks before, another FBI report said the Chin was intentionally "making himself scarce" – but federal agents apparently missed the memo. Gigante was front and center at the St. Anthony's Feast, an annual Village event that profited the local parish and the Genovese crime family. He appeared three times in six days to join in the June 1975 revelry, greeted and feted like a local celebrity, according to another FBI report.

"Vincent Gigante, who was clean shaven and cleanly dressed, appeared to be very bright and alert and was the center of attention among the group," stated an FBI undercover. His two bodyguards stood nearby, keeping the hoi polloi at bay. A trio of locals actually interrupted the FBI surveillance at the corner of Sullivan and Houston Streets, using a series of whistles to announce the federal presence.

The Chin was later spied casually sipping wine with two other men.

In addition to his Village crew, Gigante was now serving as Genovese point man for business dealings with other families. Among those who made the trip to visit the Chin inside the Triangle was Paul Vario, head of a notorious Lucchese family crew based in Brooklyn.

"Big Paulie," who stood six-three and weighed 250 pounds, occasionally traveled with an unknown young Mob wannabe from his neighborhood. The aspiring gangster's name was Henry Hill.

The 1970s

Hill was a kid born to the Mob, growing up opposite a Brooklyn taxi stand run by the Vario crew. He took instantly to organized crime, although his Irish father (despite a Sicilian mom) insured Henry would never become a made man. Hill nevertheless moved up quickly in the Lucchese ranks, aligned with another loyal Irish mobster, Jimmy "the Gent" Burke.

Though a low-level gangster, Hill was a bit of a "Zelig" among the Lucchese family, turning up in the middle of some major-league scams. He was part of the 1978 Lufthansa heist, which netted a stunning $5.8 million from Kennedy Airport. Hill was also involved in a college basketball point-shaving scandal involving Boston College in the 1978 through 1979 season. Hill also tagged along with his capo when Vario headed across the East River, twice a month, to see Gigante at the Triangle. The Chin had adopted the bizarre wardrobe that served as his business attire by now.

"Paulie was quite friendly with him," recalled Hill. "He was one of the bookmakers taking bets from Chin. It was hell getting paid from him. Paulie would bust his balls, and then they'd make arrangements for Paulie to get paid. Paulie would see him at least once every couple of weeks."

Vincent Gigante became aware of Hill when the young mobster was picked up in Nassau County with several Genovese members. Hill said it was immediately clear upon arrival on Sullivan Street that the Chin was absolutely the real deal when it came to La Cosa Nostra.

"He was a legend even then," recalled Hill. "He knew what the fuck he was doing. He didn't want the spotlight. And it was inevitable that you had to bring the Genoveses in on certain things because of who they were. You'd save a lot of grief by bringing them in from the beginning."

Hill was also aware of Gigante's already well-established prosecution dodge and the Chin's strange, bathrobed alter ego. But he had no doubts about which one was the real Gigante.

"He was a clown sometimes, but don't fuck with him," Hill recounted. "And don't fuck with anybody around him. He didn't care who you were. He knew what he was doing. He talked real sensible. Strangers would walk by him, looking, but he was already trying to fool the cops back then.

"He was a smart man, sure. That's why he lasted."

Hill didn't last as long in the ranks of organized crime, running afoul of his bosses by dealing cocaine. He famously turned federal informant in 1980, fearful that the greedy Burke intended to kill him in a bid to keep the entire Lufthansa haul for himself. His story eventually became grist for a best-selling book by Nick Pileggi and the classic Martin Scorsese movie *GoodFellas*.

Years later, Hill recalled his admiration for the way Gigante and the rest of the Genovese family took care of their business: "They were a powerful family, always were. They were quiet, not like the Gambinos, the Colombos, killing and fighting each other. There were guys running those operations, evolved into bosses—I can't believe it. Half-assed wiseguys, get a button, work their way up. It freaked me out."

The hard-living Hill, who died at age sixty-nine in 2012, recalled that Gigante's Achilles' heel was gambling. The Chin was a guy who loved the action, and Vario was just one of the mobbed-up bookies taking Vincent's action.

"He was betting with anybody who would take his bets, a real degenerate gambler," said Hill. "He'd have his good-luck spurts, but nobody is good at betting—it's a losing proposition. You get ahead a little bit, and then you go back."

As he rose through the ranks of the Genovese family, the Chin's luck turned. By the time he became head of the family, the card games among his colleagues inevitably ended with Vincent holding the winning hand. Every time.

"Biggest cheater I know," Genovese capo Federico "Fritzy" Giovanelli declared once during a bugged conversation. "Ya know, if he lived in the Wild West, he'd have to wear a bulletproof vest. That man never loses. What are you gonna do?"

In one oft-repeated tale from the Triangle, the cards were once distributed to the Genovese associates at the table. The Chin looked down at his hand, lifted his head and declared, "Gin." The other players silently tossed in their cards as he took the pot.

While the crazy Chin enjoyed his social club gambling success, brother Mario was dealt a bad hand. Mario was making his gambling money the old-fashioned way: taking illegal bets as part of a $50-million-a-year betting ring. It was a staggering amount of money in 1975. After a two-year probe Mario and twenty-four others were busted for running the ring that took bets in Manhattan, Queens and the Bronx.

Mario, forty-one, was now living in Yonkers, and was identified as the operation's kingpin. Newspapers reported that he was the brother of Louis Gigante, the South Bronx priest and city councilman.

Vincent emerged as one of the prime movers in the Mob's ban on drug money, a fast and lucrative business that was growing. Making good on his oft-stated opposition to slinging dope, the Chin became known throughout the underworld as the enforcer behind the Mob's antidrug effort. The penalty, as promised, was a death sentence from Judge Chin and his thug jurors. Their preferred method of dispatching the guilty was tossing them off a roof.

The ever-vigilant Chin was similarly merciless to those he deemed rats or violators of the Mob oath. He instituted a rule that no one in his family was permitted to utter his name—or even his nickname. The ban was later extended to the other

four New York crime families, with the same penalty for breaking the law: execution.

Gigante's home base was now firmly established inside the
Triangle, a "social club" with a decidedly antisocial look. The
storefront at 208 Sullivan Street had its front windows blacked
out. The front door, with an air conditioner just above the entrance, was similarly impenetrable to outsiders.

It was a Spartan twenty-foot-by-twenty-foot space, about ten
feet high with a metal ceiling and a tile floor. A mural on one wall
showed a French village, complete with local cafés and a park.

Two pinball tables stood inside to the right of the front door,
while a small bar with a coffeemaker was installed to the left. A
sign, hung on one wall, declared: MEMBERS ONLY. Another, placed
carefully above its pay phone, was a vintage World War II sign
with an eternal message: LOOSE LIPS SINK SHIPS. It was accompanied by a drawing of a boat going nose down into the water.

The walls held other cautionary bromides: THE ENEMY IS LIS-
TENING and TOUGH GUYS DON'T SQUEAL. A fourth sign carried a
simple and direct warning: DON'T TALK. THIS PLACE IS BUGGED.

On the off chance that his colleagues didn't read the signs,
Vincent had the club swept for bugs on a monthly basis. And
with good reason: The club's telephone was first bugged in October 1966 as part of a probe into gambling and extortion. The
feds sought information on Gigante and his brothers—or at
least the three who were not saying Sunday Mass.

The sixty-day tap of the former Italian restaurant produced
zilch, an early indicator of the Chin's savvy when it came to electronic surveillance. The NYPD and FBI somewhat routinely
repeated the process with the same results: Bug, wash, repeat.
Nothing of much use was ever recorded or played for a jury.

One of the Chin's shrinks, in a 1982 evaluation, generously
described the dingy outpost as a "small café," where Gigante
would "play pinball, which was his life." A side door allowed access to an adjoining apartment building, where particularly sen-
sitive Mob business was discussed.

There was a toilet in the rear and three tables. One held a police scanner near the rear of the club, behind a long, rectangular table about ten feet inside. In the far rear, near the bathroom, sat the circular table where Gigante engaged in his endless card games as a cadre of trusted underlings floated in and out.

Gigante's associates occasionally complained about the lack of heat inside, particularly when forced to hang out with the Chin into the wee hours of the morning.

The club's daily routine began around seven in the morning, when a gray-haired gent arrived alone and opened the doors. Genovese regulars would begin arriving within five minutes. One was typically designated to take the club's guard dog for a stroll. Traffic would continue throughout the day.

Vincent thrived in the dour environment, even as his crazy act continued to bear legal fruit. When Queens prosecutors subpoenaed him in the threatened murder of a businessman fighting off Mob infiltration, his attorney responded that the strain of testifying "might affect him mentally and physically." He was subsequently never called to appear.

There was another trip to St. Vincent's in May 1975, which was the first year Chin crossed paths with young Sammy "the Bull" Gravano. The Gambino underling accompanied his capo, Salvatore "Toddo" Aurello, to a business meeting at the Triangle.

The Chin agreed to reach out to a fellow Genovese capo to straighten out a construction business issue. He took time during the meeting to share a bit of family gossip: One of his colleagues was recently promoted from capo to consigliere. The impressed Gravano, after laying eyes on Gigante for the first time, departed with the conviction that the Chin was the complete opposite of crazy.

Those who encountered the Chin on the streets outside the club saw a different man, as detailed in a February 1977 federal document—the FBI's first written account of Gigante's deranged alter ego: *Source stated that Gigante is rarely seen on the streets, but when he is seen, it is often in such a capacity as playing a "crazy man routine." Source stated that one time, Gigante was seen walking down*

Sullivan Street unshaven and waving a chair like a madman. Source believes this is an act by Gigante to enhance his reputation as being mean so people will jump when he tells them to do something.

The shortsighted report failed to mention how the act was by now a reliable stay-out-of-jail card—another guaranteed victory for Vincent Gigante.

At the same time the Chin was handling the Genovese side of the "Concrete Club," an extraordinary operation involving four of the five families. The group cooperated on a bid-rigging scam, where only certain companies received jobs worth more than $2 million in the five boroughs. In return, the "winning" bidders provided a 2 percent kickback to the Mob.

The Genovese family was flush throughout the decade; Salerno had an estimated $80 million on the streets in the 1970s, according to a 1983 U.S. Senate report.

Further indication of the Genovese penchant for secrecy at its highest levels was illustrated in an NYPD report that same year listing the retired Lombardo as the family boss. By then, Salerno had taken over and departed, ceding his spot to the Chin.

In one of the most stunning efforts in the history of law enforcement, Agent Joe Pistone infiltrated the Bonanno family in the late 1970s, risking his life for six years as an undercover. Even observing from a distance, the FBI agent knew the Chin was held in high esteem throughout the underworld. He laughed out loud when asked about the Chin's Sullivan Street theatrics.

"The wiseguys knew he wasn't crazy," said Pistone. "I heard guys comment what a great act it was. Everybody knew it was an act. Unless you're doing business with another family, there's usually not much conversation about the other families. But when I say *everybody*, I mean all the wiseguys knew it was an act."

Mobster Phil Leonetti said the Chin's strange double life was simply accepted as part of the day-to-day business. Nobody said a word.

"Everyone knew it was fake, but nobody said nothin' about it," he explained. "What's somebody going to do, go up and bust the Chin's balls about it?"

CHAPTER 8

LICENSE TO KILL

*T*HE 1980S ARRIVED IN THE CITY OF BROTHERLY LOVE WITH A savage and unexpected spasm of violence. For more than two decades Angelo Bruno oversaw the Mafia family based in Philadelphia with a firm hand and a low-key persona, which earned him an atypical organized nom de crime: "The Docile Don." He took over in 1959, eventually becoming the longest-serving boss in the city's history.

Bruno was widely considered a good businessman who expanded the family's financial interests. This was particularly true when casino gambling came to New Jersey in 1976, when he grabbed a piece of the lucrative construction work.

His preference for settling disputes was mediation over murder, and Bruno was an absolute stand-up guy: He did two years after refusing to testify before a grand jury investigating corruption in Atlantic City in 1970. His ties to the Genovese family went back decades, including a March 1963 summons for a meeting with then-acting boss Eboli.

By the time the '80s arrived, Bruno's laid-back style—and his reticence to approve drug dealing—created friction among the new generation of gangsters, led by Bruno's treacherous consigliere, Antonio "Tony Bananas" Caponigro.

The sixty-nine-year-old Bruno, with his driver John Stanfa, was sitting in a car outside his home in a predominantly Italian-

American neighborhood of South Philly on the night of March 21, 1980, when the bloody coup began. Two shotgun-wielding killers, one of them Caponigro, blasted away at the vehicle before disappearing into the darkness.

"The Docile Don" was dispatched in brutal style—his twenty-one-year reign ended. Stanfa survived the hit. The people deemed responsible would not. Bruno was buried after a Funeral Mass at a local church.

"Angelo had money, fame and power, and he had hundreds of loyal family and friends," said priest John Dieckman in his eulogy. "Yet none of those were protection against the fate that awaits every man and woman."

As it turned out, the Philly unrest actually began at the other end of the Turnpike, with the Genovese family in New York City. Chin Gigante, his power and prestige growing, would emerge as the kingmaker of the Philadelphia Mob. The Bruno assassination was eventually exposed as a carefully arranged double cross by Gigante and the rest of his family.

"For the record, the Genovese family had manipulated a Philadelphia family member, Tony Bananas, to murder Bruno," said Gravano. "Right away, there was a commission meeting, and to cover themselves the Genovese people volunteered to track down Angelo Bruno's killer."

The move assured the Genovese power grab, but also gave Vincent Gigante a chance to flex his muscles against the cabal of killers. Murder of a boss without approval from the Mob's ruling commission was the highest of the secret society's inviolable rules—and a pet peeve of the Chin.

"When Ang was killed, Chin made it clear to everyone in La Cosa Nostra, the whole country, you can't kill a boss without permission," said Leonetti, whose Atlantic City crew reported to the Philly family.

The setup started in the summer of 1979, when Caponigro approached Funzi Tieri to propose Bruno's brutal murder. The two had a history; they were on opposing sides of a previous beef over a bookie operation that each claimed as his own. The dispute went before the commission, and Caponigro was declared the winner.

Nursing a grudge, Tieri decided this was the time to show that bygones were *not* bygones. Funzi indicated the Bruno hit was okay with New York, but never brought the plot before the heads of the other four families. The result: the Bruno murder, unknown to Caponigro, was an unsanctioned killing.

Gigante informed the other families that the Genoveses would handle the bloody payback—done with their full knowledge. The Philadelphia regime change was a huge boost to the Genovese coffers: their pal in the Philly Mob, Nicodemo "Little Nicky" Scarfo of Atlantic City, would grab control of the unions once belonging to Bruno.

The Genovese family would also now carry the Philadelphia vote when their family was brought in for commission business. Plus Tony Banana's lucrative North Jersey gambling and loan-sharking operations, worth millions of dollars, would fall into Genovese control. It was a clean sweep—unless your last name was Caponigro.

The Philly mobster reached out to Salerno in the aftermath of the murder, but Fat Tony made it clear that Caponigro's future as the new boss was not his call.

"I do not want to get involved," Salerno declared. "I do not want to hear about it. Go see Chin."

He would. It was the last trip he made while still breathing.

Tony Bananas and his brother-in-law, Alfred "Freddie" Salerno, were summoned for an April 18 sit-down in the Triangle with the Chin. They came expecting a coronation, only to arrive for their own executions.

Vincent Gigante was seated at a table in the cramped social club, where he was joined by Fat Tony Salerno—no relation—top capo Bobby Manna and the duplicitous Tieri. Caponigro immediately recounted his conversation with Tieri, where he was told the hit was approved by the New York bosses.

Tieri looked the Philly gangster in the eye: "I told you to straighten it out, not to kill him."

Hearing those words, the two out-of-town mobsters knew they were beyond their depth. Gigante made sure the two plotters were subjected to a brutal, slow and sadistic death.

Caponigro, sixty-seven, was shot fourteen times with five different guns. The first shots went into his elbows and arms, to keep him alive and suffering as the relentless assault continued. He was stabbed repeatedly, and savagely beaten. Salerno, sixty-four, suffered a similarly grisly fate.

Both of the tortured men were stripped naked, with $20 bills stuffed in their mouths and up their asses as a graphic reminder of their greed. The bodies were eventually discovered in the trunks of two abandoned cars left in the South Bronx.

But the Chin wasn't done avenging the Docile Don in venomous style.

The body of plotter John "Johnny Keys" Simone, sixty-nine, was found near a Staten Island landfill on September 18, 1980. The hit was proposed by Gigante, approved by the commission and assigned to Gravano. Before a single bullet from a .357 Magnum was pumped into his skull, the doomed man unleashed his fury against Vincent.

"[Simone told] how he now knows it was the greed of the Genovese family," Gravano recalled. "How the Chin—Vincent Gigante—had conned this Tony Bananas that the commission sanctioned the hit on Bruno. How the Chin conned the commission by volunteering to do an investigation and take out Tony."

Simone had two final requests: He wanted to be shot by a made man. And he wanted to take off his shoes. Gravano complied with both.

There was one more body: Frank Sindone, fifty-two, was discovered behind a Philadelphia variety store, stuffed inside two green plastic garbage bags. Sindone, shot three times in the head and found on October 30, was the last of the Caponigro crew to die. Leonetti was both impressed and appalled by what happened.

"They had set it all up, and now they want everyone who had a hand in it to be killed," said Scarfo's nephew. "That's how treacherous they were."

The Chin would also pick Bruno's successor. He was leaning toward the murderous Scarfo, who had done time with Manna in the early 1970s after both refused to testify in a New Jersey Mob probe. Scarfo demurred, preferring to take the consigliere spot. Aging mobster Philip Testa was installed, instead, by Gigante as the new head of the Philadelphia family.

"My uncle was very close to Phil Testa, who was the underboss, and my uncle told Chin, 'I think it should be Phil Testa,'" Leonetti recounted. "I think the Chin respected that, because my uncle respected the rules of La Cosa Nostra like he did."

Testa was now the boss. His reign was short and ended horrifically.

On March 15, 1981, the mobster known as "the Chicken Man" doubled-parked his year-old Chevy on the street outside his South Philly home. Testa was fumbling with his house keys when a massive bomb detonated on the front porch. His front door was blown thirty feet inside the house, with its doorknob finally coming to rest in its kitchen.

The explosive device was packed with thirteen sticks of dynamite, carpenter's nails and shotgun pellets. The results were beyond gruesome. "He looked like he went through a paper shredder," noted one local cop.

Carrying $10,000 cash in his pocket, Testa was pronounced dead two hours after the 2:55 A.M. blast. An internecine Mob war was blamed for the killing. And, once again, it was Gigante who would reassemble pieces of the shattered Philadelphia family.

If Chin's role in resolving the Bruno murder was in some part personal, his handling of the Testa hit was all business. Testa's underboss, Pete Casella, was summoned north to meet with Gigante at the Triangle, like Caponigro before him.

Gigante, in his bathrobe, cut quickly to the chase. Casella admitted his part in the murder plot, but the Chin spared his life. He banished the underboss to Florida and spit at the disgraced *amico nostro* on his way out onto Sullivan Street.

Scarfo witnessed the whole thing. He was now alone inside the Triangle, face-to-face with the Chin.

"Well, Nick, I don't see no one else in here," Gigante finally declared. "I guess that makes you the new boss."

Scarfo planted a pair of kisses on Gigante's stubbled cheeks to become the new head of the Philadelphia family. They would be aligned now for good with the people who put them in charge, the Genoveses.

Not everyone involved in the Testa hit was as fortunate as Casella, who died in Florida at age seventy-six. The Chin signed off on Scarfo's plan to whack two of the banished gangster's sidekicks.

Co-conspirator Frank "Chickie" Narducci, forty-nine, died in a January 7, 1982, hail of bullets in an ambush while exiting his car on South Broad Street. And Rocco Marinucci, who allegedly built and detonated the devastating bomb, was found dead in a Philadelphia parking lot. He was shot in the head, neck and chest. The message of his role in the hit was made clear by the killers: three unexploded firecrackers were stuck inside his mouth.

"Now my uncle didn't respect anybody," said Leonetti. "But he respected Chin, and Chin respected my uncle, because he knew my uncle was a no-nonsense guy and that my uncle was a real gangster like him."

Though he was loyal to the Chin, Nicodemo Scarfo proved to be disastrous. The new boss emerged as a killing machine, ordering murder upon murder during a truly insane reign atop the family. Law enforcement attention inevitably followed the trail of bodies, and Scarfo just as inevitably wound up in prison as his family fell apart.

Even worse, his reckless behavior—often in direct contradiction of the "Mob rules" that he so often cited—turned his nephew against Little Nicky. "Crazy Phil" became a devastating FBI informant, as the Chin would learn down the road.

The bloodletting, while the impetus for the Philadelphia Mob's disintegration, became songwriting fodder for others.

The Bruno murder inspired a Philadelphia-based band, Marah, to give the Docile Don a shout-out in their song "Christian Street." More memorably, the Testa assassination led Bruce Springsteen to open his "Atlantic City" with a terse summary of the murder: *Well, they blew up the Chicken Man in Philly last night/ And they blew up his house, too.*

CHAPTER 9

GOTTA SERVE SOMEBODY

*B*Y THE TIME OF THE TESTA bloodletting, THE CHIN HAD VERY quietly settled into the top spot with the Genovese family.

While the ceremony for Mob induction is fraught with symbolism—drops of blood, burning saints, vows of silence and eternal allegiance—Vincent Gigante's installation as head of the family occurred against a backdrop of bedpans and heart monitors.

In 1981 the cigar-chomping Anthony Salerno was felled by a stroke. As he recuperated at New York University Hospital, a trio of top Genovese leaders arrived for a visit: Gigante, underboss Saverio "Sammy Black" Santora and consigliere-in-waiting Manna. Oddly enough, an ailing Lombardo was recovering in the same hospital at the time.

A decision was reached at the bedside summit: The two older dons would step aside to let the Chin take command of the family. In Mob parlance Salerno was "pulled down." And Vito Genovese's Greenwich Village protégé, nearly two decades after the old man's death, would finally follow him into the family's top spot.

Gigante assigned Genovese soldier Vincent "Fish" Cafaro to serve as Salerno's right-hand man in an effort to both ease the transition—and give the Chin eyes on the outgoing boss.

In his first directive as the new don, the Chin ordered Cafaro to keep word of the change to himself—even within the Genovese family. Fat Tony Salerno would continue to stand as the public face of the family, handling commission meetings and drawing the heat from an increasing number of federal investigators.

"Gigante allowed Fat Tony to continue to front as the boss, letting the other families believe . . . that Fat Tony still controlled our *brugad* (family or borgata)," said Cafaro. "In fact, Fat Tony conferred with Chin on any major matters affecting the family."

But Vincent Gigante was now unquestionably the man. His reign would stretch into the new millennium.

He did leak word of his promotion to one family: the Gambinos, headed by the equally powerful boss Paul Castellano. The Brooklyn-born Mafioso was a businessman, too, and made a fortune from a wholesale meat business. He was widely considered a Mob success story after taking the chair when Carlo Gambino died of natural causes in 1976.

Castellano had a family tie: His sister was Gambino's wife. But there was no doubting his Mob pedigree: The six-two "Big Paul" was among the youngest attendees at the ill-fated 1957 Apalachin Mob meeting. And while he preferred peaceable settlements of Mob business, he embraced a more violent approach when necessary.

He was eventually linked to twenty-five murders as boss, including an order to murder his son-in-law after learning his daughter, Connie, was a victim of domestic abuse. The Castellano-approved divorce left Frank Amato's remains chopped up and tossed into the Atlantic.

Salerno left the hospital and returned to his farm near Morris Levy's place in Ghent. Once he felt good enough to go back to work at his Palma Boys Social Club in East Harlem, Fat Tony made sure to check with the new boss about his plans.

"I spoke to Gigante, and told him of Salerno's desire to return," said Cafaro. "Gigante told me Salerno could return after a few months, but added if Salerno was approached about anything 'serious' on his return, 'I want to know about it.' "

The Chin was now running a powerful family with tentacles

throughout the city and much of North New Jersey. There were fourteen Genovese capos, with about four hundred soldiers working for them. And he ran a tight ship: each soldier was required to check in with his captain at least once a week, and to hand over 10 percent of their earnings.

The family controlled a number of important unions, giving them power throughout the construction, shipping and concrete industries. Through capo Matty "the Horse" Ianniello, the Genoveses operated with impunity in the garbage industry. The family ran the waterfront in Manhattan and the Garden State, and made a fortune through their gambling operations.

Cafaro, for example, had seventy-two men running numbers and taking sports bets in East Harlem. He estimated taking about $80,000 a day in action, and personally cleared about $2 million in a good year.

Gigante's cold-blooded approach to Mob management wasn't limited to the streets of Philadelphia. The Chin ordered a pair of local hits around the same time: the murder of Genovese soldier Gerry Pappa, whacked in 1980 for the unauthorized murder of two Colombo made men, and the assassination of Nat Masselli, identified as a snitch in 1982.

The process in the Masselli killing was simple, and took mere days between proposal and execution.

A Genovese soldier, Philly Buono, arranged a meeting with Genovese underboss Saverio "Sammy Black" Santora. When Santora arrived, he was handed a piece of paper inscribed with a single name: *Nat Masselli*.

"No good," said Buono. "He's a rat."

"Could this kid hurt you?" asked Santora.

"Yeah," said Buono. "I did a few things with this kid."

"I am going to go down and see 'the Skinny Guy' (Manna) and the Chin," said Santora, promising an answer within twenty-four hours.

Masselli was the son of another Genovese loyalist, Pellegrino "Butcher Boy" Masselli. But his lineage was no help in this case.

Chin approved Buono's request, and Santora headed back to East Harlem with word that the hit was approved.

On August 25, 1982, Nat Masselli was found shot to death behind the wheel of his Lincoln Continental in the north Bronx, near Van Cortlandt Park. A single bullet from a .38-caliber handgun was fired point-blank into the back of his head in classic Mob execution style.

As it turned out, he was cooperating with Special Prosecutor Leon Silverman's investigation of Secretary of Labor Raymond Donovan. So was his dad, which explains why his family ties failed to win him a pass.

The Pappa hit was a case of murder as Mob business. He was suspected of killing Tommy "Shorty" Spero who went "missing" in 1980. Spero, a made member of the Colombo family, had actually recruited Gravano into the world of organized crime in 1968—although the Bull eventually landed with the Gambinos.

For Pappa, it was an opportunity to turn a quick profit. Spero was exacting payoffs or just straight robbing Brooklyn drug dealers, who in turn approached Pappa looking for a solution to their problem. Pappa took a $500,000 killing fee, and then whacked Spero.

With the help of two obscure Genovese associates, Peter "Petey" Savino and Bobby Ferenga, he buried the body in a brick warehouse on a grimy stretch of Brooklyn. Savino, also known as "Black Pete," suggested the spot; he owned the building, which was undergoing renovation. The newly poured concrete would insure Shorty Spero spent eternal rest beneath the ramp outside a loading dock, wrapped in a sleeping bag with his feet pointing toward the entrance.

Except that it didn't. And it was Savino, along with Ferenga, who would recount what happened in the most pivotal moment of Vincent Gigante's decades in organized crime—one where he wasn't even in the same borough, or aware of what was going down.

Pappa, a ferocious Genovese hit man known to his wife as "Pappa Bear," became an instant suspect in the Spero killing.

The Chin, approached by the Colombo family, signed off on his murder—even after assuring the thirty-six-year-old gangster that he was safe. The two met at a Manhattan restaurant, where Gigante questioned Pappa about Spero's "disappearance."

The Chin appeared satisfied with the answers. In truth, he was not.

On July 10, 1980, two killers carrying shotguns walked into the Villa 66 restaurant, one of Pappa's favorite hangouts for the last sixteen years. The Brooklyn eatery was owned by Tieri, who was awaiting trial for racketeering and did not appreciate the extra aggravation caused by Spero's death.

The killers arrived at 11 A.M., twenty minutes before Pappa rolled in for a late breakfast. The lone woman behind the counter was handcuffed to a sink as the gunmen waited. Pappa didn't even have time to order his eggs before the shooters delivered a serving of lead.

The employee heard five blasts before one of the two killers told her the cops would arrive soon enough to turn her loose.

His decisive and callous style only enhanced the new Genovese boss's reputation inside and outside the city. Angelo "Big Ange" Lonardo, head of the Cleveland family, recalled that word of the Chin's steady ascension was known among the Mob cognoscenti.

"In the early '80s, I knew Salerno to be the boss of the Genovese family, and I also knew that Vincent Gigante was the consigliere and was being groomed to be the boss," he recalled. The Chin also represented the concerns of the Cleveland and Chicago families on the commission, giving his family the loudest voice on the ruling panel.

The Chin's ascension coincided with the departure of one of the family's oldest hands: Frank Tieri, his partner in the Colombo hit and Pappa's death. The Funziola died in 1981 of natural causes, ending his run as the original "Teflon Don." The seventy-seven-year-old Tieri beat nine cases, and passed away before spending a day in jail after his racketeering conviction.

*   *   *

Among the most profitable businesses inherited by the new boss was the Genovese family's widespread interest on the New Jersey waterfront. One report indicated the Chin himself pulled in $2 million a year from the family's control of the docks and its unions.

It was during the 1960s, around the time of the Summer of Love, that the city's two most powerful Mob families found peace in a deal over the docks—one of the most important jewels in their crooked fiefdom.

Anthony Scotto, a politically connected union official who was friendly with Senator Robert F. Kennedy and Mayor John V. Lindsay, represented the Gambinos. George Barone, a cold-blooded killer associated with Fat Tony's Harlem crew, stood up for the Genovese family.

The two men were the perfect emissaries, serving as both union officials and organized crime veterans. The pair divided the New Jersey and the city docks evenly: Brooklyn and Staten Island to the Gambinos, the Garden State and Manhattan to the Genoveses.

The negotiations, as Barone recalled years later, were quite civil. The Genovese rep didn't even need to spring for the $24 that Peter Minuit paid for Manhattan. A bothersome Mob war was avoided, along with the accompanying investigation and bad press. Everyone was happy, and about to get happier—not to mention wealthier.

"Anthony Scotto sat down and discussed it [with me] and finalized it, and it came into effect," he said. "Anthony Scotto and I . . . came to an agreement that was the way it would be, and I reported that fact to Mr. Tony Salerno."

Control of the docks came with control of the International Longshoremen's Union's various locals. It was a momentous decision that allowed the Genovese family to turn the Jersey unions and docks into their personal piggy banks. A Mob tax was imposed on virtually every item passing through the port, resulting in higher prices for U.S. consumers—and bigger profits for the Chin's family.

Under Gigante, the family's grip on the Garden State side of the Hudson grew ironclad. Unions fell completely under the sway of organized crime, with the presidents of some locals dispatched with a bullet rather than a ballot.

There were tales of union workers told to open Christmas Club accounts, typically set up to insure the working class had a little extra cash to buy presents before December 25 rolled around. The money, instead, went to the Genovese family. It was the Cratchits kicking up to Ebenezer Scrooge.

"They had the waterfront sewn up," said Leonetti. "Chin had it all."

The crime family's tentacles dominated three International Longshoremen's Association locals: 1588, 1804-1 and 1235. Waterfront monitor Tom Gallagher recalled the days when Chin's underlings Venero "Benny Eggs" Mangano and sidekick John "Johnny Sausage" Barbato, whose aliases conjured up visions of a Jersey diner, collected a flat $25 for every container unloaded. The methods evolved, but the result was inevitably the same: the cost was passed along to the public and the profits to the Genovese hierarchy.

"Somebody pays for it, and it's always the customer," said former NYPD commissioner Robert McGuire, who was summoned in the new millennium to clean up 1588.

Leonetti recalled the Chin rather effortlessly arranging a huge favor for a restaurateur under the thumb of the Philadelphia Mob.

"We had a friend who had a restaurant with us, we controlled him," Leonetti recounted. "It was called the Deptford Tavern and it was right outside Philadelphia. We got him an appointment with somebody connected to Chin where he could buy food and fish cheap direct from the waterfront, no middleman.

"Our guy had to drive up there at three A.M., and he told 'em whatever he needed—fish, meats, whatever. He paid 'em, and they delivered. Everybody was happy."

Local 1804-1 was founded by Barone, and 1235 was run for more than three decades by Michael "Mikey Cigars" Coppola—

even after he became a suspect in a 1977 murder and went on the lam. He was linked nearly thirty years later to the killing of former local business agent Larry Ricci, a Genovese capo who disappeared in the middle of a federal trial. His body was found in the trunk of a car parked at the Huck Finn Diner in Westfield, New Jersey.

Bayonne-based Local 1588 offered the full package of organized crime corruption inside a single building on Kennedy Boulevard. Kickbacks, extortion and fraud were as regular as an annual Labor Day picnic at the lucrative Genovese outpost, where the ornate front windows were etched with an anchor and rope motif—the better to keep anyone from peering inside.

In 1954, when Marlon Brando was starring in the Oscar-winning *On the Waterfront,* a delegate from the local was already under investigation for receiving kickbacks from the rank and file. A half century later, the union leadership was accused of running things the same way—demanding cash in return for promotions, overtime and job training.

Union members were also forced to buy $500 tickets to the annual Christmas party, and then ordered to stay home unless personally invited.

John DiGilio—a former boxer turned mobster, like the Chin—was installed at the local in the mid-1970s. "He was a big moneymaker for the Genovese family," recalled Lawrence Lezak of the Waterfront Commission.

He was also a flamboyant, unrepentant gangster who once punched out a codefendant in the hallways of a federal courthouse. DiGilio liked to run his mouth, too; a federal wiretap caught him boasting, "Bayonne is mine."

DiGilio's style was seriously rubbing the crime family's leadership the wrong way by late May 1988. Unlike his boss Gigante, DiGilio seemed to relish the media attention that came with his position. It was a fatal flaw.

A Genovese hit man blasted five shots into the back of DiGilio's head in a murder so grisly that the killer was left to clean blood and pieces of teeth from the interior of the Lincoln Continental where the hit took place. The victim was later fished out of the Hackensack River.

His replacement atop the 440-member union was Genovese associate Joseph Lore, who had once threatened to take a blowtorch to a fellow mobster's testicles.

Despite Vincent Gigante's rising profile and expanding influence, the feds were no closer to putting handcuffs on the Chin in the early 1980s than the flummoxed Bergen County prosecutors a decade earlier. Gigante's visits to St. Vincent's had evolved into an annual getaway – a demented version of a week in the Hamptons.

He was prescribed medications to treat his "illness," but once the nurses left, he slipped the pills under his tongue and spit them out. Gigante, as usual, signed himself in, and signed himself back out when he felt the time was right.

Gigante arrived for a short stay on March 9, 1982. The next year he checked himself in on April 20. He stopped back in, yet again, on May 7, 1983. In each case Gigante showed the same symptoms, received the usual treatment and headed back to the Village.

There was one difference: The FBI was now waiting outside, along with the Chin's driver. Within hours of his departure on May 23, 1983, Gigante was back in the company of Dominick "Baldy Dom" Canterino, Frank Condo, Vito Palmieri (the Chin's driver) and other Genovese associates. It was like a trip to Lourdes, and then it was business as usual. As was a 1983 meeting with an up-and-coming Colombo capo who became a moneymaking Mob machine before his thirty-fifth birthday.

The 1980s

In 2014, on a fall weekend morning in New Jersey, Michael Franzese shook hands with a steady stream of guests inside an industrial park in tiny Totowa, a town where the dead (one hundred thousand in five cemeteries) outnumbered the living (ten thousand residents).

Franzese was dressed casually but neatly, with a fashionable hint of stubble. He was here to show his new movie, *From Godfather to God The Father,* a tale of redemption that the born-again Colombo capo hoped would save a few souls.

Things were far different three decades earlier, in the 1980s, when Franzese, conspiring with the Russian Mob, conjured a massive scam to circumvent federal and state taxes by peddling bootleg gasoline in several states. His personal take in the rip-off was estimated at somewhere in the area of $2 million a week, and his rise through the family ranks was meteoric.

By one account, he became the Mafia's most prolific earner since Al Capone. Franzese drove a Cadillac El Dorado, took to the seas in a yacht and flew through the skies on a private jet. He even opened a Florida moviemaking business, Miami Gold.

A 1986 *Fortune* magazine piece ranked Franzese at number eighteen on its list of the nation's fifty biggest Mafia bosses. On the other hand, they listed the long-deposed Salerno at number one, while slotting the Chin one spot behind Franzese at number nineteen.

Franzese came with an impeccable Mob pedigree: The gangster's dad was the legendary Sonny Franzese, who adopted the boy as an infant and raised the child as his own. In an oft-repeated bit of lore, Sonny was behind bars in 1974 when he heard that a Colombo soldier was hitting on his wife. The body of suitor Carmine Scialo was found buried in a cellar, a garrote around his neck and his severed genitals stuffed in his mouth.

The elder Franzese, who was a pal of Roulette Records' McCalla, hoped his boy would become a doctor. Instead, Michael followed him directly into the family business. His skills at making huge amounts of cash soon earned the younger Franzese a true 1980s nickname: "the Yuppie Don."

His dad was an old-school guy, with a standing reservation at the Copacabana in Manhattan. Guests at his table included Sammy Davis Jr. and Bobby Darin. Michael became a made man in the 1970s, and he quickly ascended through the ranks to become a captain.

It was the gasoline scam that led Gigante to reach out for Franzese. Genovese capo Fritzy Giovanelli, one of the Chin's most trusted capos, was dispatched to arrange the sit-down.

"Every family wanted a piece of the gas business," Franzese recounted. "When I first realized what I had in 1978, 1979, I told [Colombo boss] 'Junior' Persico that I would show him more money than he had ever seen before."

Other families, including the Gambinos and the Luccheses, made efforts to muscle their way into the illicit gas operation, so Franzese was unsure what to make of this summons to Sullivan Street.

"The word among all of us was that no one—made guy or not—was allowed to meet with Chin, unless he sent for you, or someone who he trusted very much would first vouch for you, qualify the reason for you to meet, and then be there when you met," said Franzese.

"In my case Chin asked to meet with me. Fritzy told me Chin wanted to meet with me about the gas business."

From the rip-off's inception, Franzese was insistent that the profits should remain for the Colombos only. He braced himself for an overture from the Chin, angling for a slice of the lucrative petroleum pie.

He was instead pleasantly surprised. Gigante, as befitting an elder statesman, wanted only to meet with the rising star and offer any needed assistance for the operation. He was more father figure than cutthroat boss to the up-and-coming gangster.

"Chin did not try to grab a piece from me," Franzese recounted. "In fact, he told me if anyone bothered me, to let him know and he would help. I believe we would have done business eventually, but we were both having issues at the time and it was best not for us to be seen together."

Franzese recalled several subsequent meetings, all at the Chin's request and all down in the Village. Whenever Gigante called, he always found time to answer.

"My father told me early on that Chin was the real power behind the Genovese family," he recounted. "In general, that was the word on the street. My dad was happy when Chin asked me to meet with him, and told me to stay close to him.

"My personal conversations with Chin were all good. I know he commanded a load of respect on the street. I knew he was feared. I know how he treated me. I believed him to be a very good boss."

Franzese also knew the Genovese boss to be absolutely lucid and deeply involved with his family's business, although he couldn't help but notice Gigante's robe and slippers.

"A dapper dresser, he was not," said an admiring Franzese. "However, I always said that in order to play crazy so well for so long, and at the same time run a very powerful operation with pretty much of an iron fist, you had to be a bit crazy—no other way to pull that off, in my view. I know I couldn't have done it."

Franzese insisted that he never knew Chin or the Genovese family to handle any of the drug trade. The Colombo capo also knew enough to make sure he kept his mouth shut about any dealings with Gigante—or even mentioned his name.

"For sure," said Franzese. "We knew he was serious about it. To me, that was very smart. More guys got into trouble, with names being dropped on surveillance equipment, than you can imagine. Chin was smart in that regard."

Franzese left the Mob behind in 1989, signing a cooperation agreement with the feds. With the help of his wife, he improbably turned to God and launched a new career, where he often referred to his old one as a tale of redemption.

His name would later surface as a potential witness against the Chin, although he never took the stand against Gigante.

CHAPTER 10

ALL ALONG THE WATCHTOWER

*T*HE FEDERAL FOCUS ON CHIN AND HIS FAMILY HEIGHTENED IN 1983, with each of the five New York families assigned a specific team of FBI and NYPD investigators responsible for identifying the top players and gathering evidence to bring down the bosses.

John Pritchard, a native New Yorker who launched his law enforcement career with the NYPD in 1965, led the law enforcement team focusing on the Genoveses. Within six years as a cop he was named to the Major Case Squad, an elite crew of detectives. He moved to the FBI as a special agent in 1976, and became head of the joint NYPD-FBI team chasing the Chin.

"What happened was the FBI thought if we created a squad for each family, it would be a little more effective," Pritchard explained in his understated style. "It was a good move for the bureau. For a long time, under (J. Edgar) Hoover, they didn't want to acknowledge the existence of organized crime.

"It was a very powerful idea, and eventually we convinced headquarters. There was a lot of work done on organized crime, but this was the first time a La Cosa Nostra family was gone after as a whole."

One of the unexpected results of the increased attention was the firsthand sightings by FBI agents of Chin's almost mythic crazy act. With their eyes now directly on Gigante at all hours, the investigators marveled at what they saw from the venerable boss.

The first tale—and still, decades down the road, perhaps the most infamous—came in 1981 when two FBI agents arrived at his mother's apartment to serve Gigante with a subpoena. They knocked on the door, and she asked the two men to wait a minute before letting them inside—possibly to give her son a little time to get set up.

By the time the agents made their way through Yolanda Gigante's home and reached the bathroom, the pair found themselves staring at the naked Chin standing in a running shower, beneath an open umbrella.

The eyes-on pursuit continued, with the FBI arriving for almost daily sessions around the Triangle. The oft-repeated images and tales sealed the Chin's reputation as a secretive, rationally paranoid man, willing to do just about anything to avoid jail.

First, of course, was the "Looney Tunes" outfit: floppy hat, dingy shoes, ratty pants and, of course, a bathrobe that had long seen sharper days. When feeling frisky, Vincent added a belt to his robe. His five o'clock shadow bristled twenty-four hours a day, and his hair was in permanent porcupine mode—unwashed and disheveled, pointed skyward like some strange divining rod.

Second was the attitude. Like a demented Marlon Brando, Vincent Gigante was a true method actor. Standing inside his mother's apartment across from the Triangle, his wardrobe in place, the Chin would slip into character. His posture would slowly slip into a slump, his face devoid of emotion, his walk suddenly the shuffling gait of an ancient man.

The show—a bit of dark nuttiness that often left the agents slack-jawed—would begin once the Chin took in the Village air. The tales, passed around endlessly, became the kind of can-you-top-this stories swapped by the agents during their downtime.

The Chin would occasionally stop during his strolls on the crowded sidewalks, turn and urinate in the street. At other times Gigante would pause during his ramblings to chat with parking meters and trees. "We're going for a walk, parking meter," he once announced. "Want to come?" He looked down to address imaginary pets or spoke with invisible friends.

There were impromptu sidewalk monologues, unleashed for no apparent reason—except, perhaps, to amuse himself or annoy the feds. One night, as Gigante walked along Houston Street, he spotted FBI surveillance. He instantly dropped to his knees in prayer before one of the religious statues outside St. Anthony of Padua Church.

"For all I know," Pritchard has said, "maybe he really was praying."

Pritchard recalled watching in disbelief as Gigante climbed inside a waiting car wearing his grungy robe, but emerged decked out in a sharp sharkskin suit. "Looked like a million bucks," recalled Pritchard.

There were occasions when the act fell into slapstick. The Chin once stood on a Sullivan Street sidewalk waiting for one of his sons to pull his car out into traffic—and an unwitting motorist honked his horn at the momentary delay. Gigante ran into the street and berated the driver: "What are you, in a rush?"

Agents watched as Chin and driver Vito Palmieri slowly exited a building on busy Sixth Avenue, arm in arm, with the aide helping his boss meander along the sidewalk. The two then bolted separately through the traffic like a pair of NFL halfbacks dodging oncoming linebackers. Once reunited on the other side of the avenue, Palmieri took Gigante by the arm, slipping into their characters of doddering old man and helpful pal.

And there were glimpses of a more cunning and cogent Chin. After shuffling through the Village, he would dodge FBI bugs by making calls from a pay phone on the street—and use a credit card to cover the charges.

The stories weren't limited to law enforcement. Trusted waterfront sage George Barone was summoned to meet with Gigante, some union officials and other mobsters before heading to prison in 1983. Barone was waiting for Gigante's appearance in an apartment when he was rattled by the arrival of an unknown and terrifying presence.

The gangster later told the FBI that the interloper "looked

like the Man from La Mancha," and that he instantly thought "this person was there to kill them."

As the person came closer, he realized it was Chin dressed in a robe with the hood up over his head, read an FBI summary of the meeting. *Gigante embraced him, told the others how much he loved [Barone], and described how they were together years ago with Vito Genovese.*

The strange tales, viewed as a whole, made one thing clear: What started as a ruse to beat a New Jersey bribery rap had somehow morphed into a full-time lifestyle for the Mob boss. For the Chin, as William Shakespeare once noted, all the world had become his stage.

Though Gigante was the undisputed star of this strange production, he needed a large cast to make it appear legit. Family members, underlings and average Village denizens each contributed to the endless charade.

"It wasn't just Chin," said Pritchard. "It was the other people around him. It was so stupid and nonsensical."

And frustratingly effective.

His Sullivan Street walking companions varied as Gigante inevitably made his way to the foreboding Triangle. Daughter Rita was sometimes asked to join her father on his stroll across the block. A famous 1988 photo caught a mumbling Chin and his brother Louis, hidden behind sunglasses, walking arm in arm through the neighborhood, with big brother in terry bathrobe, pajamas and slippers.

"He would take me. 'Let's go for a walk,'" recalled Louis Gigante. "And I would walk with him, up and down the street, different places. And he was seen. He purposely, in my mind, he wanted to be seen. And he was seen! They were taking pictures! I swear, we were on Sullivan Street walking and I saw somebody from a building—the cameras! Look at this! So what? They saw the way he was."

Gigante's method acting extended into his day-to-day non-Mob activities. The Chin appeared for appointments with his dentist and chiropractor in character and costume, remaining silent and disheveled while receiving treatment.

The feds also learned about Gigante's insistence on dead silence when it came to speaking his surname, his nickname or anything else referring to him. Genovese family members, including top capos Mangano, Baldy Dom Canterino and Quiet Dom Cirillo, spread the word that people referencing the Chin should simply point to their own chin rather than utter the *C* word.

Making the letter *C* with your hand was also deemed acceptable. So was the term "this guy." Capo Giovanelli was caught in a wiretapped conversation referring to his boss as "Aunt Julia," a nickname that likely remained unknown to his murderous chieftain. Tales quickly emerged attesting to Gigante's dead-serious no-name edict.

When Colombo member Joseph "Joe Black" Gorgone was caught mentioning the Chin's name in a wiretapped conversation, Gigante sent along word that the mobster would be killed if the mistake led to an indictment against the Genovese boss. Lucchese family associate Joe Fiore endured a fearsome beating from three of Chin's underlings after a Genovese family member learned that he invoked Gigante's name in a business deal.

Sammy Gravano was chastised for jokingly bringing Gigante's name into a discussion about Mob construction business. Genovese capo Vincent DiNapoli was hardly amused: "Sammy, you get caught on tape or you get this guy hurt, you're going to get hurt. We refer to him like this."

The capo touched his chin.

"You're gonna get me killed," DiNapoli concluded.

A wiretapped conversation between two Genovese members illustrated the fear inspired by the Chin's declaration. One mentioned how he'd met and wooed a woman, finally convincing her to stop by his house. The mobster was so thrilled that he ran outside to greet her—in a bathrobe.

"The Chin is going to be angry that you're stealing his act," his pal warned.

When he was summoned by Gigante the next day, he assumed the omniscient Mob boss had somehow learned of the accidental indiscretion and was fully expecting to be murdered once he appeared. He left with his life and a resolution to keep the bathrobe as strictly an in-home outfit.

The success of Chin's mental dodge prompted other mobsters to consider the psycho defense, but Gigante put the kibosh on any would-be imitators.

"He'd make sure a message was sent directing them to knock it off. 'Hey, get off my act, you're watering it down,'" recounted federal prosecutor George Stamboulidis, now the cohead of white-collar defense and corporate investigations for the law firm BakerHostetler.

"The mental incompetency act was unique to him. He invested a tremendous amount of time and effort in it, and perfected it over a few decades. It suited him very well."

Gigante's other ruse—installing Salerno as the family's straw boss—was equally successful. By 1983, with Gigante already two years into his reign atop the family, a U.S. Senate report identified him only as a "major contender for the position of boss." Chin was covered in a mere two sentences, about the same amount of space given to his New Jersey waterfront underling DiGilio.

A 1985 FBI report flatly identified Gigante as his family's underboss, with Salerno running the family.

The New York State Organized Crime Task Force, in response to a Freedom of Information Act query for information on Gigante from 1970–1985, said it had "conducted a diligent search and has located no records that respond to your request." The same group planted a bug inside the car of Lucchese boss Anthony "Tony Ducks" Corallo, a devastatingly successful maneuver.

Sammy Gravano, who attended a meeting between Gigante and Gambino family head Paul Castellano around this time, said there was no doubt among the Mafia cognoscenti about who was in charge.

"It was clear as a bell who was the boss," he said—and Gigante was not afraid to flex his muscles. Castellano, who fancied himself as much a businessman as a mobster, would hold "mini-commission" meetings to discuss concrete, construction and other joint enterprises.

"Paul loved that shit," said Gravano.

The Chin? Not so much.

"He was pissed," recalled the Bull. "He said that commission meetings should be just about family business, not the construction business or any other business. These things should be handled by the captains and never even reach the commission level.

"The Chin said, 'What are we doing at these fucking meetings, sitting around talking about bullshit? Does that require this? What if we take a surveillance?'"

The Genovese boss, at one of the meetings, made it clear he wasn't willing to risk anyone seeing his lucid side. "I've invested many years in this crazy act," the Chin declared.

Regarding business, Gigante was just as resolute: the bosses should only gather in matters of life or death, or to set policy that would affect all five families.

"The Chin made some good points," said Gravano. "I had to agree. He didn't sound so crazy to me."

There was another, subtler example of Gigante's expanding reach when his brother Mario was busted once in 1982, this time for extortion and loan-sharking. Mario was by now a Genovese capo, and the charges were for muscling a customer with a $20,000 debt and a late-payment schedule. The high-interest welcher received some advice from Mario about his need to get current: "I'd like to take your fucking skull and just open it up."

Mario settled for punching the man in his jaw. It took a Manhattan federal jury four days to convict him. Mario was categorized by prosecutors as a "rich and feared captain in the Genovese family of La Cosa Nostra."

Mario arrived for sentencing on June 15, 1983, bringing along a sheaf of two hundred laudatory letters, which was a move right out of the Chin's old drug case playbook. The ploy worked, to a degree.

"It's clear to me that you've done a lot of good things in your life," said federal judge Charles Stewart before imposing an eight-year jail term. Father Gigante appeared to defend a different brother, calling the allegations that Mario was a capo in the Genovese crime family nothing more than a "myth."

The sentence was substantially shorter than the twenty years max carried by the conviction, but it was still too much for the Chin and Father G. A year later the priest went calling on Senator Alfonse D'Amato with an appeal for leniency. The politician then personally lobbied U.S. Attorney Rudolph Giuliani to give brother Mario a lesser term.

The Chin simply dispatched Fish Cafaro to see notorious attorney/fixer Roy Cohn with a $175,000 payoff to get his brother a sentence reduction of two years. Vincent Gigante opted for the lower payout: three years off was going for a cool quarter-million dollars, Cafaro later said.

"I know this because we discussed it," Cafaro allowed. He acknowledged that it was unclear how the money was distributed, and no one was ever charged with a crime for the payoff reportedly made in three payments delivered to Cohn's office.

Either way, Mario's term was trimmed by two years in 1985. Father Gigante's efforts remained a secret for five years, finally emerging as Giuliani—with D'Amato's support—mounted his first run for New York City mayor.

Pritchard's pursuit of the Chin eventually led to a face-to-face meeting with Gigante that neither man anticipated, expected or particularly wanted. The FBI boss was leaving his Manhattan office on the evening of January 21, 1986, when he ran into a pair of NYPD detectives assigned to his squad: Anthony Venditti and Kathy Burke.

"We went down in the elevator together," Pritchard recalled. "I never said, 'Be careful,' because I thought whatever the hell happens out there, he will survive. Tony was a helluva detective. Kathy too."

Both detectives were longtime law enforcement hands: Venditti was a veteran of undercover work, with twelve years on the force and a history of making gambling and Mob cases. Burke joined the department in 1968, and had since worked on the NYPD's renowned Major Case Squad.

On this night, they were conducting surveillance on Giovanelli, a close Gigante associate and a regular guest at the Triangle. The pair climbed inside their vehicle, a 1977 brown Lincoln Town Car, despite their concerns that Giovanelli now recognized the car as a tail.

When they spotted the Genovese associate driving a BMW near his Queens hangout, the veteran investigators were convinced that Giovanelli had identified them, so they decided to call it a night. Venditti suggested they stop at the nearby Castillo's Diner so he could use the men's room and grab a cup of coffee.

Burke quickly noticed the BMW still driving behind them, now with its lights off, and became alarmed. Venditti brushed her concerns aside; there was a long-standing Mafia prohibition on killing anyone in law enforcement. Giovanelli apparently missed the Mob memo.

Venditti went inside the diner as Burke parked their car. She spotted another car behind her, and bolted toward the diner to alert her partner. When she arrived, Venditti was holding a paper bag with his coffee as three men stood around him. When one of the men ordered the five-two female officer to go stand alongside Venditti, she went for her gun—and a bullet slammed into her chest.

Venditti was unable to reach the weapon in his ankle holster. He was shot four times and killed.

The night after the Venditti murder, New York law enforcement turned out en masse in every organized crime hangout across the city as they hunted the killers. Pritchard was dispatched to the Triangle to grill the Chin. He walked inside and went right up to Gigante.

"We dragged Chin outside of the Triangle, right onto Sullivan Street," Pritchard recounted. "We talked to Chin separately, away from his minions. We took him outside, and we talked to him like you and I are talking right now. There was no crazy act. He was clear as a bell.

"He apologized for what happened, but he took no responsibility. He said nothing off-color, no wiseass remarks. He communicated like any other human being. This was just one more indication that he was crazy like a fox. I knew he was sane, and he knew I knew that he was sane. It only reinforced what I knew.

"I do believe," Pritchard added, "that he was concerned on some level that a cop was shot."

Loyalist Canterino, pulled in by the FBI a few days later, was outraged by the brazen confrontation of his boss. If he was there, Baldy Dom declared, he would have stopped the agents from entering the Triangle. Gigante was a sick old man, and Canterino offered to produce "medical records going back ten years" to prove that the Chin was "mentally unstable," an FBI summary of the chat reported. *Canterino explained that "The Chin" is like a brother to him,* the summary stated.

Giovanelli was nevertheless arrested the next day, along with fellow gangsters Steven Maltese and Carmine Gualtieri, setting off a nearly decade-long legal odyssey with four separate trials. Two state prosecutions ended with deadlocked juries for Giovanelli and Maltese, and an acquittal for Gualtieri.

The trio was convicted on federal racketeering charges in 1989, including the murder count—although the charge was later overturned on appeal. One final state trial ended with Maltese and Giovanelli walking on the murder rap.

CHAPTER 11

EAST SEVENTY-SEVENTH STREET REVISITED

*F*BI AGENT CHARLIE BEAUDOIN IS THE KIND OF GUY WHO BELIEVES the shortest distance between two points is a straight line.

When he transferred to New York from Erie, Pennsylvania, he bought a home in New Jersey off the interstate—a straight shot down Route 78 to the FBI's headquarters in Lower Manhattan. And once he landed on the Genovese Squad, he was among the agents who popped in uninvited at the Triangle for a closer look-see at some new faces spotted during federal surveillance.

If the Chin was stunned by the presence of the FBI in his Village hideaway, Beaudoin was equally surprised by the sight of the powerful Mafiosi decked out in a ratty bathrobe and a pair of sweatpants. Gigante immediately rose and challenged the badge-waving intruders.

"He actually stood up and started asking me, 'What are you guys doing in here? I thought we had a deal that you guys would not come into my place?'" Beaudoin recalls with some amusement. "He's speaking quite cogently."

And then, almost as if a lightbulb flicked on, the Chin considered the situation and turned off his anger. His voice and demeanor changed entirely, as did his rancorous behavior.

"He reached into his pocket and pulled out a handful of religious medals," the agent said. "He told me, 'I have change for a dollar. I can help you. I have change.' Once he went into crazy mode, I realized, 'That's it, we're done.'"

The short bit of face time illustrated the FBI's biggest hurdle in tracking the Chin. The Triangle was nearly impregnable, and anyone inside was unlikely to say anything of value—particularly about Vincent Gigante, given the sanctions involved.

Efforts to get information on the Village streets were equally ineffective, with the neighbors alerting Gigante or his minions whenever the FBI was spotted. The insular area served as a human early-warning system for the Mob boss.

"He had hundreds of eyes working for him in the neighborhood," recalled Pritchard. "The FBI was in no part a favorite in that 'hood. And Chin was a popular guy."

Pritchard recalled the feds buying a small prefab storage shed to use as a lookout point, putting it together on the roof of a school opposite the Triangle.

"It was really just an observation point to look down on the entrance to the club and see who was coming and going," he said. "We came back the next night and found the thing destroyed."

There was one tactic rejected out of hand by the investigators: trying to infiltrate the Chin's inner circle. Mangano, a valued capo and future underboss, was a longtime associate from the same section of the Village. Cirillo was a friend from Gigante's days in the fight game, and Canterino was a trusted right-hand man and bodyguard. Manna was an unrepentant killer, valued earner and a true Mob believer.

None would ever cooperate with the authorities, as one infamous tale about Manna illustrated perfectly. When jailed in the early 1970s for refusing to speak before a Jersey organized crime probe, he was thrown in jail. The gangster agreed to open wide, only after he developed a tooth abscess while inside the State Prison in Yardville, New Jersey.

The treating dentist wanted to pull the offending tooth in a painful procedure. Fearful he might speak if given a painkiller, Manna refused a shot of Novocain.

"The story is they pulled his tooth out, and he didn't flinch," recounted onetime federal prosecutor Michael Chertoff. "From the corner of one eye, there was one little teardrop. He had a rep as a stone-cold guy. Not to be messed with, and not much of a sense of humor."

The thought of an outsider infiltrating the top level of the Genovese family, a ploy used by FBI undercover Pistone with the Bonannos, was broached and quickly dismissed.

"Near impossible," said Pritchard. "You were dealing with old-timers in the Genovese family. . . . Then you look at the people who are closest to Chin. The people around him, he knew them his whole life. Somebody new was not going to get in too deep."

Beaudoin recalled the squad's growing frustration: "He had an entire network. . . . It's fair to say that every attempt at surveillance of the Chin had failed. Oh yeah."

One of those efforts included trying to track Gigante's nocturnal wanderings. This led his Mob pals to refer to Chin jokingly as "the Vampire" or "Dracula." (Never to his face, of course.)

The seemingly simple plan proved treacherous for the assigned agents. The Chin's chauffeur—the boss wasn't crazy enough to drive himself—whipped through the streets of the Village in a style more Mario Andretti than Genovese soldier. Vito Palmieri would pull up outside the apartment building where Gigante lived with his mother and wait for the boss to exit.

And then it was off to the races. Palmieri would run red lights, ignore one-way signs and accelerate like a madman.

"His driver always lost us," said Beaudoin. "But he was always heading north, toward the Upper East Side. It was decided we were going to find out where he was going."

The feds finally tailed the runaway Cadillac to its destination and found their answer: Gigante was visiting a luxury duplex at 67 East Seventy-Seventh Street, in between Park and Madison Avenues. It was, much to their surprise, the home of Chin's longtime mistress and mother of three more Gigante progeny.

The Chin—surprise!—was leading a double life inside his double life.

*   *   *

Olympia Esposito was nicknamed "Mitzi" by friends and family, but she quickly acquired a second alias from investigators—one that referenced Gigante's wife across the Hudson. Esposito henceforth become known among the investigators pursuing the Chin as "Olympia 2." Mrs. Gigante was dubbed "Olympia 1."

The feds first heard mention of the second Olympia via phone taps, only to assume their targets were speaking about Chin's long-suffering bride in the Jersey suburbs. Now, on the tony Upper East Side, they laid eyes on the matriarch of the Chin's secret extramarital family. Gigante would typically spend the night in the comfy digs, leaving early the next day to Sullivan Street and his official duties.

A little digging exposed the details of exactly how Esposito was able to move on up to the East Side. The building was once owned by Morris Levy, who quite generously transferred the property into her name for only $16,000, a year after buying the town house for $500,000. Esposito's neighbors included three-time Tony nominee Sandy Duncan, the actress best known for her work in the Broadway revival of *Peter Pan* and the television hit *The Hogan Family*.

The discovery of the high-end hideaway was great news for the feds chasing the Chin.

"Pritchard said, 'The first team to find a spot to set up [surveillance] wins,' " Beaudoin said. "Wins? They won maybe a round of beers."

The agent and his NYPD partner, Detective Bill Murnane, took an undercover scouting trip through the neighborhood in late 1985. There was a place for lease in the building next door, directly alongside the Esposito residence—a huge space with an outdoor patio.

"We walked in and pretended we were partners in a CPA firm, Bradley and Kennedy," he recalled. "I went to a local printing place and had cards printed up. I was 'Charles Bradley.' You always use your real first name. In case anybody says, 'Hey, Charlie,' you want to make sure you answer."

The fake accountant proved pretty good at real estate speculation. Beaudoin proposed the FBI buy the place for $1.2 mil-
lion, a suggestion rejected in short order by the suits in
Washington. They wound up settling for a one-year lease at
$1,400 a month, with an option to buy.

Five years later the space was worth $10 million.

The next step was finding a vantage point to watch the Chin
in his somewhat unnatural habitat. Agents settled on the Ramaz
Yeshiva, home to a prestigious Jewish school on East Seventy-
Eighth Street, after a visit under the pretense of a security check
for an upcoming United Nations General Assembly meeting in
October 1985.

To reach the spot with an optimal view, a terrace on the school's
back end, Beaudoin took the most direct route: the agent, a daily
jogger with a runner's build, simply jumped the two-foot gap from
his patio to set up surveillance from a distance of about fifty feet
away.

For the next four months, from January through April, through
the cold, rain, snow and darkness, this became Beaudoin's al
fresco office.

The eagle-eyed Beaudoin carried just a pen, a notebook and a
flashlight. The Chin would typically arrive around midnight.
The agent decided to go low-tech in his surveillance because
using a camera or binoculars could lead to complications if and
when he had to testify about all he had seen.

A second team was set up to watch the building entrance, with
another team member stationed at nearby Lenox Hill Hospital
across the street.

"Outside, he would need help walking—one guy on each
side, holding him up," the agent recalled. "He's tripping on the
sidewalk. And then, when he gets inside, it turns into *Father
Knows Best*. He would walk in, and hug and kiss [Esposito]. You
could see them talking like normal people. He takes off his cap
and puts it on the shelf. Then he takes off his old bathrobe and
puts it on a hanger.

"He changes into nicer clothes. His common-law wife brings

the paper over, and he sits at the dining-room table. He'd have dinner and a little bit of conversation. It's like the guy just came home from work. He's the boss, sitting right there at the head of the table."

The typically grungy Gigante would enjoy a relaxing shower. He would flip on the apartment's big-screen television and take in a movie, flip the light switches off when he left a room. When it was time for bed, he walked over and punched the button for the elevator and his bed upstairs. The next morning, Gigante would depart the building in the same ratty outfit that he wore inside the night before.

Beaudoin, watching in disbelief from his perch behind some planters on the adjoining terrace, recalled the thought that passed through his head: "This is crazy."

In between his arrival and bedtime, the Chin was all business in what basically served as the uptown, upscale version of the Triangle.

Various Genovese associates came through in the course of an evening. The Chin, more CEO than schizophrenic, studied the numbers presented in various ledgers. A mobster named Angelo D'Acunto, head of a taxi drivers' union, arrived one night. Gigante was spotted counting a large stack of bills just minutes later.

He would occasionally leave the town house and walk to a nearby pay phone, where lengthy calls ensued as agents watched in frustration.

The apartment's phone was bugged in short order, capturing mostly lovey-dovey phone chatter between Gigante and Olympia 2. An October 17, 1985, taped call was typical: questions from the Chin about an injury to their son, suffered while boxing like the old man, and other tidbits of domestic trivia. The mobster and his mistress more often whispered sweet nothings like a pair of lovestruck teens.

"I love you," said a laughing Gigante in one gooey exchange.

As Esposito begins coughing, the Chin advised her to stop smoking.

"All right," she said before Gigante started making kissing noises into the phone.

"I love you," declared Esposito.

"I love you," the Chin responded.

"Toodles," said Esposito before hanging up.

Constantly worried about intrusive federal ears, the Chin conducted some of his conversations in code. He used a series of whistles to communicate. One night, for instance, agents listened in as Gigante whistled and whistled at his son, who clearly had no idea what any of it meant. The exasperated Gigante, determined not to speak on the phone, handed the receiver back to underling Cirillo and barked, "I don't want him to catch a cold. Tell him to put a coat on!"

The tale still brings a smile to Stamboulidis.

"They weren't always proficient on the secret-decoder act," he cracked. "It was those rare and unguarded moments of truth that helped to reveal Chin's mental incompetency for the act that it was."

Other calls were more comical. Pritchard recalled one of Gigante's daughters calling a beauty salon for a price on getting her legs waxed—and balking at the price.

"And then she asks, 'Well, how much for one?'" he said. "We laughed so hard! We had tears coming out of our eyes."

There were snippets of tantalizing conversations—an order to "give Morris a call," an apparent reference to Levy; another instruction to "tell Benny to be there at three-thirty," possibly an order for underboss Mangano to show up in the middle of the night.

"Starting to rain," Gigante once declared. Was it code or weather forecast?

After four months of Beaudoin's eyes-on surveillance, the FBI—with plenty of probable cause—moved to get a bug placed inside the apartment. Beaudoin, who took some high-school drafting classes, did a bit of figuring and thought installation of the mike in the same room as the Chin's dinner table was doable.

He whipped up an impromptu blueprint, illustrating how a hatch from the rental's patio led to a boiler room, providing access to the Esposito apartment.

A top-flight, high-tech surveillance expert was dispatched from Washington to handle the particulars. Disaster ensued.

"Now a guy shows up—I call him 'Mr. Black and Decker,'" said Beaudoin. "He's got big trunks full of gear. He arrives in the daytime, because Vincent is only there at night. We waltz into the building, and he's carrying all this stuff like he's the Fuller Brush man with a bagful of samples. He gets all his things out, and then he says all non-FBI personnel have to leave the room."

A special drill was employed, with the capacity to suck out the debris as it went and a sensor allowing the tool to reach within a fraction of an inch with the wall on the other side. Mr. Black and Decker went to work.

"We come back and he's like, 'Uh-oh,'" said Beaudoin. "And I'm asking, 'What do you mean?' He says, 'I busted through the wall.' There's a hole, and this red sludge dripping down the wall. It's the size of a .38-caliber bullet, and it looks like a gunshot wound. Now I realize there's nothing we can do to salvage this. The whole caper's gone."

Sure enough, when Beaudoin next jumped to the yeshiva's terrace, the party was over. Every blind on every window facing out of the East Side sanctum was drawn tight. The lights were out, and the inside of the duplex was pitch black.

It wasn't the only bit of bad luck to beset the squad in their chase of the Chin: another bug in Olympia 2's home wound up behind a refrigerator, where the hum of its working parts rendered impossible any attempt at listening to conversations.

A bug was installed, after much effort, inside Gigante insider Baldy Dom Canterino's car. Within days word leaked that another Mob boss's car was wired, eventually providing investigators from the Lucchese Squad with reams of recordings. Conversation in Canterino's vehicle ceased almost instantly.

There was another aborted attempt to install a camera at the duplex to record the Chin's rational behavior around his mistress's home. Even the Reverend Al Sharpton, a rabble-rousing local civil rights leader destined for the national stage, was recruited to tote a recorder into meetings with Genovese soldiers. He carried a specially fitted Hartmann briefcase equipped with a microphone.

One FBI official recalled Sharpton as a very willing participant, albeit with one quirk. Before he was wired up, the rotund reverend would apply a large dose of extra-strength antiperspirant beneath both arms.

In addition to the taps on Olympia Esposito's home phones, bugs were installed on Baldy Dom's phone and Levy's Manhattan office with information provided by Sharpton's surreptitious work. All of these turned up nothing incriminating on Vincent Gigante.

The surveillance was now over on the Upper East Side, but the details of the adventure would stick with Beaudoin for decades.

"Our instructions were 'don't pay attention to the normal behavior,'" Beaudoin said. "Watch for the criminal behavior. Performing normally isn't evidence against him."

Not for another decade, anyway.

The generous town house deal with Olympia Esposito wasn't the only real estate transaction handled by music man Morris Levy on behalf of the rapacious Vincent Gigante and his Mob minions.

By now, the feds chasing the Chin were after the record business legend, too. Levy's sprawling empire now included three record labels, along with forty retail record stores known as Strawberries. And a confidential informant told the FBI that Levy, like any Genovese capo, was kicking up cash to Gigante from his dealings in bootleg records.

One of Gigante's brothers became a part owner of the record and tape emporiums, so the family was also bleeding Levy for a piece of his legitimate cash income, according to secretly taped conversations with Gambino family associate Joseph "Joe Bana" Buonanno.

[The Chin] developed and maintained a stranglehold upon Morris Levy's recording industry enterprises, turning Levy into a subservient source of ready cash for the Genovese LCN family and its leaders, Agent Gerald King wrote in an FBI application for yet another fruitless bug inside the Triangle.

After his years of consorting with the Mob, Levy wasn't above calling in a favor or two. Buonanno, speaking with the wired Sharpton, recounted how the music mogul tried to arrange a hit on the mobster's brother for stealing from Levy. The request was shot down at a commission meeting.

Levy was also used as a front for the family to purchase other properties, moving their illegal cash into legitimate real estate. The East Seventy-Seventh Street transaction, exposed by the FBI, was the most obvious deal, but not the only one. Buonanno, in another taped chat, revealed that the Chin and his crew had Levy front the cost for real estate investments—to "buy buildings," as he bluntly stated about their arrangement.

"You Jew cocksucker," the Chin ranted at one sit-down with Levy, "you buy those two pieces of property or I'll bury you."

The properties, once purchased, were to be transferred into the names of two Genovese members close to Gigante.

In a show of generosity laced with greed, the Chin had actually spared Levy from a 1982 Mob hit. Genovese member Joseph Pagano, a force in the family's entertainment rackets, and the overseer of the family's operations in the city's northern suburbs, flew into a rage after Levy interceded with Gigante on behalf of a Pagano pigeon targeted for extortion.

Pagano wanted Levy whacked, but the Chin brokered a deal where Levy would, instead, pay Pagano $100,000 to settle the beef. Once he was cooled down, Pagano—in perhaps a first in the Mafia's long history—forgave the debt. That was more than the Chin was willing to do.

Gigante told Levy that he was responsible for the music executive's free financial pass, and informed the record maven that the cost of living was $10,000 for a down payment on an unidentified property.

The hapless Buonanno, prattling on during the taping in May 1984, made it clear that Levy's position in the family had grown tenuous with time. Worn down by decades of Mob association, and with his old partner Eboli long dead, Levy was looking to find a way out of his business ties with the Genovese family.

The problem, Buonanno said, was that Levy "has only one way out"—and then mimed someone pointing a gun and pulling the trigger.

CHAPTER 12

HARD TIMES IN NEW YORK TOWN

*I*T WAS AN AMBITIOUS ITALIAN-AMERICAN PROSECUTOR WHO FINALLY brought the case that forever altered the decades-old war against the Mafia—and forever tilted the playing field toward the government. As word spread of the case against the Mob's ruling commission, Gigante was left silently twisting in the wind as his Mafia contemporaries kept running their mouths.

Rudolph Giuliani was the U.S. Attorney for the Southern District, perhaps the most prestigious job in the Justice Department, short of attorney general. The Brooklyn-born Giuliani came from a family with its own Mob ties: his father had worked for a brother's mobbed-up loan-sharking business.

But Harold Giuliani moved his family to the Long Island suburbs to keep his son away from the Mob influence. Giuliani arrived in the Manhattan office in 1983, and quickly allied himself with the new FBI squads targeting the five families. The prosecutor became one of the earliest proponents of a powerful, if still obscure, legal cudgel: the Racketeer Influenced and Corrupt Organizations (RICO) Act. Mobsters convicted of even two crimes linked to their organized crime families were now facing decades in prison.

Wiretaps soon provided the most damning evidence. The bugs were everywhere, from Salerno's once-impregnable Palma Boys Social Club, on East 115th Street, to the dashboard of the

Jaguar used by Lucchese boss Anthony Corallo to make his daily rounds.

Authorities collected hours of devastating conversations involving the highest echelons of the Mafia's ruling hierarchy. The unexpurgated chats quickly established the existence of the commission and its powers to settle disputes, cut up illegal profits and discuss various mutual interests. But almost no one mentioned Gigante's secret bedside ascension as head of the Genovese family, and the FBI and federal prosecutors pursued Fat Tony with the four other bosses.

There were some glaring exceptions ignored by the Mob's pursuers when it came to Gigante's lofty position.

Tapes from a 1983 meeting in a Brooklyn restaurant linked the Chin to various Mob activities, including a declaration from Colombo family boss Gennaro "Gerry Lang" Langella about problems that were raised "before the commission meet with Chin."

A May 22, 1984, recording from Salerno's headquarters was even more revealing.

The demoted Salerno, griping about the list of proposed candidates for made membership in the Genovese family, said he was unsure of the new members because "they didn't put the nicknames on there."

"They should have the nicknames down," agreed the legendary family capo Matty "the Horse" Ianniello.

"But, anyway, I'll leave this up to the boss," said Salerno. "Send it, ah, to the Chin."

Word of the impending commission prosecution was on the minds of the Mob's ruling class, as Salerno noted in a February 1985 conversation with confidant Giuseppe Sabato, which exposed the Chin's position atop the Genovese family.

"If they get the Chin, they're all wrapped up," said Sabato. "All the finagling, manipulating, manipulating, manipulating to fool the government . . ."

"He's got to worry," said Salerno, unaware of the recording

device or his own imminent demise. "If he gets pinched, all them years he spent in that fucking asylum."

"That's what I'm saying," agreed Sabato.

"For nothing," Salerno declared.

One of the bugged chats captured in the Jaguar came as Tony Ducks Corallo headed to a commission meeting at a pizza supply house.

"But is Chin gonna be here?" asked Tony Ducks. "And Bobby [Manna]?"

"Oh yeah," replied Lucchese consigliere Christopher "Christie Tick" Funari. "Gotta be there. Everyone's gotta."

The Chin was unsure what the feds knew, or whether he was a target of this unprecedented assault on the Mafia. But Gigante, despite his long and successful dodge of prosecutors, knew nothing lasted forever in his chosen profession. The Mob veteran braced for the worst and hoped for the best.

His answer came on February 25, 1985, when the heads of the five families—with Salerno representing the Genovese operation—were indicted in the federal government's most far-reaching assault in the long history of the Mafia's secret society. There were nine named defendants in the fifteen-count racketeering charge—and nary a one named Gigante.

Charged as the Genovese kingpin, Salerno was immediately held without bail.

"Chin fully expected he was going to be in the commission indictment," said one federal prosecutor. "He was completely surprised when he wasn't."

His ruse of keeping Salerno as the nominal head of the family, plus his street theater and the impregnability of the Triangle, had spared Gigante. It would also create problems for other federal prosecutors still chasing the Chin a few years down the line.

Salerno was cuffed in his East Harlem apartment just as a food delivery order arrived; Fat Tony was taken away still suffering from hunger pangs. He was joined by Tony Ducks, Bonanno boss Philip "Rusty" Rastelli, the Colombos' Langella and family member Ralph Scopo, Lucchese underboss Salvatore "Tom

Mix" Santoro and consigliere Funari, along with Gambino head
Paul Castellano and his underboss, Aniello "Mr. Neil" Della-
croce. A superseding indictment later added Colombo boss
Carmine "the Snake" Persico.

Among the charges: the commission had sanctioned the 1979
hit on Bonanno boss Carmine Galante and four family associates. Galante's bullet-riddled corpse was famously photographed
with his ever-present cigar still in his mouth.

"This is a bad day, probably the worst ever, for the Mafia," said
Giuliani.

And a very good day for Gigante and the rest of his family.

After he dodged the indictments, the ever-careful Chin checked
back into St. Vincent's on March 4, 1985, for a two-week stay.
Within five days of his release, it was back to business as usual:
the FBI watched him meet routinely with a who's who of the
Genovese top echelon, including Canterino, Manna, Mangano
and Cirillo.

His Gambino colleague Castellano quickly hired famed defense attorney James LaRossa, one of the New York bar's best, as
the heads of the five families prepped for trial. Big Paul's wait
was complicated by one renegade crew within his fractious family, and they were already plotting to ensure Castellano never
heard the verdict. The Queens gang run by John Gotti was ready
to impose its own sentence on the Gambino boss. And they didn't
intend to ask Vincent Gigante, Castellano's close pal and the
most powerful commission member, for his approval.

"They were too tight," plotter Sammy "the Bull" Gravano said
later of the Chin and Big Paul. "They had all their big money
arrangements. So we decided, 'Fuck Chin.' If it comes down to
it, we'll go to war with them."

The genesis of the Castellano takedown was the insistence of
the Gotti crew in dealing heroin—an absolute no-no with the
Gambino boss, who was trying to move his family into the legitimate business world. He had the full backing of Gigante.

"It's Paul . . . him and Chin made a pact," said Angelo "Quack

Quack" Ruggiero, a member of Gotti's crew who seemed comi-
cally inept at avoiding federal wiretaps. "Any friend of ours gets
pinched for junk, they kill 'em. They're not warning nobody, because they feel the guy's gonna rat."

Another taped call captured Ruggiero discussing a summons
for Gotti to meet with Castellano over the drug dealing of Peter
"Little Pete" Tambone.

"Johnny, you know that anybody who's straightened out that
moves babania (heroin) faces execution," he said.

The problem was much closer to home for Gotti: His brother
Gene, along with Ruggiero, was indicted for dealing heroin. The
case included incriminating wiretaps, and Castellano wanted to
hear the conversations before moving forward with any decision
on their fate.

Strike one.

There were other disputes between the boss and his capo
about money and Castellano's purported greed. The Gotti group
was also outraged when Castellano allowed Genovese killers to
whack a Gambino capo in Connecticut. The Chin complained
to Big Paul that Frank Piccolo was becoming a pain in the ass
and needed to go.

Castellano, in a violation of La Cosa Nostra rules, quickly gave
the okay for Piccolo's killing. The move only raised Gambino
capo Sammy Gravano's admiration for Gigante.

"The Chin would never do that," the Bull said later. "Nobody
fucked with him. He ran a tight ship."

Strike two.

The last impediment to Castellano's execution went into the
ground with the body of commission codefendant Dellacroce, a
respected Gambino executive and Gotti mentor. Dellacroce,
seventy-one, was a voice of reason in the family, and he had
urged the Gotti faction to come clean with their boss. In a tape-
recorded June 1985 conversation, the mobster, aka Mr. Neil, advised Gotti and Ruggiero that they had no choice under the
rules of La Cosa Nostra but to surrender the tapes.

"That's what I'm telling you," Dellacroce said flatly. "That's

what we want to hear. You see, that's why I says to you before—
you, you don't understand La Cosa Nostra."

"Angelo, what does 'Cosa Nostra' mean?" Gotti demanded of
Ruggiero. Dellacroce interrupted before the other mobster could
speak: "Cosa Nostra means that the boss is your boss."

When Dellacroce died on December 2, 1985, Castellano
couldn't be bothered to pay his respects at the wake.

Strike three.

Two weeks later, on December 16, the Gambino boss came
into Manhattan from his Staten Island estate, known to the rank
and file as "the White House," for a mix of business and pleasure. Castellano, chauffeured in a black Lincoln Town Car by
loyal driver/capo Tommy Bilotti, stopped by the Manhattan law
offices of lawyer LaRossa. The two men said their farewells, and
Bilotti drove his boss toward a dinner date with five other mobsters at Sparks Steak House on East Forty-Sixth Street.

Castellano's favorite cut of beef awaited: prime rib. But Big
Paul had already eaten his last meal.

The pair drove through the brightly lit city, festooned with
holiday decorations, hanging a right turn just a few blocks south
of the Rockefeller Center Christmas tree. Mingling amidst the
tourists and holiday shoppers were four men in matching winter
wear: black Russian fur hats, pale trench coats.

In lieu of gifts, they carried loaded handguns as they waited
for the Lincoln to arrive. Half a block away, Gotti and Gravano
sat anxiously in a parked car. As Castellano's Lincoln drove past,
Gravano switched on a walkie-talkie to alert the shooters that
their target was headed their way.

The day shift surrendered to nighttime in newsrooms around
the city as twilight descended on Manhattan. A large contingent
of law enforcers gathered at New York University for a lecture by
the godfather of the RICO Act, Notre Dame professor G. Robert
Blakey.

The quartet in their pseudo-Siberian getups watched as the
Town Car ignored a NO PARKING sign and nestled against the
curb outside the restaurant at 5:30 P.M. The hawk-nosed Castel-

lano, wearing a business suit, was unarmed and carrying $3,000 cash. Red meat and old friends awaited.

One of those friends, Gotti loyalist Frankie DeCicco, emerged as the Judas with a taste for T-bone—Brutus to Castellano's Julius Caesar.

Bilotti stepped out of the driver's-side door as his boss exited the backseat. The street suddenly echoed with the deafening *rat-a-tat-tat* of gunfire as the four shooters opened fire with lethal accuracy. When the gunshots stopped, beepers began chirping at NYU and fax machines whirred in newsrooms around the city: two white males, shot to death in Midtown Manhattan.

Confirmation came quickly: Paul Castellano was dead. Police sirens howled and radios crackled as authorities rushed to the crime scene, where twin red rivers of blood now flowed from the Mob boss and his slain bodyguard.

The killers shot Big Paul first, watching as the mortally injured Mob boss collapsed. Bilotti, staring in disbelief, was gunned down as he peered through the car's windows. One of the killers walked casually toward the bleeding Castellano and fired a final shot, point-blank, into the boss's head.

DeCicco, alerted by the gunfire, abandoned his table and exited the restaurant as the killers walked casually past the bodies. They walked, followed rapidly by DeCicco, toward a prearranged getaway on Second Avenue.

Before the cops arrived, in a car driven by Gravano, Gotti cruised past the chaotic scene to admire the handiwork of his hit team. Shooter Eddie Lino later described the perfectly executed execution to Gotti in great detail, right down to the one shooter's gun jamming.

When the Chin awoke nine days before Christmas, 1985, he was greeted by an early and unwanted present: John Gotti, the self-appointed new boss of the Gambino crime family, who landed in his lap like a frothing pit bull and lingered like a chronic disease.

CHAPTER 13

MASTERS OF WAR

*I*F THE CHIN WAS NOT TOO WELL VERSED ABOUT THE OUTER BOR-
ough thug who had just whacked his pal Castellano, Gotti was
fully in the know about his Genovese family counterpart.

John and his brother Gene Gotti told a confidential informant in 1984 that Gigante was used by the commission during
the 1970s to execute Mafiosi caught violating the ban on dealing
heroin.

An FBI agent summed up the Gottis' beliefs this way: *Those ap-
prehended and/or convicted . . . normally met with individuals associated with Gigante, and these meetings were usually their last.*

The Gotti brothers specifically referred to Carmine Consalvo,
tossed from the roof of a twenty-four-story building in Fort Lee,
New Jersey, while facing a heroin trial in 1975. His brother
Frank suffered the same deadly fate three months later after a
shorter fall: five stories from a building in Little Italy.

Among law enforcers, the two murders were dubbed "The
Case of the Flying Consalvos."

Gotti's renegade crew not only feared the Chin—they respected him. Charlie Carneglia, one of Gotti's most trusted contract killers, was caught on another bug calling Gigante "smart"
for his ongoing mental-health routine. (Proof of Chin's high-
quality act: Carneglia was convicted in 2009 after prosecutors
said he unsuccessfully pulled the same stunt.)

To Bill Bonanno, former Bonanno family boss and son of

Mafia founder Joseph Bonanno, Gotti and his ilk were hardly men of honor.

"They're a product of 'the opera generation—me, me, me,'" scoffed Bill Bonanno. "It is a different Mob."

The Chin was a padrone, taking care of local problems in a low-key fashion reminiscent of "Godfather" Don Corleone on the day of his daughter's wedding. Gotti, however, in a typically showy move, hosted a massive Fourth of July party in Howard Beach—complete with illegal pyrotechnics.

The annual event was held despite Gotti's unknown past as a draft dodger; "the Dapper Don" avoided wearing olive drab by blowing off his draft board on the very day that President Kennedy was assassinated in Dallas.

Gotti, a guy from Queens, was hardly part of the Mob's upper echelon; his base of operations was in far-flung Ozone Park at the Bergin Hunt and Fish Club, where the rods came equipped with silencers. Hijackings at Kennedy International Airport were their bread and butter. Gotti was hardly a subtle guy; when the threat of violence wasn't enough, he simply turned to violence.

To a made man with Chin's pedigree, Gotti was an outsider and unworthy of respect—even after the Castellano hit. Gigante was unappeased by Gotti's public denials of the murder or his immediate "election" by Gambino captains as the family's new leader.

Gotti's disregard for both Mob management and his late boss was captured on a particularly bilious recording made in an apartment above the Ravenite Social Club after the Castellano assassination.

"Hate, really hate Paul," Gotti ranted. "He sold the borgata out for a construction company. He was a piece of shit. Rat, rat cocksucker. Yellow dog!"

His feelings toward Gigante, while not as colorful, were equally dismissive. Gotti sneered at the Chin's bread and butter, the crazy act: "I would rather be doing life than be like him," the mobster once told his son John "Junior" Gotti.

The Dapper Don and the Oddfather did share some similarities. Both men were first-generation Italian Americans. Both would prove, in Mob parlance, to be stand-up guys: they did their time and kept their mouths shut.

Gotti, like Gigante, made his bones with a Mob hit after a none-too-bright Irishman named James McBratney "masterminded" the kidnapping of boss Carlo Gambino's nephew, Emanuel "Manny" Gambino.

Gambino paid a $100,000 ransom, but Manny was already dead. So was McBratney, although he didn't know it yet.

On May 23, 1973, Gotti and two pals found McBratney drinking in a Staten Island bar. He was shot three times and left to die on the barroom floor. A generous plea deal cut by Mario Gigante's future benefactor, attorney Cohn, left Gotti to serve less than two years for the killing.

Gotti was a guy who nursed a grudge, like the one he held toward Castellano, and he cared—a lot—about making money. Gigante took a more benevolent approach to the cash generated by his illegal operations and his loyal staff.

"Chin was very well-liked by his crew because he didn't ask for a lot of money from his capos, his soldiers," said former federal prosecutor Greg O'Connell.

Gambino underboss Gravano agreed: "He ain't that interested in the money. He already had a ton of money. His biggest problem was where to hide it. He didn't take money from most of his captains."

Gravano saw that move as evidence of Gigante's well-honed instincts toward proper Mob rule and self-preservation. "I guess he didn't want some captain to flip and say, 'I been giving him money,'" the Gambino underboss explained.

Gotti, on the other hand, appeared jealous of right-hand man Gravano's assorted moneymaking operations—and at one point said as much on secretly recorded FBI tapes that convinced the Bull to seek out the FBI.

Three different law enforcement sources said the murderous Gambino boss was petrified of the ruthless Chin.

"John Gotti was terrified of Gigante," said FBI agent Bruce Mouw, once the head of the agency's Gambino Squad. "He knew that the Genoveses were the most powerful family, very tough, a vicious family."

"I'm sure he was," agreed O'Connell, noting the Chin was apparently afraid of nothing.

Former Bonanno capo Michael Franzese echoed the law enforcement assessment. "I believe everybody feared Chin, even when Fat Tony was the [supposed] boss," said the born-again gangster. "It was pretty much common knowledge that Chin was no fan of Gotti's."

Gotti led the lifestyle of a celebrity, flaunting his sudden wealth. He wore $1,800 Brioni suits, hand-painted ties and monogrammed socks. As Gigante stumbled through the Village and angled to stay off government tapes, Gotti was profiled in *People* magazine and appeared on the cover of *Time* magazine—in a portrait done by Andy Warhol.

Gigante surreptitiously assumed control of the family in his secret bedside takedown of the hospitalized Salerno, and remained happy to let Fat Tony endure as a figurehead. Gotti's bloody ascension was followed by his reckless embrace of the limelight, which virtually ensured his rapid downfall. He almost dared federal officials to take him down, taunting his FBI pursuers.

"I give you three-to-one odds I beat this case," he told reporters after his indictment for ordering the shooting of a union boss. He was right: Gotti walked after fixing the jury.

The rumpled Chin remained content to wear rags despite his riches, crossing Sullivan Street to hold court in the Triangle. The ever-preening Gotti, typically dressed to the nines, would arrive at his Little Italy headquarters in a chauffeur-driven luxury car that picked him up outside the door of his Howard Beach home. He lacked the Chin's nose for sniffing out federal surveillance—or maybe he was just too arrogant to care.

FBI agents staking out the Ravenite Social Club in the days

after the Castellano hit watched intently as a steady stream of Gambino members arrived for the annual family Christmas party to pay fealty to their new leader. Each hugged and kissed Gotti as the agents along Mulberry Street watched in amazement.

"Gigante believed that organized crime should be a secret society," said Mouw. "Nobody should know who the boss was, and he shouldn't be on the front page of the *Daily News*. John had his own feelings."

While the Chin's gambling was now limited to fixed card games with his Triangle cohorts, Gotti was a wild bettor who couldn't get out of his own way. Secretly recorded tapes found the Dapper Don bemoaning his leaden touch while betting football, including a $53,000 beating in a single weekend.

"I bet the Buffalo Bills for six dimes ($6,000), they're getting killed, ten to nothing," he griped on a wiretapped November 11, 1981, conversation. "I bet New England for six dimes, I'm getting killed with New England. I bet six dimes on Chicago, they're losing. I bet three dimes on KC, they're winning. Maybe they'll lose, those motherfuckers."

Despite the decades of federal pursuit, the Chin was never heard discussing his multimillion-dollar business or any other matters of organized crime. Long after he was caught yapping on the Ruggiero tapes, Gotti talked his way into a life sentence after the Castellano hit.

Yet, when the feds secretly planted a bug in an apartment upstairs from the Ravenite, they captured nary a bad word from Gotti about Gigante.

"All the conversations in the Ravenite, John Gotti bad-mouthed everybody—the Colombos, the Luccheses," said Mouw, who listened to hours and hours of tapes. "And every time it got around to Chin, he almost lowered his voice like the old E.F. Hutton commercial—'Well, the Chin says . . .'"

Even when alone with his most trusted Gambino associates, Gotti would never admit to any complicity in the Castellano killing. He seemed haunted by the thought that somehow, someway, word of his treachery would reach Gigante.

"Whoever done it, probably the cops done it to this guy," Gotti said during one conversation recorded by the feds. "Whoever killed this cocksucker, probably the cops killed this Paul. But whoever killed him, he deserved it."

In another chat in an apartment above the Ravenite, Gotti offered his grudging endorsement of the Chin's inspired lunacy. He recounted a conversation where another mobster began speculating about Gigante's mental health.

"You don't like the idea a guy wears a bathrobe," the Dapper Don said dismissively to the flunky.

When Gambino associate Joseph (Joe Glitz) questioned the Chin's sanity on another occasion, Gotti quickly told him to keep his mouth shut.

"He says, 'John, isn't he a fucking nut?'" Gotti said in yet another taped conversation from January 4, 1990. "He says, 'Why should I be subject to follow a nut?' And then he said, 'If he ain't a nut, he's faking it. He'll do this to stay out of jail. He'll do anything, you know?'

"So I told him, 'Listen, Joey, you said it and you got it off your chest, okay? That's that. Don't say it no more.'"

Gigante was "the anti-Gotti, to the extent that Gotti brought law enforcement attention, couldn't avoid electronic surveillance, promoted people he shouldn't and created internecine warfare," said Ronald Goldstock, the former head of the New York State Organized Crime Task Force.

"Gigante was exactly the opposite. No matter how we tried, there was no electronic surveillance," continued Goldstock. "People in the family respected him. He resolved problems, rather than fomenting them. The people surrounding him were tried and true."

Mouw said Gotti yearned for the kind of reputation and respect accorded the Chin.

"I'm sure he was envious," said Mouw. "The one thing John respected was power . . . power and money."

Atlantic City mobster Leonetti, in a conversation with Gam-

Vincent Gigante leaves
the Federal Courthouse
in December 1958,
where he was on trial
with sixteen others
on narcotics charges.
(Courtesy New York Daily News)

Olympia Gigante kisses
her husband Vincent
after his May 1958 acquittal
in the attempted murder
of mob big shot Frank Costello.
(Courtesy New York Daily News)

A 1958 photo of Vincent Gigante during the trial for the attempted murder of Frank Costello.
(Courtesy New York Daily News)

Frank Costello leaving Roosevelt Hospital, bearing blood stains on his jacket after a "mystery gunman" shot him in the lobby of his Central Park West apartment building, on May 3, 1957.
(Courtesy New York Daily News)

Gigante, flanked by his parents, mother Yolanda and father Salvatore, on trial
for the attempted murder of Frank Costello, May 13, 1958.
(Courtesy New York Daily News)

Mafia boss Vito Genovese (in passenger seat) after being arrested by federal narcotics agents.
Vincent Gigante was also arrested, July 8, 1958.
(Courtesy New York Daily News)

Vinnie Gigante — not looking
too concerned — after being
arrested on drug charges,
July 9, 1958.
*(Courtesy New York
Daily News)*

What, me worry? Gigante,
accompanied by his attorney
Maurice Edelbaum (center)
on his way to traffic court,
September 19, 1957.
(Courtesy New York Daily News)

Vinnie "Chin" being booked
for the shooting of Frank Costello
at the West 54th Street
police station, August 20, 1957.
(Courtesy New York Daily News)

August 14, 1957: Mario Gigante,
Vinnie's brother (center)
handcuffed to NYPD detectives
as he enters court.
Vinnie was still on the lam
at the time.
(Courtesy New York Daily News)

"Vincent Gigante — where is he?"
So read the caption on this mug shot
dated July 18, 1957.
(*Courtesy New York Daily News*)

Gigante strolling in Queens with Dominick "Quiet Dom" Cirillo, a high-ranking member of the
Genovese crime family, who briefly served as acting boss for Vincent when he was in jail, April 10, 2005.
(*Courtesy New York Daily News*)

Vinnie "Chin" Gigante, second right, huddles with his members of the Genovese crew: Frankie Condo, right; Bruce Palmeri, second left, and Dominick Canterino.
An undercover NYPD detective testified that Gigante, who claimed to be mentally ill, functioned normally when off his guard—dodging cars on a busy street and asking an impatient driver if he was "in a rush."
(Courtesy U.S. Attorney's Office)

The April 5, 1990 cover of the *NY Daily News* with a bathrobe-clad Gigante being led away in the $143 million windows scam. Peter Gotti, John Gotti's brother, was also pinched.
(Courtesy New York Daily News)

The robe makes the man: Gigante being placed under arrest in the multimillion-dollar windows scam, May 30, 1990. *(Courtesy New York Daily News)*

A clean-shaven Vincent Gigante, with his son Vincent, leaves the Upper East Side home of his longtime mistress (or "goomare") on June 27, 1997.
(Courtesy New York Daily News)

bino underboss Gravano, got the lowdown on the feud between the nation's two top mobsters.

"Sammy told me that John hated the Chin," Leonetti recalled. "But I think it was because John knew that he would never have the power that Chin had. I mean, the newspapers and the media made him the Dapper Don. But to guys on the street, guys in the Mob, they knew it was the Chin who was the real power in New York. And I think that irked Gotti, that as regal as he was, he couldn't trump this guy in a bathrobe."

When Gotti ascended as the new Gambino boss, Chin never regarded him an equal, a partner or a friend. Gigante viewed the interloper as a rule-breaking cop magnet and general pain in the ass.

The Chin treated the so-called Teflon Don with a certain faux deference, sitting with him at commission meetings and even once tipping him to the coming testimony of Genovese turncoat Cafaro in an upcoming Gotti trial.

But if the two appeared friendly on the face of things, their contrasting approaches to leadership became obvious at a sit-down held just months after Gotti took the seat atop the Gambinos. The freshly minted boss proposed violating another long-standing Mob protocol: killing someone in law enforcement.

And not just anyone: Gotti targeted federal prosecutor Giuliani, the Mob-buster who went on to become mayor of New York and a GOP presidential hopeful. Gotti was backed by Colombo boss Carmine Persico, who was one of the defendants in the case when the commission met in the fall of 1986.

Cooler heads prevailed, with Chin casting the deciding vote to spare Giuliani. In November, Persico and three other bosses, along with five of their top aides, were all convicted and sentenced in Giuliani's Southern District.

The bosses of the Lucchese, Bonanno and Genovese families rejected the idea despite strong efforts to convince them otherwise, read a memo on the meeting from FBI agent Lindsey DeVecchio.

Things were different behind the scenes. As he did when Philly boss Bruno was whacked in an unsanctioned hit, Vincent

Gigante wasted no time in plotting his payback on the plotters. A murder contract was placed on John Gotti's head after the Chin—accompanied by his brother Ralph—ventured to the wilds of Staten Island for a sit-down with Lucchese boss Tony Ducks Corallo.

The men, sitting in the home of Christie Tick Funari, agreed that Gotti had to go.

The new Gambino boss, apparently unaware he was now the target of Chin's wrath, blithely went about his business as if he was the new king of New York City. In reality, the first interfamily bloodletting since the Castellammarese War was festering in the Big Apple. Gigante was poised to strike the first deathblow.

Gotti wasn't alone in his cluelessness: Gigante had also ordered hits on the treacherous Frankie DeCicco, who was now the Gambino underboss, the capo and co-conspirator Sammy Gravano, Bartholomew "Bobby" Borriello, who was Gotti's driver/ bodyguard, and shooter Eddie Lino.

Longtime Lucchese soldier Alphonse "Little Al" D'Arco recalled the Chin's initial plan was to deliberately not whack Gotti in a quick strike, the way Castellano was taken down. The fuming Gigante wanted to eradicate Gotti's friends and fellow plotters, leaving the Gambino boss with the feeling of a noose tightening around his disrespectful throat.

"Vincent Gigante wanted John Gotti," said D'Arco, who would eventually become boss of the Luccheses. "He just didn't want him killed first."

One of the things that Gigante most despised about Gotti actually kept the Gambino boss alive: Johnny Boy's constant attention from the FBI and the press wrapped him in a security blanket, making it hard to hit the new boss. The storefront Ravenite in Little Italy was tucked amid cramped and crowded streets, which made a Mob killing almost impossible in the neighborhood.

"He's all the time being watched by the government and the

news media," griped Lucchese underboss Anthony "Gaspipe" Casso. "John Miller's feet are sticking out of his ass half the time."

Miller, then a local television reporter, would leave the media for law enforcement and become the NYPD's antiterrorism czar.

"He loves the attention," Gigante replied. "He thinks he's in show business."

"Yeah," said Casso. "Seems so."

"What I wouldn't do for a little privacy," replied the oft-surveilled Chin.

The meeting ended with hugs and a kiss on the cheek.

On April 13, 1986, almost four months to the day from the Castellano hit, the Genovese family received word that Gotti and DeCicco would visit a Brooklyn social club for a sit-down with the Gambino family's new hierarchy. The Chin's plan of a slow death for Gotti was instantly jettisoned.

It was a cloudy, overcast day when DeCicco parked on a Bensonhurst street and headed inside. When DeCicco emerged, he was accompanied by a man who had a close resemblance to Gotti—but was actually a Lucchese family soldier named Frank "Frankie Hearts" Bellino. In a cruel twist it was the Luccheses who agreed to handle the hit for Gigante. It was decided to use a bomb fashioned from the plastic explosive C4.

Using a bomb was against the usual Mafia regulations, and was typically a method left to the Sicilians. The bomb was chosen precisely because an explosion would point the finger away from the Chin, who was a noted nitpicker for Mob protocol, murderous or not.

The killers swung into action, affixing the package of plastic explosives beneath the Buick Electra. Gravano was inside the Veterans and Friends Social Club with DeCicco as the killers worked outside.

When DeCicco returned to his car with Bellino, the bombers watched and waited, with one finally pressing a remote control from a toy car purchased at a Toys "R" Us. DeCicco was killed instantly, blown right out of his shoes, which still held his toes. Bellino miraculously survived.

After nearly four months of quiet following the Castellano murder, Gotti never saw it coming.

"I don't know what the fuck is going on," he told Gravano, "but we've got problems."

Gotti, as Gigante had hoped, never suspected the Chin was behind the bomb blast.

"Our first thought was the Genovese family," said Gravano, who was bumped up as the new underboss. "But the Chin was a real stickler for the rules of our life, and one of the rules was you don't use bombs."

Gotti even reached out to the Philly Mob for help in figuring out what happened.

"They were looking for us to help, to figure out who made the bomb and who planted it, because of how Phil Testa was blown up," said Leonetti. "But we didn't know much about that bomb, except it was loaded with nails."

The patient Chin crossed one name off his list. It took another four years, but Castellano killer Eddie Lino was next on the hit parade.

The Gambino soldier was driving home from a Mob social club in his black Mercedes on the morning of November 6, 1990, when an unmarked police car flipped on its lights and pulled the gangster over on the Belt Parkway in Brooklyn.

The routine traffic stop quickly became something else; the men inside the police vehicle were a pair of crooked NYPD detectives collecting a monthly $4,000 retainer from Gaspipe Casso. They had followed Lino until they reached a section of the highway where he could pull off onto a grassy stretch of shoulder.

Gaspipe "wanted to be involved in retribution for that [Castellano hit] because it was unsanctioned," his old friend and illegal business associate Burton Kaplan later testified. The Lucchese bigwig reached out to Louie Eppolito, a highly decorated NYPD detective who grew up in a Mob family before launching a career in law enforcement.

Eppolito checked with his partner, the equally mercenary Steven Caracappa, soon to live in infamy as "the Mafia Cops," the most corrupt officers in the NYPD's long and storied history. The two decorated detectives signed on as Mob hit men, although not without some difficulties.

The cops, unwilling to use their service revolvers in service of Mob murder, asked if Gaspipe could provide two guns. The mercurial and murderous Gaspipe exploded at the request.

"Jesus!" he snapped. "Don't these two guys do anything for themselves?"

Casso eventually provided the weapons. The "Mafia Cops" did the rest.

The two cops pulled up behind Lino's car. Before getting out of their own vehicle, the detectives put on their NYPD badges so Lino would know they were cops, not killers. The gregarious Eppolito did the talking, and the taciturn Caracappa handled the shooting.

"Hey, Frankie, how are you?" asked Eppolito—a reference to Eddie's cousin, a member of the Bonanno family.

A smile of relief came about Lino's face.

"I'm not Frankie Lino," the doomed man said. "I'm Eddie Lino."

Eppolito pointed to something on the passenger-side floor, asking Lino if he could pick it up. When the made man leaned over, Caracappa opened fire, and didn't stop until Lino's bullet-riddled body slumped down in the front seat. Eppolito blithely explained why Caracappa handled the actual killing: "Steve is a much better shot."

On April 13, 1991, Bobby Borriello pulled into the driveway of his Brooklyn home at about 7:30 P.M. His wife, Susan, and their two-year-old son were waiting for Daddy inside, but Borriello never made the front door. A fusillade of bullets followed, with the Gotti loyalist struck ten times in the head, back and arm.

His wife rushed outside to find her murdered husband face-down in a pool of his own blood. She later charged that Cara-cappa and Eppolito fed the killers inside information culled from the NYPD to target her husband.

This murder struck Gotti particularly close to home. He had once assigned the trusty Borriello to his son John Jr.'s crew to keep an eye on the Mob scion and future Gambino boss. Gra-vano said later that Gotti never suspected the deft hand of the Chin in any of the killings.

Gotti learned in 1987 about the Chin's plans for his death after the DeCicco hit, after the FBI planted a bug inside the ladies' room of Casella's, a Hoboken restaurant owned by mob-ster Martin "Motts" Casella. The details of the plot, ostensibly for Gotti's unwanted intrusion into Genovese business in North Jersey, emerged from the women's room in the summer of that year. The man organizing the murder was old Genovese hand Bobby Manna.

"Remember I told you it was a big hit?" Manna said on one tape. "John Gotti."

Two unidentified voices chimed in with suggestions and pre-dictions.

"The only way to do it is in Rockefeller Center," said the first. "Make your hit solo."

Manna was typically joined in the bathroom sessions by Ca-sella, retired police lieutenant Frank "Dipsy" Daniello and Mob enforcer Richard "Bocci" DeSciscio. Before one of their conver-sations began, a female customer walked in to answer nature's call.

"Go piss in the street, lady," one of the gentlemen advised her. "This is a fucking business meeting."

Manna was among the Chin's most trusted aides, with a his-tory of violence and an unshakeable belief in his sworn oath of omerta. A 1972 New Jersey report on organized crime tied Manna to the late Tommy Eboli, and identified him as the Genovese family's man on the waterfront—responsible for bookmaking, loan-sharking and numbers operations.

When subpoenaed that year in a Mob investigation, the Hudson County hard-ass not only refused to testify, but he refused to be sworn in. His silence landed him in the state Correctional Center in Yardville, where he first met fellow true believer Little Nicky Scarfo. The two became fast friends, walking the yard and discussing their Mafia ambitions.

He had one other qualification for the job, recounted Genovese Squad head Pritchard: "Bobby Manna was a stone killer." The gangster shared one other characteristic with his boss, Vincent Gigante: He didn't like people throwing his name around. The skinny Manna, sometimes known as "the Thin Man," preferred his associates to raise one pinky finger when referring to him.

Manna's suggestion was to take a shot at Gotti in his natural habitat, out near the Bergin Hunt and Fish Club in Ozone Park.

"Wear a disguise," the consigliere advised. "It's an open area."

"Do you know where you're going to hit him?" asked Daniello.

"Yeah," said Casella. "On that corner."

Daniello later declared, "The godfather . . . ain't getting home."

The Gambino Squad, as required by law, visited with Gotti on September 30, 1987, to deliver news of the planned killing. Mouw recalled that the agents never mentioned Gigante by name during a short session with the Gambino boss outside his Howard Beach home.

"We didn't say Gigante," he recalled. "We just said the West Side—the Genovese family." Gotti read between the lines, so he began traveling with a bodyguard.

The bathroom tapes indicated that the Hoboken plotters were undeterred by the FBI heads-up, and continued scheming until they were indicted and arrested.

"Hey, John Gotti knows," Casella said on a later tape.

Manna even upped the ante by mentioning Gotti's dope-slinging brother Gene as another target. "Gene Gotti's dead," he declared in a bugged January 12, 1988, chat.

"When are you going to hit him?" asked co-conspirator James Napoli.

"Gene Gotti's dead," Manna repeated evenly.

"We're gonna be paying for this, you know, for the rest of our lives," Napoli replied.

Gotti ordered a hit of his own on Gigante, but the purported retaliation was more pipe dream than pipe bomb. There was a single Gambino response to the Chin's offensive: Vincent "Jimmy" Rotondo, a Genovese waterfront racketeer, was found shot to death inside his car. In an old-school touch, a bag of fish was left on the dead man's lap.

But Gotti remained improbably clueless about the Chin's lethal and laser-like focus on taking the Gambino boss down. In a secretly taped November 30, 1989, conversation with Gravano, the Dapper Don recounted how one of his underlings had praised him for an era of Mob goodwill.

"He says, 'Since youse was here, this is the first time that they could remember in years that the families ain't arguing,'" Gotti boasted. "'Nobody's arguing. None of the families are arguing with nobody.'"

"No," agreed Gravano.

"Everybody sedate," Gotti replied.

The ultimate meeting between the pair came in 1988, when the two bosses were undisputedly the most wanted figures in organized crime. They sat together, the slovenly Gigante and the impeccably attired Gotti, to discuss the state of the city's crime world. It was the Mafia equivalent of Ali and Frazier breaking bread.

Gigante sported a five-day growth of wild stubble. He wore a robe and pajamas. His skin was so filthy that white flecks of dirt fell to the ground. And yet the old-timer schooled the younger, more aggressive gangster.

First was the meeting's location: an apartment in Lower Manhattan, in a building that was home to a Gambino capo. The sitdown was arranged by Benny Eggs and the Bull, with Gravano later acknowledging he was surprised by Gigante's agreement to meet there.

It turned out the Chin had a relative in the building. The perpetually paranoid Gigante spent the night in his apartment, and walked through the building to thwart any hit teams waiting outside. Lucchese boss Vittorio "Little Vic" Amuso and Gotti, in contrast, met on the street, leaving both men wide open.

Gotti proposed recognizing the Bonanno family, a recovering collection of dopes and dope dealers reeling for the last decade since FBI undercover Pistone infiltrated the family. They were now headed by acting boss Vittorio "Little Vic" Orena, with Gotti's ally and Howard Beach neighbor Joseph "Big Joey" Massino among the family's up-and-comers.

The Chin, backed by Amuso, vetoed the idea until the next commission meeting, denying Gotti an ally on the ruling board.

Gotti next suggested opening the books to induct new members, including forty spots in the Genovese family. The Gambino boss figured any new Genovese inductees would learn the openings came courtesy of Gotti, who hoped to make inroads into Gigante's family. The Chin nixed that one, too.

"Chin stared straight at John and said, 'When the time comes, I'll make those moves inside my family. I appreciate your concern, but I'll do it when I'm ready,' " Gravano later recalled.

There was some small talk during the ninety-minute meeting. At one point Gigante lifted his pajama top to display the scar from his recent aortic valve replacement. He warned all involved that these types of get-togethers were not destined to become a regular feature of his schedule.

"I've put a lot of time into this crazy act, and I don't want to get caught in any of these meetings or picked up or bugged," the Chin told them.

D'Arco, a top Lucchese capo, later revealed that Amuso and

the Chin only allowed Gotti to attend in an effort to dupe the Dapper Don into believing he was a welcomed equal at the commission meetings.

Gigante delivered the coup de grace when Gotti boasted about his son's Christmas Eve induction as a made member of the Gambinos.

"Jeez," the Chin replied. "I'm sorry to hear that."

Gravano, in the room as his boss's second, left astounded by everything he had just seen and heard.

"So here was the Chin, who's supposed to be crazy, saying who in their right mind would want their son to be made," Gravano recalled. "And there was John, boasting about it. Who was really crazy?"

Gotti called Gravano the next day to praise the Chin's deft handling of everything. Gigante was "smart as a fox," said the Chin's bête noir.

Police found a crude bomb outside Gotti's Ravenite Social Club after an anonymous phone call, a year later, reporting a "gift for John Gotti" left on Mulberry Street. Officials were unsure if it was a pointed message or some kind of stunt. Chief of Detectives Robert Colangelo opined that both were possibilities.

"It's either a warning to Gotti that he is vulnerable or his club is vulnerable," he said. "Or it could have been a prank."

There was one more failed plot to kill Gotti. In 1990, when Chin was under indictment, Amuso and Casso approached D'Arco about contacting a mobbed-up Pittsburgh cousin to provide a "remote control bomb" to blow up the Dapper Don.

D'Arco was concerned that the bomb might be traced back to him, because his relative had ties to the Genovese family.

"Don't worry about it. 'The Robe' knows about it," Gaspipe told him, using his own alias for Gigante.

The two warring Mob bosses were once on the same side, albeit under strange circumstances. An undercover Drug Enforcement Agency agent was posing as a cocaine dealer when he went for a Staten Island sit-down with a mobbed-up drug dealer in 1989.

Everett Hatcher, a forty-six-year-old father of two, arrived in the desolate section of Staten Island and never returned. The DEA agent was shot to death inside his car, his body left slumped over the steering wheel. The cold-blooded execution sent the city's law enforcement community into an all-out, no-holds-barred manhunt for the killer, Constabile "Gus" Farace.

The suspect's Mob ties ran deep: Farace had an uncle in the Gambino family, and cousins in the Bonanno and Colombo enterprises. DEA investigators immediately put intense pressure on the city's five families to turn Farace in, with appeals made to Gotti and Gigante to exert their influence on the underworld in closing the case. Robert Stutman, the head of the DEA, personally appealed to Gotti in a visit to the Mob boss's Howard Beach home.

"We tried everything," Stutman acknowledged.

There was precedent for the unusual move: Genovese capo Ianniello agreed to help authorities searching for a six-year-old named Etan Patz after the boy disappeared on a Manhattan street in 1979.

Farace, though never arrested, did receive a death sentence. He was sprayed with sixteen bullets to the head, neck, back and leg in a November 17, 1989, Mob execution. Two Lucchese family associates later pleaded guilty to performing the Mafia-sanctioned murder.

John Gotti survived the Chin's assorted murder plots, although he couldn't escape arrest. When his son assumed command after the Teflon Don was busted on December 11, 1990, the Genovese hierarchy—in a final slap at the elder Gotti—refused even to meet with the Mafia novice.

CHAPTER 14

IT AIN'T ME, BABE

*T*HE COMMISSION CASE FINALLY WENT TO TRIAL IN 1986, WITH A brilliant young prosecutor named Michael Chertoff winning convictions across the board after a ten-week trial that drew unprecedented media attention. All nine defendants were found guilty, with the jury forewoman brushing away tears as she read the lengthy verdict.

Salerno and the rest showed no emotion during the twenty-minute recitation. The triumphant Chertoff declared the newly convicted Mafiosi were "directing the largest and most vicious criminal business in the history of the United States."

Salerno and the other bosses were sentenced to the max: one hundred years, with no possibility of parole. He would die three years later after suffering a stroke at the federal prison medical center in Springfield, Missouri. By then, the rest of the world would know the secret that Fat Tony took to the grave: Vincent Gigante was the true head of the Genovese family.

Salerno, while awaiting the commission trial, was indicted again that same year in another RICO case, with fourteen other defendants, including old pal Fish Cafaro. But the two had a falling-out over cash, and Cafaro became the first Genovese family made man to turn government witness since Valachi more than two decades earlier. He proved every bit as chatty as his infamous Genovese predecessor.

With Salerno placed in prison, Gigante's name began surfacing in random news stories speculating about the new boss of the Genovese family. But the Mob power remained a cipher to most of America; those aware of the name most likely recalled apocryphal tales of the old mobster wandering the Village as if dressed by a color-blind homeless man.

The Chin's long subterfuge was presented to readers of the *New York Times* in February 1988, when the newspaper exposed his strange existence in a 2,300-word piece by longtime organized crime chronicler Selwyn Raab. The exposé ran just two months before Fish Cafaro exposed the inner workings of the Genovese crime family before the U.S. Congress.

Almost every afternoon, a graying, unimpressively dressed man emerges from an apartment building on Sullivan Street in Greenwich Village and gingerly crosses the street to a dingy store, where he spends several hours playing cards and whispering to confidantes, Raab wrote to start his piece.

Although he behaves oddly at times in public, law-enforcement authorities say the man, Vincent (the Chin) Gigante has created one of the most impregnable mob strongholds in the country.

The story noted: *[Gigante] was lightly regarded by law enforcement mob experts as a potential candidate for the hierarchy of the Genovese family. He was generally viewed as an old-fashioned capo who was so distressed by the fear of arrest that he feigned mental illness in an attempt to discourage attention from the authorities.*

And it quoted Goldstock, the former head of the state Organized Crime Task Force, about Gigante's strange reign—unlike that of any Mafia chieftain dating back to the creation of the five families in 1931.

"It is like a Howard Hughes syndrome," Goldstock observed. "He locks himself up in a small area, and it is hard to understand what enjoyment he gets from being a mob boss. The only pleasure appears to be the pure power that he exercises."

Vincent Gigante was into his seventh year atop the powerful Mob enterprise when the story appeared. Anybody who missed the *Times* piece was treated to a far more colorful, and personal, recounting of the Chin's rise when Fish Cafaro came to Washington directly from no-man's-land.

The Genovese family veteran, in the nineteen months since betraying his Mob brethren, had flipped and flopped more than a catfish on the end of a fishing line. He wore a wire for five months; and then, a year later, he changed his mind about cooperating.

Cafaro, initially a prized catch as the first Genovese family soldier to flip since Valachi sang for the U.S. Congress in 1963, didn't deliver as authorities initially hoped. His efforts were widely denigrated as disappointing and disjointed.

Pritchard acknowledged that Cafaro tipped the FBI to Liborio "Barney" Bellomo, a suburbanite who was the hottest young star in organized crime.

"We didn't even know he existed," said Pritchard. "He was the ultimate sleeper."

Overall, however, Pritchard said, the Fish was a poor catch.

"To me—and now again, I don't want to hurt anyone's feelings—I don't think he gave everything," the ex-FBI man said. "I don't think he gave one hundred percent. When he did turn, a lot of people were blinded—'Oh, wow, the Fish! Wonderful'—but he didn't cooperate as fully as he could have. He was clever about what he coughed up or fessed up. He was given some reverence, misplaced, because he was the first Genovese guy to get on the bus."

A federal prosecutor who encountered Cafaro in the late 1980s was more blunt: "He was a bitter, broken former capo with a lot of anger and a lot to drink."

A different Cafaro arrived to sit before a congressional panel investigating organized crime. The Fish had finally decided his odds at survival were better with the feds than the goodfellas.

"Hundreds, if not thousands, of La Cosa Nostra members wanted him dead," announced Cafaro's lawyer, David Eames. One was son Thomas, who followed his father into the Mob family; the FBI (somewhat ironically) learned through another informant that the younger Cafaro was given a contract for the old man's murder.

Cafaro's disloyalty had almost cost Thomas his life, too. Bonanno family associate Joe Barone, whose father was a made man with the Genovese family, said the powerful but forgiving Barney Bellomo decided not to impose the sins of the father on the son. Thomas Cafaro, like Barone Jr. and Bellomo, had followed his old man into the Mafia.

"Fish had a son, and they were going to whack him," Barone Jr. recounted, "but Barney gave the order to let him go. He gave him a pass. The kid was a good kid, you know?"

Those were the circumstances when Cafaro came to Capitol Hill on April 29, 1988, to offer his reflections on a Mob life that had begun in Fat Tony Salerno's numbers operation in 1958— and finished under the rule of the Chin.

"Do you swear the testimony you give before this subcommittee will be the truth, the whole truth, and nothing but the truth, so help you God?" asked U.S. Senate Permanent Subcommittee on Investigations chair, Senator Sam Nunn, a Georgia Democrat.

"Yes, Senator," the gangster replied. "My name is Vincent Cafaro, known to my friends as the Fish."

The hypersecretive Chin's domain was laid bare to the nation by Cafaro—especially Gigante's long, successful psychiatric dodge, dismissed by the Fish as pure ruse by a respected boss determined to remain on his lofty perch.

"To the outside world, Gigante is known for his sometimes bizarre and crazy behavior," Cafaro began. "In truth, he is a shrewd and experienced family member who has risen through the ranks from soldier to capo to boss. His strange behavior, insisting to the outside world that he's crazy, helps to further insulate him from the authorities. In the meantime his control of the family's activities is as strong and calculated as ever."

"Could you give us an example of his so-called crazy behavior?" asked Senator Nunn.

"Well, he walks around with the robe and pajamas. He—"

Nunn interrupted: "You mean outside?"

"Outside, yes," Cafaro continued. "By the club where he stays. He is always in his robe and pajamas, and says crazy things. He does crazy things."

"You are saying he is not crazy?" asked Nunn.

"I do not think so," replied the understated Cafaro.

The Fish recounted Chin's nod for the 1980 whacking of Caponigro and the 1982 murder of Masselli. He testified about Gigante's closed-mouth approach to Mob business, detailing how the Chin never confirmed his 1981 ascension to boss to most of the Mob's ruling hierarchy in the Big Apple. Cafaro touched briefly, without details, on the Chin's long association with Morris Levy and Roulette Records. He detailed the family's sources of income: bid rigging, the 2 percent kickback on concrete, construction, gambling.

"But our real power, our real strength, came from the unions," he declared. "With the unions behind us, we could shut down the city—or the country, for that matter—if we needed to, to get our way. . . . I would say at least half the locals in the city is run by wiseguys—carpenters, laborers—so that is all wiseguys involved."

He made it clear that the no-nonsense Chin, who boasted a personal crew of thirty to forty hard-core loyalists, ran a tight ship. The Genovese family was a "very disciplined organization," where the street soldiers were mandated to check in weekly with their captains. Those capos received a 10 percent kickup on all scores.

The family had fourteen capos, with approximately four hundred total members. Chin was the boss, with "Sammy Black" Santora serving as the underboss and Bobby Manna as the consigliere. When Gigante called, the capos came running—no questions asked, day or night. Or middle of the night, the Chin's preferred hours of operation.

"When you were a captain, you have to be there," he testified. "You're on call twenty-four hours a day in case there's problems or beefs or whatever."

He was unwavering in his assertion that the Chin imposed a total ban on drug dealing within the Genovese family. "No way in hell they would fool around with junk," Cafaro said. "There might be some sneakers. But as far as I know, no."

The soldier recounted his own introduction to the Mob, back when he was a teenage heroin dealer growing up in the shadow of the Palma Boys Social Club in East Harlem. Cafaro was busted with two ounces of heroin, and his grandparents brought him to see Salerno—a Mafia version of the Scared Straight program.

"Fat Tony took me aside and gave me some advice. 'Leave the junk alone. If you need money, go out and steal,'" Cafaro recalled.

When Cafaro was twenty-four, Salerno reached out to offer an entry-level job in his numbers operation. "I said yes, and stayed with Fat Tony for the next twenty-five years," Cafaro said. "In the end Fat Tony had become, in many ways, like a father to me."

In 1974, at a ceremony in the Il Cortile restaurant on Little Italy's Mulberry Street, the Fish was inducted as "a true *amico nostro*" at a ceremony overseen by underboss Funzi Tieri and consigliere Salerno.

"This is not something you ask for," he made clear. "This is something you are offered by the family, if they feel you are worthy."

Cafaro provided a quick lesson in Mob economics. When he became partners with Fat Tony in the West Harlem numbers operation, they handled about $80,000 a day in bets collected by seventy-two runners. In a good year he and Salerno split $4 million from the gamblers between 110th and 153rd Streets.

Nunn was somewhat incredulous about Cafaro's income, which went out as fast as it came in.

"You said in some good years you made one million, two million a year. . . . Did you save any of it? Did you put it up?" Nunn asked.

"Nope," said a rueful Fish. "I spent it, Senator. Just gave it away. I never got it all at once. I never had a big lump of money. As I was making it, I was spending it: women, bartenders, waiters, hotels. Just spending the money . . . If I had it to spend, I'd spend three million. I used to go out with five thousand to ten thousand in my pocket."

It was money that finally fractured his near-lifelong friendship with Fat Tony, a sad insight that neatly encapsulated the Mob's true loyalty: cold, hard cash trumped everything.

The Fish owed Salerno a $65,000 debt, but he was unable to pay it from his cell inside the Metropolitan Correctional Center after an arrest. Salerno was angry, and so was Cafaro. When the Fish was sprung, he made good on the debt. But he brusquely informed Salerno that he would no longer kick up the lucrative proceeds of his slot machines. Fat Tony had collected a hefty one-third of the take in the past.

"So he says to me, he says, well, he says, 'I'll pick this cane up and I'll hit you with it,'" Cafaro recounted. "So I says to him, 'Well, that's the biggest mistake you'll ever make, if you pick up that cane to me.' And that's how I think I turned."

Nunn inquired about Cafaro's health—or, more precisely, how worried the Fish was about it.

"So, if you were to get on the streets right now, you think you'd be a marked man?" the senator asked.

"Think?" replied the bemused Cafaro. "I know."

Cafaro also recounted three meetings of the Mob's ruling commission, an assembly of leadership from all five New York families, in 1984 through 1985. On the first two occasions Gigante, ever fearful of a tail or a wiretap, sent Fat Tony as his representative.

Both times, Cafaro served as Salerno's chauffeur from the Palma Boys to a Staten Island luncheonette, where they were met by the doomed Gambino capo Tommy Bilotti as Gambino boss Castellano's go-between. From there, they were driven to a house in the city's smallest borough, the home turf of the imperious Castellano, for a business meeting about construction and concrete.

The attendees included Castellano, Lucchese underboss Tom Mix Santoro, and Colombo capos Dominick "Donny Shacks" Montemarano and Ralph Scopo. The Bonannos, still in post-Pistone disarray, were not invited.

Bilotti, Cafaro and four or five other *amici nostri* stayed up-stairs while the meeting went on below. When it ended hours later, Cafaro was briefed about the topics.

"Every time there was a commission meeting with Paul, it was about business—money and business," he recounted, echoing Gravano's recollections. Gigante preferred to ignore such get-togethers.

The second time, Cafaro was ordered to wait in the lun-cheonette. On both occasions, Salerno had no fears about the prying eyes or ears of the FBI as they sailed into Staten Island.

Meeting number three was an unmitigated disaster.

The get-together was held close to the Chin's Village base, at Bari's on Houston Street, a business that sold restaurant equip-ment. Fish Cafaro drove Fat Tony to meet with Gigante, and they headed for the sit-down with Corallo, the Gambinos' Castellano and Joe N. Gallo, and the Colombo family's underboss Langella and Montemarano.

With the notoriously paranoid Chin involved, security was ramped up. Genovese capo Baldy Dom Canterino was dis-patched to keep an eye on the street as Cafaro waited nearby to drive Fat Tony home. He was stunned to see a disheveled Sa-lerno reappear far too soon. The rotund, cigar-chomping mob-ster was sucking air.

"Usually a commission meeting lasts four or five hours, six hours," Cafaro explained later. "And he come back to the neigh-borhood [early] and I seen him. He's huffing and puffing. I says, 'How come you're back so early?' He says, 'There were agents down there. . . . We had to get out.' So rather than to get pinched or the agents go in, they all ran."

Escape was easier said than done for the portly, poorly condi-tioned seventy-four-year-old Salerno.

"He says, 'They had to push me out through the window to get out.' He couldn't fit," Cafaro recounted, oblivious to the scene's comedic value. "He was too fat. He got stuck in the window."

Gigante, with the help of Donny Shacks, rushed to Fat Tony's aid. With a few well-placed shoves from the Chin, Salerno finally popped through to freedom like a cork loosened from a champagne bottle. Fat Tony then ran to meet up with Cafaro and head for safer ground.

When they returned to the Palma Boys, "he was still out of breath over his escape," Cafaro added.

"Who knows if there was an agent or there wasn't an agent?" the "Fish tale" concluded. "I really don't know."

The Cafaro testimony made headlines, but was more of a petty annoyance to the Chin. The year 1988 proved crucial to Gigante's reign for another reason: There was a real and very active rat within the Genovese family. And he was there at the Chin's invitation.

CHAPTER 15

WANTED MAN

VINCENT GIGANTE HAD NO IDEA WHAT HIS FUTURE WOULD HOLD the first time he sat in a room across from Genovese family associate Peter Savino.

Savino, on the other hand, was pretty certain that he was about to take his last breath. The summons came two months after Pappa had already done the same.

It was 1980 when Savino walked inside Ruggero's, a Mob-owned restaurant on Grand Street in Little Italy, to answer the call from on high. It was dark inside, and he was directed to an office upstairs.

"As we were walking up the stairs, there were no lights on, and we came to the top of the stairs, and I expected to be shot at any moment," he later recalled.

To Savino's surprise, he was still alive after reaching the landing. He walked into the office and his heart almost stopped: There was Gigante, along with Funzi Tieri and other high-ranking members of the Genovese hierarchy. He knew the Chin only by reputation, and found Gigante in the flesh to be even more terrifying.

Their first request proved almost impossible: "They asked me not to be nervous."

The next question involved his street boss, Genovese capo "Sally Young" Palimieri: Did the captain take control of Pappa's street business, including a lucrative loan-sharking operation? Savino conceded that he had.

Gigante spit on the floor in disgust.

"Are these the new rules?" asked the defiantly old-school boss. "We take money from widows and orphans?"

Savino then confirmed the capo was handling drug money. Young was instantly demoted, and Savino learned he was about to be reassigned. "They said to me that I didn't have to be with Sally Young anymore, if I wanted to pick someone I would be comfortable with," Savino said.

In a strange and ultimately life-defining decision, Savino landed with the guy who made him most uncomfortable: Vincent Gigante. In an equally unlikely choice, the Chin, whose Mob radar was generally unerring, eventually took a shine to the quivering Savino.

But business would come before friendship. Though Savino was attached to the Chin, he would report to Genovese capo Joe Zito.

"We will tell you what to do through Joe," Gigante announced.

Savino would also need to repay a $1 million debt owed Vic Amuso and Gaspipe Casso as the Genovese family took over the business that he shared with the two high-ranking Luccheses. The two soldiers, a pair of wild cards who would share a murderous rise to the top of their family, had invested $500,000 with Pappa in a scam involving four Mob families.

They wanted the money repaid—plus another $500,000 in profit for their troubles.

Savino considered the 100 percent markup a reasonable price to pay for his life. He sold $250,000 in bonds to make the first installment on his debt, delivering the cash inside a Sunkist orange crate during a meeting inside a Brooklyn bar. Zito tagged along with his new recruit.

"They were upset that the money was in fives, tens and twenties," Savino said.

Zito rose quickly to his defense: "What is the difference? You got two hundred fifty thousand. That is what is important."

* * *

The payoff was linked to what became known as "the Windows Case," a massive Mob conspiracy concocted by the crafty Savino in the late 1970s. At the time the federal Department of Housing and Urban Development (HUD) launched an ambitious program to cut heating costs dramatically in public housing through the installation of new windows.

Tall, dark-haired and handsome, Savino looked into the double-glazed windows and saw millions of dollars in ill-gotten gains. To pull it off, he would need the full weight of New York's families working in concert.

The Brooklyn-born Savino, a World War II baby, was involved with both organized crime and Local 580 of the Architectural and Ornamental Ironworkers Union during the 1960s. Both affiliations proved quite lucrative as the 1980s approached.

The Genovese family, through Savino, served as the lead group. The Luccheses controlled the window workers union, so they were given a piece. The Gambinos and the Colombos owned window-manufacturing companies, as did Savino—Arista Windows and American Aluminum. The bumbling Bonannos were frozen out.

"There are too many junk guys," sniffed Salerno.

His partners in the business were Casso and Amuso, who made a single contribution to the operation: they built a handball court behind the Brooklyn offices, as Little Vic Amuso was an aficionado.

The operation was simple yet ingenious: Thirteen Mob-run companies rigged the bidding process, insuring the low bidder would win the contract at an outrageously high price. Any non-Mob window companies would pay a $2-per-window Mob tax for a piece of the installation action. The union, in addition to installing windows, would shatter any glass put in place by outsiders. Bribes paid to city officials kept everything running smoothly.

Savino once explained to a Colombo associate that winning a bid was like flipping a coin among the families.

"All right, you won this toss," he said. "Now you get that one. The next one, I get."

Savino wasn't afraid to get his hands dirty to keep things running smoothly. When a Genovese-affiliated window manufacturer began listening to Lucchese overtures about switching affiliations, Savino and a second mobster turned up at their storage yard.

The pair, armed with machine guns, opened fire. When the bullets stopped flying, two hundred windows were reduced to glass shards.

Prosecutors later said the Mob won $151 million of the $191 million in window replacement contracts from the New York City Housing Authority between 1978–1989, turning a crooked profit estimated in the tens of millions of dollars.

The case offered yet another peek into the Gotti-Gigante dynamic—and their relative spots on the Mafia food chain. While the Chin and the Genovese family were making millions off the window scam, Gotti complained that his group—specifically, his brother Peter—were getting short shrift.

"Joe 'Piney' (Armone) and Sammy (Gravano)—he made my brother Pete get involved with that fucking asshole with the 'Windows,'" Gotti moaned in a December 12, 1989, conversation above the Ravenite. "Never made a dime. He's going to jail for it."

Benny Eggs Mangano, by now the Genovese underboss, had previously rebuffed a Gambino family bid for a bigger piece of the multimillion-dollar action.

If their first meeting was fraught with terror on Savino's part, his well-deserved reputation as one of the biggest earners in the Genovese family soon won Gigante's admiration and respect. He dealt mostly with Mangano, who provided a quick primer on the family rules.

Number one: "Point to your chin and say 'This guy.'"

Number two: "If anyone asked about the Chin's act, reply only that 'Vincent's crazy.'"

Savino became a habitué of the Triangle, embraced by the Chin and welcomed into the boss's tight inner circle.

"Savino is directly with Chin, face-to-face," said ex-federal prosecutor Greg O'Connell. "The Chin took Petey under his wing. He loved Petey. Petey was a charismatic guy who was a huge moneymaker for the family."

Although Savino was never inducted as a made man, his new status came with some strange and scary turns.

On one Triangle visit for a discussion of the labor racketeering business, the perpetually paranoid Gigante brought him into the back bathroom and turned on all the faucets. Only then did the Chin put his unshaven mug against the guest's ear and whisper.

He asked, with unusual concern, if anybody in the Genovese family or the union was hitting Savino up for free windows. (Chin later asked for installations in Old Tappan for his wife and on the Upper East Side for his mistress.)

"Okay, I wanted to know if anyone was taking advantage of you," the Chin said. He paused before continuing.

"Don't be afraid to tell people I'm crazy, because you know I am crazy, right?" he said.

"Yes, I know you are," Savino wisely responded.

He was summoned again in June 1982 to hear a request just as terrifying as Gigante's call for Savino to chill out during his first trip to the Triangle. This time he was led through the side door connecting to the adjoining apartment building and taken to a first-floor landing to freeze out even the social club's regulars.

Gigante, joined by consigliere Manna, had Savino in mind as a hit man. Could Savino, they wondered, get close enough to do the job? The target was a seventeen-year-old suspected of killing Edward Lanzieri, the father of a Genovese made man named Edward "Eddie Buff" Lanzieri.

"Take him out," the Chin ordered icily.

The unnerved Savino, though a veteran of Mob murder from his days working alongside Pappa, knew the target. Instead of killing teenager Enrico "Eddie" Carini, he procrastinated until the plot eventually disappeared from the Chin's radar.

There were lighter moments. Savino was invited back to Ruggero's, this time to dine with Gigante. Capo Zito—owner of the restaurant—took a shot at his crew member's lack of sartorial style, which ran to burgundy track suits and spotless white sneakers. The words were barely out of his mouth when the Chin rapped Zito between the eyes with the wooden duck's head handle of a nearby umbrella.

"He dresses okay for me," Gigante declared.

Savino was perhaps never as rattled as the time he was rousted from slumber and summoned to the Village by a 3 A.M. phone call from Canterino. "Get down here, right now," growled Baldy Dom. It did not sound like a social call.

The two men met in the darkness on an empty Sullivan Street, walking through the stillness to a barbershop near the Triangle. Savino was certain he was about to get killed; why else avoid the endlessly bugged and FBI-monitored Triangle?

He arrived to find Vincent Gigante clutching a clothes catalogue in his hands. A light went on for the suddenly relieved Savino, who recalled giving Chin the catalogue, along with a promise to get Gigante any items that he desired.

He desired three jogging suits, in red, blue and green.

"It's not for me," Gigante allowed. "It's for my kids. You can go now."

Things turned heavy when Savino's old body-burying buddy Ferenga was busted on a drug rap in 1987. The arrest of the truly obscure crook, in a truly unexpected turn, would lead prosecutors directly to the Chin. And it was all because the drug-slinging Bobby Ferenga believed chivalry was not dead.

Bobby Ferenga was a wisecracking mobster with a rapid-fire "dese and dose" style of speech honed on the streets of his native Brooklyn. Nobody considered him among the sharpest tools in the Mafia's shed—not even Ferenga himself.

On Mob trips to Vegas with Lucchese associate Peter "Big Pete"

Chiodo and other gangsters, Ferenga would visit the roulette wheel and plop down $50,000 on a single spin.

"I just want to get the losing over with," he would moan.

On another occasion a prosecutor offered Ferenga a "Queen for a Day" deal—lawyer-speak for a one-time-only sweetheart plea bargain.

"Now dis guy's calling me a queen!" the insulted mobster complained.

Ferenga was lying in bed one night in November 1987, warmed by both the presence of his girlfriend and a $20,000 windfall in a coke deal, when the FBI bashed down the door of his apartment. Agents waved guns and a warrant. Ferenga left in handcuffs.

The feds were steered to Ferenga by another low-level crook, David Negrelli, a confidential informant for Brooklyn assistant district attorney Mark Feldman. The ADA shared his snitch with the FBI, and Negrelli steered them toward Ferenga, among others.

Negrelli was an unlikely candidate for the first falling domino in the probe. His strange ways led investigators at the Drug Enforcement Agency to blackball him, leaving Negrelli adrift until Feldman recognized his usefulness. He implicated Ferenga in a drug gang operating in Brooklyn.

More than twenty codefendants were busted, mostly organized crime guys, but the haul also included Ferenga's girlfriend and her mother. There was even worse news for Ferenga: The coke deal was a sting, and he was caught on wiretaps discussing his illegal exploits. Ferenga was facing a twenty-five-year jail term. His leverage at this point was less than zero.

"Bobby Ferenga was a mess," recalled O'Connell. "But being a chivalrous guy, Bobby had a guilt complex about the women."

U.S. Attorney Charles Rose initially played hardball with the gangster.

"He was brought into our office, and we laid out the law for him," Rose recounted four years later. "I told him, 'You're going to jail for the rest of your life. What can you tell us?' "

After a bit of back-and-forth, Ferenga confessed he was most bothered by the arrests of his gal pal and her mom. An offer was made: The charges against the women, peripheral figures at best in the case, would disappear if Ferenga agreed to flip. He briefly pondered his position, and reached a decision.

"Mr. O'Connell, I wouldn't do this except for my girl and her mother," said Ferenga, who was soon going steady with the Brooklyn prosecutors. Oddly enough, Ferenga's beloved wound up dating another mobster, who landed in jail based on Bobby's testimony two years later.

A street crook like Ferenga was never any closer during his life to Vincent Gigante inside the Triangle than he was to Pope John Paul II inside the Vatican. But O'Connell and the feds decided to roll the dice, squeeze their new informant and listen to his tale.

"Once you have a chance to poke your nose into the tent, good things happen for law enforcement," O'Connell explained. "It wasn't a shot in the dark for us. We knew this guy was connected, and could become a great source. When we were debriefing him, it was crystal clear that narcotics were secondary to a potential organized crime investigation.

"He opened the window, so to speak, for us."

O'Connell recalled his first meeting with Ferenga, a super-secret session in the DA's office. The prosecutor and his colleagues were joined by the FBI, a couple of Brooklyn DAs and two NYPD homicide detectives. While the feds were looking at the big picture, the cops' concerns were more immediate.

"Greg," said one cop, an inch of ash hanging from a still-burning cigarette, "we're looking for bones. Give us some bones."

Ferenga did just that, steering the squad to Savino's old Brooklyn warehouse for a gruesome nighttime dig that was by parts macabre and comical. A search warrant was obtained, and Ferenga accompanied the law enforcers to Scott Avenue to point out the seven-year-old concrete graves.

The building's head-turning current owner appeared to let the investigators inside.

"She's wearing a cocktail dress—bright red—and she's got

her lawyer and the keys," O'Connell recounted. "The lady in red stumbles as she steps into the building, and Bobby catches her arm. She says, 'Thank you, you're a gentleman.'

"And Bobby, without missing a beat, says, 'Lady, I ain't no gentleman. I am a criminal.'"

The digging commenced near the loading dock ramp, with the NYPD team using a backhoe and jackhammers in their search for Tommy "Shorty" Spero. The first bones they came across were too small for human remains, but Ferenga recognized them immediately: he, Savino and Pappa shared a take-out order of fried chicken while burying Spero's body.

This was the right spot. When Spero's body was found, Ferenga solemnly looked to the heavens as if in prayer.

"What are you looking up for?" asked an FBI agent.

"You're right!" replied a tickled Ferenga, instantly tilting his head toward the hole.

Next was Richie Scarcella, buried beneath a urinal in a bathroom. How was Ferenga so sure of the location? The burial site became a running joke among the killers, who would use the bathroom and announce, "I'm pissing on Richie."

Scarcella's body came up, too. And so did the name of Peter Savino, who was joined at the hip with Ferenga in a variety of ways that would land him in jail, too.

"That night a decision was made to arrest Savino and try to roll him," said Rose.

Savino, the Mob moneymaker and Chin comrade, was bizarrely enough already on the FBI books as an informant. Busted in 1973 on a New Jersey rap for smuggling bootleg cigarettes, he became among the most uncooperative of cooperating witnesses in history over the next fourteen years.

"I never volunteered information," Savino later admitted. "I answered questions when they called, but withheld important information."

This time, with two bodies attached to his old warehouse and Ferenga pointing the finger, Savino faced a far more troubling

situation. Rose wasted little time in explaining the situation. He
made no threats and provided zero wiggle room. Rose, instead,
offered a simple recitation of the facts over coffee in a diner on
East Twenty-Third Street. The whole thing lasted twenty minutes.

Rose later recalled his pitch—a fastball, high and tight: "I told
him he was going to be indicted for homicide and racketeering,
and he would go to jail for the rest of his life. I told him there
was only one way out. Plead guilty, wear a wire against whoever
we directed him to . . . and that he would have to testify against
whoever we caught.

"He was in shock. I told him it was a 'take it or leave it' deal.
There are no negotiations. I gave him forty-eight hours to make
a decision."

Savino was out of options. He agreed, for real this time, to go
undercover for the government. And he reached the decision
with hours to spare.

"He knew we had him dead to rights," recalled O'Connell.
"There was no need to persecute him. As we used to say, 'When
you've got 'em by the balls, the hearts and minds soon follow.'"

As O'Connell recalled, the directions to their new informant
were simple: "We told him to talk to every wiseguy he saw, and
we'll see what happens. Now he's going out to talk to people
who would kill him in a heartbeat. He was seeing these guys all
the time, and he was at risk of dying every day.

"It's a very ballsy thing to do. Not many people in the history
of organized crime had the balls for that."

Not only did the feds need to protect Savino, they needed to
keep Ferenga's cooperation a secret. O'Connell recalled the
crafty Benny Eggs, smelling a rat (or two), monitored Bobby's case
closely in search of even a tenuous link to Savino or any level of
law enforcement.

Adding to Savino's stress was a strict ban on FBI backup as he
met day after day after day with high-ranking associates of the
four families involved in the "Windows" operation. The operation
went on for sixteen months, with Savino capturing hundreds of

hours of incriminating Mob chatter—all while worrying that each day would be his last.

The pressure of his undercover work, hobnobbing with murderous mobsters, literally left Savino scared shitless. A report discussing his time as an informant noted that he was victimized by "periods of diarrhea" that were "associated with his undercover work."

The case was almost blown up by a turf war between the Manhattan U.S. Attorney's Office, headed by Giuliani, and the Brooklyn office, where Rose and O'Connell were based. Giuliani's crew, fresh off the commission victory, caught word of Ferenga's arrest and decided to claim the witness as their own. They arrested Ferenga on a mail fraud charge and threw him in jail.

O'Connell recalled receiving a collect call from Ferenga, made from the federal lockup across the East River in Lower Manhattan.

"Mr. O'Connell," the witness began, "you're never going to believe what happened today. These guys just arrested me. And they said, 'The only reason you're in handcuffs, Bobby, is those two fucking scumbags, Rose and O'Connell.'"

Ferenga paused for effect.

"I don't like these guys, Mr. O'Connell," the loyal informant continued. "If they think my prosecutors are fucking scumbags, what do they think of me?"

The Brooklyn team sprang their witness from his cell, and the dispute was settled by a grand meeting at the FBI's Manhattan headquarters in Federal Plaza. Giuliani was there, along with Brooklyn federal prosecutor Andrew Maloney. Both sides gathered to make their case to FBI officials in the crowded main conference room.

O'Connell told the tale of the phone call, and the Brooklyn office carried the day. Afterward, Chief Assistant U.S. Attorney Larry Urgenson of Brooklyn came over to O'Connell, who still remembered his boss's one-liner: "That was really cool, the way you got 'fucking scumbags' in there twice."

Now the work began. Savino signed off on a deal admitting to his part in the Spero and Scarcella murders, along with four other killings, and pleaded to a racketeering charge. He would face a maximum of twenty years in prison if he held up his dangerous end of the bargain.

Bugs were placed inside Savino's Brooklyn office in early 1988. And he began wearing a concealed body mike to an assortment of Mob get-togethers, including meetings in the Village with Mangano. By now, Benny Eggs had developed a strong distaste for the high-rolling Savino, who, flush with the window cash, was living in a bigger Staten Island home and driving a black Rolls-Royce with a sand-colored leather interior.

During one March 1988 conversation Mangano sharply shut down a Savino line of inquiry.

"Vincent said when it comes time to . . . ," Savino began.

"Don't mention that guy," Mangano snapped.

"Okay, I won't mention him," Savino apologized. "All right, he said to go out and bid the work."

"Yeah," grunted Mangano.

A few months later, back in Ruggero's restaurant again, Savino delivered the news to Mangano that Gaspipe Casso of the Luccheses and John Gotti's brother Peter were looking to make more cash off the window scam.

"It's all ours," said Mangano, reminding the man who started the scam exactly who was in charge. "Nobody's supposed to touch it."

The investigation soon settled into a routine: Savino would hit the streets and make his multiple Mob meets. He would make a secret tape drop every few days. The prosecutors would review the tapes, which were stored inside a safe in the U.S. Attorney's office. Then every two to three weeks, Savino and the prosecutors would get together for a full review of what the latest round of death-defying cloak-and-dagger work had turned up.

"He couldn't come see us at the U.S. Attorney's office or at FBI offices for fear that someone would notice him," said O'Connell. "So we'd find these mountain retreats and go away for the weekend. We'd be living together, debriefing him and strategizing, asking him what was important.

"We were one hundred miles away in these secure mountain retreats. We always took circuitous routes to get up there. Every turn was part of keeping the secrecy of the investigation."

One thing became immediately clear: The Chin had emerged as their number one target. The feds even fitted Savino with a special miniature device, a recorder designed specifically to capture Gigante's customary whisper.

Not everyone agreed that Gigante, doddering through the Village in his nightclothes, was worth the effort. Many in law enforcement believed that the Chin was now the "capo di tutti-frutti," with his crazy act the real thing based on his age and legitimate health woes. The Brooklyn prosecutors pressed on despite the naysayers.

"When we were running Peter Savino on the street with a wire, Charlie and I met with a lot of skepticism about Chin's competency," said O'Connell. "There were a lot of people who thought he was already living in his own jail. They didn't want to proceed, but our office did."

While Savino worked the streets, FBI agent Tom Rash began assembling a two-decade history of Gigante's twisted tarantella with law enforcement. Poring through FBI surveillance reports and Gigante's medical history, he pieced together a chronology demonstrating that Chin's well-timed "tune-ups" were inevitably followed by a hasty return to the Triangle.

There was never a single public episode of Gigante breaking down during his daily walks or his late-night wanderings. He was never taken to nearby Bellevue Hospital, but, rather, always to the leafy, suburban facility to walk the grounds, see the same doctors and expand his résumé of mental-health woes.

Chin's old prison records were fodder for the mill, and turned up no history of psychiatric issues. The resulting chronology, so obvious it seemed impossible that nobody assembled one earlier, was incredibly damning for Gigante. O'Connell remembered how blatantly obvious everything was once laid out by Rash.

"Family members would bring him to the hospital and say he was hallucinating," the prosecutor recalled. "After a week he was cured. We looked at this and it was like, 'St. Vincent's has done its magic again!'"

Savino captured other incriminating conversations, including one featuring representatives from all four families and Local 580 head John "Sonny" Morrissey. The outraged labor leader griped that a non-Mob company had actually managed to land a NYCHA contract, and recounted how he handled the situation: threatening to smash every installed window, and banging them for $14 kickback per window in the future, instead of the typical $2.

In another taped conversation Colombo family associate Vincent Ricciardo proposed a similarly violent solution to handling a contractor who flinched at the $2 payoff.

"I'm throwing him out that window," the enforcer declared. "I'm telling you, he's getting it. He don't want to pay nobody."

The tapes were astounding, but Savino's high-wire act of walking among the Mafiosi was reaching its end. Incredibly, despite the suspicions of Mangano and others, the first word of his defection came from inside the NYPD.

The leak came through Burton Kaplan, the old Casso friend and associate. A crooked officer from Brooklyn's Sixty-Second Precinct—Eppolito of the "Mafia Cops"—delivered Kaplan a police report that seemed to insure Black Pete's lifespan was growing short. Kaplan delivered the damning paperwork directly to Gaspipe, who had archly taken to describing Eppolito and Caracappa as his "crystal ball."

"It said Pete Savino was cooperating with the government. . . . [The] whole Sixty-Second Precinct was involved with Savino," Kaplan later recounted. Casso quickly went to the trusted Mangano, who returned to Gaspipe with assurances of Savino's trustworthiness.

"Benny Eggs came back a week later and said that they took

Black Pete down in a basement and they put a gun in his mouth," Kaplan recounted. Savino apparently convinced Mangano that he was on the level.

"He believed, and other people in the Genovese family believed, that Pete wasn't an informant," Kaplan said.

Casso claimed that he also asked for a sit-down with the Chin. It was agreed they would meet at 3 A.M. in Yolanda Gigante's Sullivan Street apartment.

Casso, accompanied by Amuso, recalled meeting Mangano. The underboss climbed into their car and took the pair on a circuitous tour of the Village to insure they weren't the targets of a tail. Once satisfied, Mangano had the two park the car and follow him into the basement of a tenement on the same block as Mrs. Gigante's home.

They trekked through the underground passageways between buildings, a subterranean world of vermin and raw sewage. "It's like *Wild Kingdom* down here," Casso said.

When they finally arrived, the Chin was sitting at the kitchen table in a bathrobe. A bottle of good cognac sat in front of the Genovese boss. Amuso was the only one drinking. Gigante sat impassively as Casso insisted that Savino was wearing a wire for the feds. There was a moment of silence before the Chin spoke.

"I'll take care of it," he said.

End of discussion.

Gravano and Casso later approached Mangano a second time to reiterate their concerns and arrange for Savino's murder.

"I don't like him," Mangano told his two business partners, "but Chin loves him. We're not going to be able to do nothing."

Lucchese boss-in-waiting D'Arco recalled that Gigante had an unexplained blind spot when it came to Savino.

"Vic (Amuso) told me he was trying to tell the Robe that Petey Savino was a rat," D'Arco recounted. "But he said Gigante wouldn't hear of it. He defended the guy to them."

When the rumors and concerns about Savino were finally confirmed in 1989, Amuso vented his disgust with the Chin: "That asshole should shoot himself now."

Gigante, late as it was for the realization, decided shooting Savino was the more prudent move. The Chin inquired with the Lucchese family about killing the informant—a hit that never happened.

Savino learned that his cover was blown in a chilling June 1989 phone message.

"We know you're a rat," said the voice, recorded by authorities. "We saw you with federal agents."

It was Negrelli, who had since dropped out of the federal Witness Protection Program and had returned to his old friends and evil ways.

It was time to shut Savino down. The investigation was officially over, with Rose and O'Connell left to put together their sprawling prosecution. The authorities prepared search warrants for more than a dozen window manufacturers. They convinced a half-dozen businessmen to cooperate with the probe about extorted payments.

For the first time in three decades, federal prosecutors were preparing an indictment for Vincent Gigante.

As the peripatetic Savino kept busy bouncing between families with his ever-present wire, prosecutors were already taking down other members of Chin's inner sanctum as the federal Mafia crackdown of the 1980s finally reached the Genovese family—and beyond.

The Chin's handpicked man atop the Philadelphia family, Scarfo, was busted in January 1987 for a $1 million extortion plot on the City of Brotherly Love's waterfront. The next year he was charged in a massive RICO indictment, and was sent off to serve a fifty-five-year term in 1989. It was an almost guaranteed life sentence, with Little Nicky's earliest release date set for January 2033.

Even worse, the Atlantic City mobster's once-loyal crew was flipping against him; his disgusted nephew Phil Leonetti, Scarfo's born-and-bred right-hand man, went to work for the FBI and became one of their star witnesses.

*   *   *

The news was just as bad for longtime Genovese associate Morris Levy, the music industry maven who was at one point under investigation by federal grand juries in Los Angeles, New York and New Jersey. The focus was a deal to peddle bootleg albums between Levy and a company called Consultants for World Records.

Among the "consultants" were Fritzy Giovanelli and fellow Genovese member Rocco Musacchia. Baldy Dom Canterino was eventually implicated as well. "An interesting combination," Levy deadpanned in a 1986 interview about the company's top echelon.

That same year, FBI agents visited with Levy and his lawyer in the record executive's Manhattan office. Their mission became clear: They wanted to convince Levy that cooperating with federal investigators against his Mob cohorts was now in his best interests. Prosecutors had served Olympia 2 with a subpoena regarding the town house sale, a move guaranteed to irk the Chin.

It was pointed out to Levy the possibility that his life may be in danger, read an August 1986 FBI document recounting their sitdown with the music mogul. *Levy stated he was not in fear of his life and was not concerned about this investigation because he has been federally investigated numerous times in the past without success.*

When the agents urged Levy to turn informant, the veteran businessman turned a deaf ear: *He replied that the witness security program was a joke and could not adequately protect witnesses.* The agents left their business cards and headed back to Lower Manhattan.

The music executive's decades-long dodge of prosecution ended on a very sour note: Levy and Canterino were convicted in May 1988 for conspiracy in a $200,000 extortion, which was relatively small change for the colorful record company mogul.

Five months later, Levy was sentenced to ten years in prison by federal judge Stanley Brotman at a hearing in Camden, New Jersey, far from the Broadway lights where the kid from the Bronx had found his calling. Canterino received a dozen years.

Levy appealed his conviction, and was freed on $3 million bail. He died of liver cancer in May 1990, his lips still sealed, without spending a day behind bars.

The law enforcement noose had tightened much closer to home, a harbinger of the uncertain future for the Chin and his crime family. Federal prosecutors in New Jersey unveiled a damning 1988 indictment, the result of a staggering 2,500 hours of wiretaps, charging trusted consigliere Manna with a plot to kill Gotti and brother Gene, along with another pair of Mob murders: hits on the obese con man Irwin Schiff one year earlier, and Frank Bok Chung Chin, who was killed in January 1977, after agreeing to testify against family waterfront power John DiGilio.

The trial was a long time coming for Manna, who had operated in North Jersey for decades with little concern for law enforcement. Manna was so feared and respected that his July indictment and incarceration did not stop his underlings from continuing to pay him tribute: the cash was delivered to his wife, Ida.

In the 1960s and early 1970s, Manna ran the family's loan-sharking and gambling operations in Hudson County. He was implicated, but never charged, in the 1962 Tony Bender Strollo hit, and was reportedly a witness to the 1960 murder of Salvatore Malfetti, who was shot eight times at close range after authorities identified him as a witness to a 1959 Mob hit. Nearly thirty years later, the authorities finally had Manna in a courtroom.

Schiff's association with the Genovese family dated to 1964, when he met family associate Joseph Pagano behind bars. Once released, Schiff was soon providing family-run clothing stores with bogus designer-label pants.

Schiff was executed on August 8, 1987, just after putting down a $30 tip on dinner at the Bravo Sergio restaurant on the Upper East Side. He never saw the gunman, who was wearing a dark suit, enter through an emergency exit. Neither did his comely, young and blond dinner companion.

Schiff took two bullets to the back of the head. Authorities suggested his fatal mistake was skimming cash owed to the Genovese family in a $25 million money-laundering scheme. It was later revealed that the big man, who stood six-four and weighed in at 350 pounds, had also worked as an FBI informant.

The prosecutor, three years off his commission triumph, was Chertoff, who was now working the other side of the Hudson River. The case boasted star power beyond its notorious lead defendant: Chertoff's boss in Newark was future U.S. Supreme Court justice Samuel Alito, and the federal trial judge was Maryanne Trump Barry, the older sister of billionaire developer Donald Trump.

Chertoff, in the new millennium, would go on to become a federal appeals court judge and the head of the nation's Homeland Security office.

Once again, Gigante—although the power behind the Gotti plot—avoided prosecution as an unindicted co-conspirator. New Jersey authorities flatly said the Chin needed to okay any and all murders committed under the Genovese banner, but Gigante remained a moving target.

"I don't think we had him," Chertoff explained years later. "He wasn't on tape, and the evidence in the case was driven by tapes. But the way it worked, murders had to be approved by the top three guys in the family. And Gigante was the boss."

The Oddfather still loomed large over the case, even if his name (as the Chin preferred) was never mentioned. Chertoff invoked the infamous Triangle at one point while addressing the jury, presenting the dingy outpost as the epicenter of the unforgiving Genovese universe.

"It's not pretty to think of a world where disputes are adjudicated in front of the Sullivan Street social club, where life and death were decided," Chertoff told the jurors.

Jury selection began on February 27, 1989, to assemble an

anonymous panel—an effort to keep the jury free of Mob tentacles.

The prosecution announced its witnesses would include the recently rehabbed Fish Cafaro in his courtroom debut. But the case swung mostly on the tapes, which captured a pair of Mob associates heaping praise on the gunman who blasted Schiff in the middle of a crowded restaurant.

"It takes guts to do it like that," said Frank Daniello, a former Hoboken cop. "This kid is a . . ."

"Stone killer," interrupted co-conspirator Casella, the restaurant owner.

"He was sitting there with a blond bitch, and they hit him," said Daniello.

One of the key defense claims was that Manna was attending his son's twenty-first birthday party on the day he was caught on tape discussing the Gotti hit. Photos from the event were produced. Chertoff pointed out to jurors that the clock in the background showed the defendant arrived ninety minutes after the incriminating conversation occurred.

"What was so important to Bobby Manna that he would be late for his own son's twenty-first birthday party?" Chertoff asked now. "The only thing that important would be plotting John Gotti's death."

The trial stretched across four months, with the jury returning after five days of deliberations: Manna and the rest were guilty. The Thin Man showed not a flash of emotion as the devastating cascade of "guilty" verdicts echoed through the Newark courtroom.

The jury foreman, completely shaken by his four-month crash course in Genovese business practices, held the hands of two fellow jurors for support as he announced their decision.

"This is a tremendous verdict, and a tremendous blow to organized crime in New Jersey," said Alito. "Any organization that can plot to kill John Gotti is a powerful force."

Manna, sixty at the time, returned to court three months later for sentencing. Dressed sharply in a dark suit, he sat at the defense table with his head held high and his mouth shut tight. The implacable gangster flatly rejected a chance to address the court, and took his eighty-year prison term the same way he took his visit to the prison dentist—without flinching.

There was one final twist to the trial: Years later, Manna, who was now working as his own attorney, claimed that Barry was prejudiced before meting out his sentence after learning of Mafia death threats against her, Chertoff and the future Supreme Court justice. Manna's court papers indicated that he was the source of those threats.

"That's news to me," Chertoff said with a laugh. "I completely missed it. I'm still alive. I spent the last ten years dealing with terrorists. In a way you're almost nostalgic for the days of that kind of criminal."

The only other legal action involving the Chin was brought by his brother Louis just prior to the Manna trial. The Gigante family petitioned a New York State judge to declare Vincent as mentally incompetent to handle his own affairs. It was a bold move as prosecutors moved in on the Mob boss; the petition could not be challenged by the federal or state investigators pursuing Gigante.

A finding of incompetence would give the Mob boss a permanent stay-out-of-jail card to play.

A psychiatrist retained by the Gigantes provided an affidavit declaring that the Chin "suffers from auditory and visual hallucinations," as well as from "delusions of persecution." Father Gigante asked Manhattan State Supreme Court acting justice Phyllis Gangel-Jacob for the appointment to manage his brother's affairs.

According to an affidavit from the priest, he and his mother now served as primary caregivers for the troubled Vincent. The Chin was living full-time with his eighty-eight-year-old mother in her Village apartment. Father G. further stated that his older brother owned "no real or personal property." A court-appointed guardian was appointed to submit yet another report on Gigante's mental health.

Law enforcement sneered at the family's petition—which was filed one day before federal prosecutors in New Jersey named him in a civil RICO suit intended to cut off Gigante's control of the Garden State waterfront. The feds flatly identified the alleged "daffy don" as the current boss of the Genovese crime family, and drily noted that a finding of mental incompetence would spare the Chin from any government seizure of his assets. They assessed these as far more valuable than the priest did.

"As far as we're concerned, he's still the boss of the family and this could be a legal move to avoid an indictment," snapped Jules Bonavolonta, head of the FBI's organized crime operation in New York.

In an old familiar move by this point, Gigante's attorney had already moved to have his client declared mentally incompetent to answer the Jersey suit. But one year after he filed, Father Gigante dropped the legal effort on his brother's behalf.

"I wish to spare my brother and members of his family from the probability of a circus-like atmosphere that would attend a hearing on my petition," the priest said in an affidavit.

Court-appointed guardian Peter Wilson said he believed the original effort was not a scam, but "was brought in good faith." Attorney Barry Slotnick, speaking for the Gigantes, said the decision to drop the mental-incompetency case had nothing to do with Vincent's faltering competency.

"His mental state is such that he couldn't be the boss of a candy store," Slotnick declared in a remark quoted endlessly over the next several years.

Father G. made headlines in another unrelated case. The city was shaken to its core in 1989 by the alleged gang rape of a white jogger by a pack of black teens in Central Park, a crime with repercussions that lingered for decades. The woman was sexually assaulted and beaten so savagely that she was comatose and almost unrecognizable.

The outrage was immediate and palpable, and only escalated when five local teens were arrested for the attack. Billionaire Donald Trump took out full-page ads in four city newspapers calling for the return of the death penalty.

Gigante posted $25,000 bail for one of the defendants, Kevin Richardson, creating a media firestorm.

"An angel came to us," said the young suspect's attorney. "Rich people and gangsters shouldn't be the only ones who are freed on high cash bail." The irony of his comment was apparently lost on the lawyer.

The priest broached the decision with his South Bronx congregation during Mass. Kevin Richardson deserved a chance at rehabilitation, he contended. The fourteen-year-old and his codefendants were eventually cleared of the charges, after years in jail, when another man confessed to the crime.

Years later, Louis Gigante shrugged off the personal attacks that followed his financial backing of the jailed teen.

"That's the newspapers," he says. "I don't think of the newspapers. You think I thought about the newspapers, publicity? I'll tell you what I was thinking—I'm a priest."

CHAPTER 16

CAN YOU PLEASE CRAWL OUT YOUR WINDOW?

*I*T WAS SEVEN O'CLOCK ON A WEDNESDAY MORNING WHEN THE FBI came banging on the door of the Sullivan Street apartment shared by Vincent Gigante and his mother. The agents brought along a battering ram on May 30, 1990, and were in the process of using it when the man they wanted finally appeared.

He was, unsurprisingly, wearing a blue hooded bathrobe and pajamas. Somewhat surprisingly—and yet somehow perfectly—he turned down an offer from FBI agents to change into more appropriate attire.

"He took so long answering, agents thought he was trying to escape," said FBI New York office head Jim Fox. "He finally answered the door, and refused to put clothes on."

"Where are we going?" the Chin asked one of the arresting agents.

"We're going to see the judge," he replied.

"Oh," Gigante deadpanned.

He then handed over a card containing a phone number to reach his brother Louis. The Windows Case, simmering for three years, had finally come to boil. Agents across the city made arrests, and a Brooklyn federal judge awaited. For once, the Chin was entitled to a flashback – his last arrest—as he was led to a waiting FBI vehicle.

Gigante was fingerprinted and photographed at the FBI offices, where he was a bit more forthcoming. Asked about his late brother Pat, the mob boss pulled out a Mass card. "He's with God," Gigante said somberly.

He also reminisced briefly about his days in the ring: "I was a heavyweight, then I lost weight and became a light-heavy. It was a long time ago. I don't remember."

Once across the East River in Brooklyn, the Chin put on a show in his holding pen. The Genovese boss, behind bars for the first time in twenty-six years, stomped madly across the cell "as though stamping out cockroaches," according to a federal marshal.

A codefendant recalled Gigante looking around the crowded courtroom in apparent confusion. "What a nice wedding," the Mob boss finally announced.

Named in the sprawling sixty-nine-count indictment, along with Gigante and his underboss Mangano, were thirteen top officials of the other three participating "Window Case" families: Peter Gotti of the Gambinos, Colombo underboss Benedetto "Benny" Aloi and Lucchese boss Amuso, along with his sidekick Casso.

The latter two were on the lam, tipped off in advance to the coming arrests by dirty cops Eppolito and Caracappa. There was one more missing defendant: union boss John Morrissey.

The takedown was a big-enough deal that Attorney General Dick Thornburgh made the trip from D.C. to downtown Brooklyn to trumpet the assault on organized crime.

"Today's indictment closes the cash window on this lucrative enterprise," the punning prosecutor declared, calling the case the most significant attack on organized crime since the successful commission prosecution four years earlier.

"We intend to keep the heat on," he concluded.

The Chin, dressed in his robe, striped PJs and ratty hat, was steered into the courtroom, where prosecutor Charles Rose first laid eyes on their slippery adversary. Rose took in the full spectacle of the deranged don, from his unruly mop of hair to the well-worn brown shoes poking out from beneath his pajama bottoms.

This was their target? The all-powerful head of the Genovese crime family?

"Have you looked at him?" a suddenly concerned Rose asked O'Connell. "Are you sure he's not fucking nuts?"

"Sit tight," Greg O'Connell assured him.

When all the defendants finally arrived in the jam-packed courtroom, the defense table lacked enough space to accommodate the mobsters and their attorneys. About one hundred people, many of them supporting Gigante, filled the courtroom seats around Father Louis.

The Chin wound up in the jury box, alongside Benny Eggs, his old friend and underboss. As O'Connell watched, the two men cupped their hands over their mouths and began conversing amid the hubbub. The prosecutor realized that something he'd heard once before was true: the ever-careful Gigante, convinced the FBI was employing lip-readers in its efforts to take him down, wouldn't open his mouth if there was a chance someone else might see him speak.

"He's deranged, and he's nuts, but he's definitely against lipreading, right?" O'Connell recalled years later. "And he's convinced Benny Eggs to do the same thing."

O'Connell quickly addressed the Chin's mental health in a preemptive strike: "If he's competent to run the family, he's competent to stand trial."

At the arraignment the federal prosecutor Rose echoed his associate, succinctly summing up the Chin's long-running ruse: "He acts crazy in order to avoid arrest."

Father G. was accompanied by lawyer Slotnick, who preened like a peacock, but stung like a scorpion. The priest, as usual, picked up the tab for his brother's counsel.

Barry Slotnick was the city's hottest defense attorney, with a client roster that had included Mob boss Joe Colombo, Meir Kahane of the Jewish Defense League, crooked congressman Mario Biaggi and Panamanian president Manuel Noriega.

The son of Russian immigrants won an acquittal for subway

gunman Bernie Goetz by demonizing the four youths shot on a downtown train, turning the geeky shooter into an urban folk hero. And he was part of the defense team that helped John Gotti and six codefendants beat a Brooklyn federal rap.

Like Gotti, he was a clotheshorse: Slotnick favored $2,500 Fioravanti suits. A mugger once relieved Slotnick of a $15,000 Piaget watch. There were rumors the attack was actually payback ordered by the Dapper Don over a financial disagreement.

The paths of the defendant and the defense attorney had crossed previously, and Slotnick found the Chin's current incarnation at complete odds with their previous encounters.

"I actually had met him before I was hired to represent Vincent," Slotnick recalled years later. "I'd known Vincent for a very long period of time. Absolutely, I saw that Vincent was not doing well. It was clear to me that he was not a candidate for trial."

Slotnick remembered Gigante as the padrone, a man treated with deference and respect in the Village.

"Vincent was a very popular person in his neighborhood," Slotnick said. "He was an extremely popular person. He'd been a boxer, and he was well known and well liked."

Although this was the era of mobsters flipping like so many pancakes on a grill, O'Connell said the feds never considered cutting a deal with the Chin. His notoriety made him an unlikely candidate. Gigante would make a huge pelt on any prosecutor's wall.

But his life as a make-believe mental patient had also destroyed all of Chin's leverage. A witness with a history of purported psychiatric treatment and psychotropic drug prescriptions would prove a disaster on cross-examination.

There was one other thing: nobody on either side of the law ever believed that Vincent Gigante would become a rat.

Slotnick entered a plea of not guilty before mentioning his client's mental and physical ills. "Any stress could cause sudden death," he informed the U.S. magistrate John L. Caden.

Gigante found quick refuge in one of his favorite old haunts:

St. Vincent's Hospital in leafy Harrison. Slotnick requested the accused Mob boss head to the Westchester County facility for a psychiatric exam, foreshadowing Gigante's enduring defense strategy.

Fugitive codefendants Amuso and Casso went with a different defense tactic: Mob hit and run. They had already ordered the execution of union boss Morrissey, who was taken for his last ride to a housing development under construction in rural Jefferson Township, New Jersey.

Sonny Morrissey, the loyal Lucchese associate, was expecting to meet with Amuso, only to meet with his demise inside a cramped construction office.

"It was a heavily wooded area," recounted Big Pete Chiodo, who escorted Morrissey to his death at the hands of two waiting gunmen. "The next thing that happened was I heard four shots."

Morrissey departed in a state of disbelief. After the first bullet grazed the union boss, he uttered his final words: "I'm not a rat." Though absolutely true, his entreaty fell on deaf ears. In the end he asked the gunmen to finish him off quickly. They complied.

The four-hundred-pound Chiodo and the killers wrapped Morrissey's remains in a carpet and buried him deep in the Jersey soil. "The Morrissey thing is done," he reported to Casso.

The union boss's remains went undiscovered until August 1991, when Chiodo—now a government witness, too—led authorities to the burial site. Chiodo flipped only after landing in the crosshairs of the bloodthirsty Lucchese leaders. The increasingly paranoid Amuso and Casso became convinced the big man was going to flip, so they ordered his execution.

Fate—and many folds of skin—would intervene.

Big Pete was at a Staten Island gas station when a black sedan appeared, with two shooters emerging in May 1991. Chiodo, though shot in the neck, chest, stomach, arms and legs, managed to pull a pistol and return fire. He survived only because his enormous girth served as a beefy bulletproof vest, stopping the flying bullets from hitting any vital organs.

The murder try came as no surprise to the Mob-wise Chiodo. "I had become a liability," he later explained blithely.

The failed assassination convinced the tight-lipped Chiodo it was time to start talking, and with little hesitation he joined the parade of Mafia turncoats now working with the FBI.

His former Lucchese associates weren't done with Big Pete. In blatant violation of the once-immutable laws of the old-school Mafia, Gaspipe and Amuso went after his family. Chiodo's mother and father received death threats—and that was the least of it.

His sister Patricia Capozzalo, thirty-eight, was shot in the back and neck and seriously wounded in a 1992 Brooklyn hit by two masked men who fired into her car. The married mother of three had just returned home after driving her son to school. And his uncle Frank Signorino turned up dead inside a car trunk on Staten Island—shot to death.

It was a move more in line with Colombian drug lords than any Italian-American men of honor. The Luccheses were light-years away from the days when Lufthansa plotter Jimmy "the Gent" Burke delivered a Mother's Day bouquet to the mom of every incarcerated family member.

With Petey Savino safely in the arms of the federal government, the Mob turned its attention to his wife and her six-year-old son. Savino's third bride had turned down a shot at the Witness Protection Program so that her boy could still see his biological father—a strict no-no under federal regulations.

In August 1990 the woman received an anonymous phone call describing Savino as a "rat" and urging her to "drive carefully." When she went out to check her car, the woman found a crude gasoline bomb in the front seat. Only a balky fuse prevented an explosion outside the family's home.

Fearful for her life and that of her son, she ran to her car to drive to collect her son, who had been staying with another family member at the time, O'Connell wrote in a memorandum. *As she reached to open the car door, she saw the device in the front seat. She immediately contacted law-enforcement authorities.*

Vincent Gigante returned to St. Vincent's yet again on August 6, 1991, complaining that he was agitated and hearing voices. Family members reported they had difficulty managing Gigante around the house. The admission papers noted this was his twenty-third visit, dating back to 1969.

For the first few days, the patient remained in his room, did not leave, nor did he go to the dining room, read a report from Dr. Eugene D'Adamo, Chin's exclusive psychiatrist at the suburban facility. *Gradually, he began going on the grounds with his family during visiting hours.*

After a two-week stay, the Chin was escorted home on August 23 by family members. He returned the next June for another two weeks with the same symptoms and results. But the Chin, like the Lucchese bosses, was thinking he might need more to beat the rap this time around.

The 1990s.

With the defections of Cafaro and Savino, paranoia was high among the Genovese clan about informers in the family business. Longtime soldier Joe Barone Sr., working with a crew headed by precocious young capo Barney Bellomo, was stunned to discover his fellow gangsters believed that he was running his mouth to the FBI.

It was the start of an unlikely saga that began with a lethal decision by the ruthless Chin—and finished, when the dominoes stopped falling, with the lives of a federal judge and a Mafia prosecutor spared from a Mob hit.

The FBI, as required by law, reached out to Barone Sr. in 1989 with word that he was marked for death. An intercepted phone call contained a chilling threat: "We gotta get JB."

"The FBI came to his house and said there was a hit on his

life," recalled Barone's son, Joe Jr. "They gave him a card, and said, 'If you want to come in and talk, call us.'"

The elder Barone, who did a 1970s jail term for dealing drugs in violation of Genovese policy, was a Mob lifer with four murders under his belt. He knew any federal knock on the door would echo loudly across the already-suspicious family, his years of loyalty disappearing like the morning mist.

"My father knew a lot of things," said Joe Jr. "He was a pretty tough guy. He was no joke."

On the face of it, there was no reason to suspect the elder Barone, a Genovese veteran made in the mid-1980s. Barone was summoned by Bellomo to meet at 2:30 A.M. in a remote, designated spot. The pair then drove together up the Brooklyn-Queens Expressway before pulling over for a quick walk and talk. Bellomo, like his boss Gigante, was obsessed with avoiding law enforcement.

"Barney liked meeting at crazy hours, because the chances of being tailed—especially on the BQE at two A.M.—would be unlikely," recalled Joe Jr., who followed his father into organized crime, landing years later with the Bonanno family. "Barney said, 'I know what happened in the past, but you're with us.' So he got straightened out before he got killed."

Bellomo's reference was to Barone's drug bust, which could have eliminated him from consideration. He went home and spoke to his son about the invitation.

"He said, 'What do you think? It's a lot of responsibility, but it's a big show of respect,'" Joe Jr. remembered. "We talked about it, but, of course, you can't turn it down."

Bellomo, like the younger Barone, was the son of a Genovese veteran, Salvatore Bellomo. Barney took his first bust at age seventeen for a gun charge, with a slap on the wrist of three months' probation. His father Salvatore was tight with Salerno; and before passing away of natural causes, the father asked the Mob bigwig to look out for his boy. The youngster wound up working for future family underboss Sammy Santora.

Bellomo, one of the youngest made men in Mob history, was the rare next-generation gangster to fully embrace the old ways of the Mafia: omerta, loyalty, respect. Barone Jr. recalled his surprise when Barney appeared at the 1988 wake for his mom. It was the kind of thing that boosted Barney above and beyond in the eyes of his crooked contemporaries.

"It's rare to see made guys at any funeral, least of all a captain—someone so high up as Barney," said the younger Barone. "They know the FBI will be there taking photos of potentially made guys. And the Genovese family is very secretive about who's who in 'the Life.'"

Bellomo also helped Joe Jr. land a job at the Javits Convention Center, the massive Mob-controlled Manhattan convention hall. The payroll was heavy with Genovese associates, including capo Ralphie Capolla. Most paid a $20,000 fee to land their gig, but Bellomo brought Joe Jr. aboard for free in a nod to his old man.

Joe Jr. was groomed from a young age for the Mob life, sometimes shadowing Joe Sr. on his daily rounds.

"I used to tag along to pool halls and their clubs," the younger Barone recounted. "I remember walking in and one of the guys said, 'Hey, whaddaya got? Who's that, your bodyguard?' I was seven years old. These guys give you money and they give you a hug. They feed you. They say, 'Hey, kid, ya hungry? Ya want somethin' to eat?' When you're a kid, it seems like such a good thing. But it turns out they're all cutthroat.

"You emulate your father," Barone continued without regret. "My father was who he was. So, what do you do as a kid? Who do you emulate? You try to be tough. You try to be strong. My father was a Genovese solider, and I was supposed to be in that family."

Barone Jr., instead, ended up with the Bonannos, working in a notoriously murderous crew headed by future family boss Vincent "Vinnie Gorgeous" Basciano, a fastidious Bronx thug and unlikely proprietor of the Hello Gorgeous beauty salon. The younger Barone became a Mob handyman, handling all sorts of business: a little muscle, debt collection, whatever came up.

In his younger days Barone Jr. and his pals would rob lobster pots in the Long Island Sound and sell their fresh catch to the restaurants along Arthur Avenue in the Bronx.

The Barones' world went cockeyed when the FBI knocked on the door of Joe Sr.'s New Rochelle, New York, home. "I'm sure the agents thought they could flip my father," Joe Jr. has said now.

As the elder Barone pondered his options, he was called to escort Genovese associate Vincent "Vinny" Matturro from suburban Scarsdale to Brooklyn for a sit-down. The soldier was suspected (accurately, it turned out) as an informant. When the meeting ended, Barone drove Matturro home, where Vinny was soon found hanging from a rope.

The official ruling was suicide, but Joe Sr. knew better. He was in on the Mob-ordered execution. Worried that he might be next, Barone Sr. decided to go on the run. He was headed south to Honduras, and summoned his son to deliver the news.

"I asked him, 'Why are you gonna leave?'" Joe Jr. recalled. "And he said, 'Maybe they think I'm gonna say something, and this will put their minds at ease if I'm not around.'"

In the elder Joe Barone's case, absence made the collective Genovese heart grow blacker. The Chin was fighting the massive Windows Case indictment, with his pal Savino set to tell all. Gigante was still playing the crazy card, but there was a need to tie up loose ends if the psychiatrists failed the Chin and he landed before a Brooklyn federal jury.

Joe Sr. settled into a Honduran villa, staying in touch with his son by telephone. The FBI was still tracking the mobster, still hopeful of turning Barone Sr. The Genoveses were tracking him, too, with more sinister intent.

Barone Sr. told his son in late 1991 that he was coming home to undergo triple-bypass surgery—and would take the Fifth if he was summoned by the feds. The next time Joe Jr. laid eyes on his fifty-four-year-old father, he was staring at a series of gruesome autopsy photos in the hands of the FBI.

Three Genovese hit men had somehow traced Joe Sr. to the Honduran village, where he was holed up, and savagely stabbed the mobster to death on January 12, 1992. The FBI showed up in Honduras the next day to find their target was already dead.

The body was held in Central America for several weeks while the FBI attempted to get the remains shipped back to the States. But prior to the body's release, the Honduran government conducted an "autopsy" done specifically to cover up the wounds, with a large V-shaped incision made in Barone's chest to mask the stab wounds.

Joe Sr. was finally buried alongside his wife in New Rochelle. Three months later the FBI had the body exhumed and the agents went to visit the slain gangster's son in prison, where he was locked up for loan-sharking and gun possession.

They laid a two-inch-thick stack of photos in front of the younger Barone, graphically illustrating how the father's loyal years of service ended with a steel blade instead of a gold watch. The son immediately flew into a murderous rage.

"You want to grab a gun and kill everybody," he said. "But I'm not a killer."

Barone Jr., after examining the photos of his father's decomposing corpse, decided to enlist with the feds. For the next eighteen years—triple the length of time spent undercover by the legendary Pistone—Barone moved in a shadow world between the FBI and the Mob.

"It was always about my father," he said. "It was always about that. 'How could you kill a guy like my father?' My father lived and died for this, and they leave him like that? He stayed loyal to the end to do what he believed, and right or wrong he was still my father and so I respect him for that."

In 2007, while working for the FBI, Barone Jr. caught wind of a plot that sounded both ominous and incredible: his old street boss Basciano, now head of the Bonannos, had ordered hits on U.S. District Court judge Nicholas Garaufis and federal prosecutor Greg Andres.

Barone went to his FBI handler with the information, and the plots were thwarted. And so it was that Joe Jr., fifteen years after

Chin Gigante ordered Joe Sr.'s death, spared the lives of two federal officials.

Joe Barone Jr., now out of the FBI and Mob business and living with his wife far from the city, reflected on the decision that put it all in motion: the hit on his father.

"I don't know if they ever really thought he was a rat," said Barone. "It was more like a Jimmy Burke thing, 'Let's get rid of everybody.'" Joe Jr. was referring to the Lucchese associate who methodically executed his co-conspirators in the infamous 1978 Lufthansa heist at Kennedy International Airport.

"It's funny how this really set the wheels in motion," he continued. "It's amazing how one moment can change your life forever—that moment for me was seeing the man I had looked up to my entire life, the man I had tried to emulate, lifeless and alone. It set everything in my life on a different course. It's crazy what happens in life. Look what I did. I saved people's lives. I musta done something right."

CHAPTER 17

IDIOT WIND

*T*HE CURTAIN ON VINCENT GIGANTE'S LATEST INSANITY DEFENSE rose way, way, way off-Broadway, before an audience of one in a hospital just a short subway ride downtown from Sullivan Street.

Gigante was suddenly facing his most serious charges since the long-ago drug case, and this time there was a witness far more legitimate than Cantellops waiting to identify him. Beating the Windows Case would rely on the Chin's ability to sit down with four renowned psychiatrists and convince the quartet that he was not a Mob boss who helped arrange an ingenious scam to loot tens of millions of dollars for organized crime, but rather a paranoid schizophrenic prone to religious-themed outbursts and averse to razor blades.

What followed was a star turn unseen in the annals of either psychiatry or law enforcement, a twisted mingling of *Rain Man*, *GoodFellas* and *Groundhog Day*. It was the role that Gigante had waited a lifetime to play, and he delivered a four-star performance that managed to channel both Olivier in *Hamlet* and Groucho in *Duck Soup*.

Hallucinations? Check.

Voices in his head? Done.

Improvisation? Outstanding.

Federal judge Raymond Dearie ruled the four experts would determine whether the wily Chin was cogent enough to face the racketeering charges. The defense chose Dr. Stanley Portnow

and Dr. Abraham L. Halpern, while Dearie picked Dr. Jonas
Rappeport and Dr. Daniel Schwartz.

Across nine months in 1990 through 1991, Gigante was examined twenty times by the psychiatrists across more than thirty
hours. The show went on the road: Gigante met with the doctors
at his mother's apartment on La Guardia Place, the psych unit
at Kings County Hospital, his old rehearsal hall, St. Vincent's in
Westchester, and the Beekman Downtown Hospital.

Never once did he break character. Opening night came on
June 14, 1990, with Portnow in a front-row seat at Beekman.

Chin's wardrobe was basic: plaid pajamas and three-day stubble. Portnow, who characterized the patient as extremely depressed, detailed what happened next.

*He was always very frightened and mistrusting of me, although this
improved as time went on,* his report to the court declared. *At times
he remained mute for long periods and could be observed mumbling to
himself. This sometimes took the form of looking off at the ceiling or
turning his head and looking at the floor.*

*When asked what he was doing his responses were chiefly of a reli-
gious nature. He was either talking to God or engaged in some ambiva-
lent struggle between good and bad voices.*

There were visions: *He would suddenly see religious symbols on the
wall or misinterpret what was in fact on the wall as a religious message
to him.*

During one of his eleven visits with the Chin, Portnow asked
about the pending racketeering case.

"Windows," he replied. *"They can have my mother's windows."*

The Chin also delivered one of the most quoted lines in Mafia
history. Asked about his legal situation, the Mob boss offered
this divine dodge: *"I don't need an attorney. God is my attorney."*

Amen.

He was less kind toward the federal attorney handling his
prosecution: *"He lies about everything."*

Dr. Schwartz arrived on June 15, spending forty minutes of
the twelve hours that he eventually invested in evaluating the

Chin. He was greeted by an "affable but reserved" Gigante, who—when asked about the Windows Case indictment—allowed that, yes, he was accused of breaking a few windows.

The court-appointed shrink described Gigante as "fully alert and reasonably cooperative." The doctor also described the Chin as "reasonably well oriented in naming the location and approximating the date." Other statements were "unresponsive, irrelevant and psychotic."

The mobster asked several times to go home and see his mother. When Gigante faced an uncomfortable question, he offered a stock answer: *"God told me not to answer that,"* the report revealed.

There were infrequent flashes of the real Chin.

All too rarely, his statements have a mature quality, Schwartz noted. *Asked, for instance, why he was in [Kings County Hospital], he responds after a long pause, "I wish I knew."*

When discussing Gigante's notorious claim that "God is my lawyer," Schwartz pointed out that Gigante had a lawyer three decades earlier when he went on trial with Vito Genovese.

"And look what happened!" he announced. *"I went to jail."*

Schwartz remained skeptical if this was a "surreality" show or something scripted.

As to malingering, I have learned long ago that this is always a possibility, he wrote. *Indeed, with Mr. Gigante, I am still somewhat puzzled by the fact that he mumbles while he is allegedly hallucinating; one would expect a person to remain silent during a "conversation" so he can hear what God or the [D]evil is saying.*

Dr. Halpern, asked by defense attorney Barry Slotnick to evaluate his client, found the Chin "appeared dazed, perplexed and bewildered" during both his examinations.

Not enough, however, that he didn't repeat the line about his mother's windows and his celestial legal representation. *[Gigante] verbalized with preservative consistency that he was hearing God's voice telling him nice things and at other times voices telling him bad things,* reported Halpern.

Court-appointed psychiatrist Rappeport, like colleague Schwartz, sat across from the Chin with a bit of a "show-me" attitude.

"There still remains some question in my mind whether Mr. Gigante may be willfully refusing to repeat the charges against him, which were explained to him," said Rappeport.

During one session with Rappeport, Gigante jumped up and walked out of the room—exactly as he did twenty years earlier during his session with Dr. Henry Davidson during the Old Tappan cop scandal. Gigante mentioned the good and bad voices that echoed in his head.

"Tell me about the bad voices. What do they say?" asked Rappeport.

"God helps me a lot. He tells me nice things," replied Gigante.

"Yes, but what about the bad voices?" the psychiatrist pressed.
Silence.

There were lighter moments. Rappeport was greeted with a perplexed look when he asked the Chin to spell "world" backward. The punch line came after a long pause.

"We'll be here all day," Gigante finally replied.

The Chin, during his session with Rappeport, did allow that he never used the telephone. When asked about his nightly excursions to see Olympia 2, Gigante said he had gone as far uptown as East Seventy-Seventh Street. However, he offered nothing more about the homey nocturnal visits monitored so closely by Agent Beaudoin.

There was one more interesting point, mentioned by each of the doctors: Gigante's personal history, as given by family members to the doctors, now included some previously unheard details. He was twice hit by cars while running through the streets of Greenwich Village as a kid, and was knocked unconscious by the first accident. There was also mention of massive head trauma from a pair of head butts during his boxing career.

In fact, his mother had long ago discussed his boxing career

with no mention of head trauma. And Louis Gigante did not recall his brother taking any severe beatings during his time in the
ring: "He got hit, hurt, but he never got seriously hurt."

A former federal prosecutor, even twenty years later, shook
his about the twin car crashes.

"It's probably all bullshit," he declared.

The four doctors disagreed, and independently came to a
consensus: Gigante was unfit for trial. Not just now, but ever. It
was a sweeping victory for the defense after the Chin delivered
like he was chasing an Oscar.

Mr. Gigante suffers from a chronic form of mental illness, wrote
Portnow. *Mr. Gigante's irreversible mental illness causes him to be incompetent to stand trial now or in the future.*

Halpern echoed the finding: *Mr. Gigante is not mentally competent to stand trial because of an organic mental defect.*

Rappeport actually cited the Chin's two decades of faux delu-
sion and his years in organized crime in finding that Gigante
was afflicted with schizoaffective disorder, organic personality
disorder and antisocial personality disorder.

*It is very difficult for me to believe that any individual would malinger
mental illness by allowing himself to be hospitalized on at least 21 occasions over a 20-year period, even in a private psychiatric hospital, for the
purposes of preventing some legal action,* he wrote. *Also, mental illness is
not generally acceptable in Mr. Gigante's cultural and social circles.*

Even the skeptical Schwartz was swayed by what he saw.

*While Mr. Gigante has apparently been hallucinating for many, many
years, he does not show the kind of mental deterioration or thinking disorder one would expect to see in a chronic schizophrenic,* Schwartz noted.

And yet, despite a diagnosis that mentioned "possible malingering," Schwartz declared Gigante was unfit for trial.

More than two decades after those reports, defense attorney
Barry Slotnick insisted the doctors absolutely got it right.

"It was clear to me that the government was going after Mr.
Gigante," the veteran lawyer said. "The U.S. Attorney's Office
had been going after him for many, many years. It was quite
clear to me that he was not competent to stand trial . . . and I

was backed by the psychiatrists, who also agreed that he was unable to assist his defense and incompetent to stand trial."

There was one dissenting voice among those who spent time with Gigante during this period. Lenny DePaul was a federal marshal in Brooklyn, assigned to keep an eye on the Chin while he was hospitalized at Bellevue. Given their respective positions, the two hit if off fairly well.

"He was fine, never caused any problems," said DePaul. "I do remember him talking to me about his fighting days, about some fights. I said, 'This guy is about as crazy as a fox.'"

One quiet Saturday, Yolanda Gigante appeared to visit with her son.

"His mother was great, a real sweetheart," said DePaul. "She came in with a box of cannolis, and asked if it was okay to bring them inside. I told her sure, as long as I get one. She was very, very nice. His brother the priest came by, and three of his sons. Gigante never gave us any problems. Whatever his deal was, that was his deal."

DePaul, who knew all about the Chin's crazy act, never saw a hint of lunacy from Gigante.

"He knew what he was doing," said DePaul. "He would tell me stories. I thought, 'He's not doing too bad for whatever he had.' He was actually kind of a funny guy."

The results of the months of testing were made public in a March 1991 hearing before Dearie, who severed the Chin's case from the other ten defendants facing trial the next month in the Windows Case.

And then prosecutors Rose and O'Connell tossed a legal "Hail Mary." What if they could produce evidence that Gigante was rational during the 1980s, when the scam was initiated? Wouldn't that trump the psychiatric reports?

Slotnick dismissed the bid as a "last-ditch attempt to put off the inevitable finding that Vincent Gigante is incompetent to stand trial as of March 1991."

The judge agreed to let the prosecutors proceed. And the whole case against the head of the Genovese family boss, almost buried beneath a pile of psychiatric reports, was suddenly resurrected—although it was a slow and daunting comeback.

The delays would last another six years, a bitter and seemingly endless battle waged as Gigante remained the unquestioned overlord of the Genovese family.

None of the lawyers on either side of the contentious March sanity hearing would be around at the end of the Chin's traipse through the legal system. Neither would the judge. Bill Clinton would serve most of his two terms in the White House, and Rudy Giuliani—the old prosecutor—would become mayor of New York.

A rookie shortstop named Derek Jeter debuted in pinstripes, and the Yankees hired a washed-up ex-Mets manager named Joe Torre to run the franchise. O.J. Simpson was arrested, tried and acquitted for the savage killings of his ex-wife and her waiter friend.

What the defense could not foresee was the sudden flood of Mafia turncoats eager to save their own skins by tossing aside their oaths of omerta like these vows were so many half-eaten pastries. This new breed of Mob informants weren't like Cafaro—low on the Mob food chain, hedging their bets when meeting with the feds. They were bosses and underbosses, and they were willing to talk with authority about the highest levels of organized crime.

"Our case only got stronger," said O'Connell. It was the opposite of the old defense saw: justice delayed is justice denied.

Prosecutors were soon getting the skinny on Gigante from the unholy trinity of Mob informants: Sammy Gravano, Alphonse D'Arco and Philip Leonetti. The three, who were once among the truest believers in the world of Cosa Nostra, came to the feds with their own reasons for walking away from the Life, to incriminate their friends, crime partners, bosses.

And, in Leonetti's case, family.

*   *   *

Phil Leonetti was a kid from Atlantic City, born to the sister of the renowned and feared Scarfo. He was groomed from a young age by his uncle to join La Cosa Nostra; Leonetti grew up with a reverence for the Mob that most kids his age might hold for their favorite football team. His first bit of Mob business came when at age nine, he rode as a decoy in Uncle Nicky's pickup truck.

In its bed was a murdered corpse, headed to Philadelphia for butchering and disposal.

Leonetti killed with the zeal of a true believer—participating in ten murders, including a pair where he pulled the trigger. Crazy Phil's decision to flip came in a holding pen where Scarfo, a less-than-model father, tried to place the blame for his son Mark's suicide attempt on Leonetti.

"I made up my mind right there in that split second . . . that I was going to live the rest of my days for me, for my son, for my mother, not for my fuckin' uncle and not for his La Cosa Nostra," Leonetti later recalled.

Testifying against Gigante was a big deal for Leonetti, who once considered the Genovese boss as the ultimate man of respect.

"As far as gangsters go, Chin was my kind of guy," Leonetti said. "He was a very honorable, very well-respected man. Nobody would utter a bad word about him."

There was another reason that taking on Gigante was a big deal.

"He was a stone-cold killer," said Leonetti. "He'd have a guy whacked like ordering a sandwich, that's how easy it was for a guy like Chin. He was a no-nonsense motherfucker."

Convinced his old boss Gotti was going to sell him out to beat their upcoming federal racketeering rap, Gravano reached out to the FBI from the Metropolitan Correctional Center. He turned the Dapper Don's betrayal upside down, joining the federal forces and providing information gleaned as Gotti's powerhouse number two man.

Meanwhile, D'Arco was perhaps the most unlikely of the trio to go rogue. He was older than the other two, and his entire identity was rooted in the Mafia life. D'Arco spoke of his years of service for the Lucchese family with a gangster's hard edge and a poet's turn of phrase.

"I was a man when I was born," Little Al once bragged. He committed every crime except pimping and pornography, which he deemed beneath his dignity. Murders? He committed eight while rising through the Lucchese ranks.

D'Arco grew up near the Brooklyn Navy Yards, a neighborhood of heavyweight mobsters—some his relatives. His childhood, D'Arco once recalled, was "like being in the forest and all the trees were the dons and the organized crime guys."

He walked into the woods without hesitation. And he didn't leave until September 1991, when he had risen to the position of acting family boss—and learned that the Luccheses' fugitive boss Vic Amuso and underboss Gaspipe Casso had added his name to their ever-expanding hit list.

D'Arco was called to a September 18, 1991, meeting at the Kimberly Hotel on East Fiftieth Street—and quickly became convinced his summons to the Lucchese get-together was actually an invitation to his funeral. After a sweat-soaked sit-down, D'Arco walked out quickly, happy (and surprised) to be alive.

He cold-called the FBI office, and a star witness was born. Little Al later said he believed that Gigante—an old friend—was in on the plot to murder him.

"I know that they would have to ask Mr. Gigante, being that I was in the administration of the family," D'Arco said. "The only way they could kill me is they have to okay it with the other bosses, and he was one of the bosses. And he still is a boss. And that's why Mr. Gigante is just as guilty as Vic and Gaspipe."

The Chin's betrayal rankled a bit more than the involvement of the other two.

"Mr. Gigante knows my whole family," D'Arco said. "His daughters hung out with my daughters, and everything else. He knows the kind of family we are. . . . He's supposed to step up and say, 'Hey, hold on. What do you mean that Al is a rat?' But he was part of the plot. That's what it is."

Before any of them took the stand against the Chin, "Fat Tony" died behind bars in July 1992, his oath of omerta unviolated. But the new generation of turncoats sent many more of Gigante's Mob compatriots headed off to die behind bars, even as the Chin's fight to avoid joining them dragged on.

By the time the turncoats stopped talking, hundreds of their associates landed in federal prisons. Leonetti, Gravano and D'Arco were personally responsible for scores of convictions.

First to go was Chin's underboss Benny Eggs, convicted in the Windows Case in October 1991 after Savino spent two months on the witness stand. Going down with him were Colombo consigliere Benny Aloi and a family capo, Dennis "Fat Dennis" DeLucia.

John Gotti, after surviving the Chin's wrath, was convicted of racketeering and murder on April 2, 1992, buried by Gravano's damning recollections from the witness stand and his own voice on an assortment of wiretapped conversations in the apartment above the Ravenite. He would die behind bars a decade later.

Lucchese boss Little Vic Amuso was finally tracked down and brought to the Brooklyn Federal Courthouse. A jury, after hearing from Chiodo and Savino, found him guilty of all fifty-four counts in his racketeering indictment, including nine murders. His underboss Casso pleaded guilty on March 1, 1994, to fourteen murders—and improbably agreed to become a government witness, too. (Casso was later tossed after lying to investigators).

The first verdict on the Windows Case was a split decision; five of the defendants, including Peter Gotti, were acquitted. The jury decision led to speculation that the Chin's insanity defense might have finally come back to bite him. If he had taken his shot in the first trial, perhaps he would have walked with his accused co-conspirators.

The odds of acquittal were better than anyone knew. O'Connell said prosecutors later learned of jury tampering, with two members of the panel recruited by the Mob to fix the case. One was dismissed; the other was "strongly suspected," but stayed on through deliberations, he said.

The juror was later placed under FBI surveillance and spotted dining with a Genovese associate. O'Connell recalled that Rose was still upbeat about nailing Mangano and the other two.

"Look at it this way," Rose told him. "Any prosecutor can win a conviction with a regular jury. But you've got to be great to do it with a tampered jury!"

Working off information from the informants, old and new, Rose and O'Connell assembled a new grand jury to consider new charges against the Chin—including counts of murder. On June 10, 1993, a federal panel returned a streamlined six-count superseding indictment with Gigante as the lone defendant.

The confident feds flatly declared that Chin was the quite rational and quite lethal head of the Genovese crime family. Its members eagerly joined with Gigante in creating the image of the doddering old man with more than a few screws loose. The indictment charged: *Gigante . . . and his fellow members and associates of the enterprise engaged in elaborate efforts to conceal Gigante's role in the Genovese crime family. Those efforts included defendant Gigante's affecting an appearance of incompetency, ordering members and associates never to utter Gigante's name, conducting meetings in early morning hours, and limiting direct contact with Gigante to only a few trusted subordinates.*

In the end none of it worked. In addition to the Windows Case charges, Gigante found himself accused of murder and murder conspiracy in the Philadelphia Mob war killings. He was accused of ordering the shotgun hit on Pappa, of plotting to murder the turncoat Savino and of ordering the revenge hit on Gambino boss Gotti.

For good measure the feds threw in charges of extortion and labor payoff conspiracy—with a list of twenty-nine alleged payoffs to the Ironworkers Union, most funneled through Savino's American Aluminum.

"It's all bullshit," sighed Father G.

When the indictment was made public, Gigante was ensconced at St. Vincent's for another well-timed tune-up. Under his strange bail arrangement, the accused murderer was allowed to stay at his mother's home, provided that he remain within a ten-block radius of her apartment. At this point, after six decades as a Village fixture, nobody considered the Chin a flight risk.

Gigante's case, once severed from the other Windows defendants, wound up before Federal Judge Eugene Nickerson, one of the most respected jurists in the Brooklyn courthouse. Nickerson's twenty-four years on the bench included his deft handling of the Abner Louima police brutality case and the John Gotti prosecution. His wife would eventually end up struggling with Alzheimer's disease.

Her illness would provide yet another detour in the Chin's endlessly winding trip to trial.

While there was a new indictment, Gigante was sticking with the same old defense—and additional psychiatric evaluations ensued. Halpern, at the request of the defense, conducted two more sessions with Gigante, on October 6, 1993, and January 19, 1994. The psychiatrist offered a medical opinion to boot: Gigante's failing health alone was enough to spare him from trial.

The Chin's blood pressure was high (unsurprisingly, given his legal woes). And his heart problems were well documented.

"Mr. Gigante is not only mentally and physically unfit to stand trial, or participate at a hearing, but is extremely unlikely to regain competence," he concluded.

Dr. Schwartz, on behalf of the state, evaluated Gigante on August 15, 1995, during one of the mobster's getaways to St. Vincent's.

"I don't want to go to no court," the Chin declared. "I didn't do nothing wrong. God knows, I didn't do nothing wrong."

The psychiatrist also noted that Gigante's son, Andrew, told him the old man's relapses became evident through nervous be-havior, body shakes and the silent movement of his lips.

There were five more visits to St. Vincent's, bringing Gigante's total to twenty-eight. He was once again under the care of Dr. Eugene D'Adamo after arriving on July 23, 1996—the same period when Nickerson was holding the hearings that would de-termine the Chin's competency to face prosecution.

He was visited there by Dr. Portnow, one of the defense psy-chiatrists. The Chin took just a single shower during his stay, and complained about his mother's failure to visit. Twenty-three days later, a reinvigorated Gigante was sent home—unaware that his decades-long bluff was about to be called by Judge Nickerson.

After six fitful years of stops and starts, prosecutors would fi-nally get their chance in court to demonstrate the Mob boss was anything but demented. A two-part process was involved: First, they would need to demonstrate that Gigante was the rational and undisputed head of the Genovese family during the time covered by the indictment. Second, if part one was proven, the four psychiatrists who examined the Chin way back at the start of the decade would consider—given the new information about his criminal exploits—how the news would affect their diagnoses.

The government, at long last, was ready to pull back the shower curtain and expose the true Chin.

A new lead federal lawyer, George Stamboulidis, had stepped in to replace the departed O'Connell and Rose, gone on Labor Day, 1994, to launch their own Fifth Avenue law firm. The new guy, coming off a winning Mob prosecution of Colombo family head Little Vic Orena, knew this was a case like none before—or since.

"The competency hearings were a real challenge," recalled Stamboulidis. "For years this was the battle of the forensic psy-chiatrists, forensic psychologists and Chin's cardiologist. At one point the Chin fooled even the government-retained psychia-trists who examined him. The biggest hurdle was getting to trial."

Stamboulidis began work as a federal prosecutor with the

Newark Organized Crime Task Force, joining the U.S. Attorney's Office in Brooklyn in 1989 as acting chief of the organized crime section. His résumé would come to include three citations from the Justice Department for superior performance.

The prosecutor's first close-up look at the mythic mobster did not disappoint.

"There he was, obviously with his act in full swing," said Stamboulidis. "He came in looking like his disheveled self. The Chin put a lot into his act. And it served him well for decades. He played the part exceptionally well. If he was an actor, his performance may have earned him an Academy Award nomination. It worked so well for so long."

The hearings began in the first week of March 1996, with Gambino family turncoat Gravano taking the stand for the first time since slipping into the Witness Protection Program. The Bull, in rebutting claims of the "crazy act," recounted his first meeting with Gigante a full twenty years earlier—and he detailed four other Mob-related get-togethers over the next two decades.

Not even the Chin's standard business outfit of bathrobe and nightclothes gave Gravano second thoughts about Gigante's sanity.

"If I thought he was crazy, how would I know what he was doing?" Gravano asked. "He could walk right into a police station after the meeting. . . . I wouldn't be at a meeting if I knew somebody was crazy."

Under questioning by Assistant U.S. Attorney Andrew Weissmann, Gravano testified that he never saw the Genovese boss mumble incoherently, appear unsure or otherwise exhibit a single instance of strange behavior.

"Not at all," he told AUSA Weissmann. "I thought he was pretty sharp."

The Bull added that his impression was Gigante didn't have much use for his predecessor, Salerno.

"They weren't real tight," said Gravano. "He made faces behind Fat Tony's back and it was pretty obvious they didn't get along."

The real fireworks ignited when fiery bantam D'Arco took the stand. His testimony under questioning from prosecutors was damning, and it provided a bit of rarely heard Mob history as D'Arco emerged as a witness with uncanny recall of details and dates.

D'Arco was unflinching in his recounting of Chin's job description: "He ran the whole show there. He was very capable."

The ex-Lucchese acting boss, asked about the Mob's handling of the mentally ill, said it was standard practice to simply whack the afflicted Mafiosi in the interest of insuring their everlasting silence.

"If someone developed mental illness, they would be killed," he said flatly. "It's like a mercy killing."

He even provided two examples, both from the Chin's own family: Genovese capo Willie Moretti, who began running his mouth after contracting syphilis, was executed. Ditto Genovese soldier Anthony "Hickey" DiLorenzo, killed after he "flipped his lid."

DiLorenzo drew attention for associating with suspected informants while behind bars, and then began jabbering about Mob business following his release from prison. His freedom was short-lived, as DiLorenzo kept speaking out of turn about various Mob pursuits.

Hickey's bullet-riddled body was found on the patio of his West New York, New Jersey, home on November 25, 1988.

D'Arco's cross-examination displayed the combative, volatile nature that earned him the fear and respect of his fellow mobsters during his decades in the Lucchese family. Defense attorney Michael Shapiro began grilling D'Arco about the terms of his cooperation deal with the feds.

"I have no control of what I am going to get," said D'Arco, his face turning red.

"I understand," said Shapiro. "But that's not my question."

"I hope to get nothing, if you want to know," shouted an enraged D'Arco, nearly bolting from the witness stand. "I hope to get nothing. But if I get life, that's it. I didn't do this for that."

Nickerson interrupted—"Gentlemen, stop"—and Stamboulidis objected. D'Arco ignored them both.

"Don't break my chops," D'Arco told the defense attorney. "I didn't do this for that. I'll break yours, too."

"I'm sure you would," replied Shapiro.

D'Arco offered an apology of sorts: "First time I ever blew up like that, but this is the first time I ever had anyone like this ball breaker. Excuse me, he's disrespecting . . ."

"In my courtroom," Nickerson chided the witness, "you shouldn't do that."

The defense, scurrying to undo the damaging testimony, filed a posthearing memo with an interesting argument.

Even if there were something to the government's contention that the defendant sometimes feigned psychiatric symptoms in the past . . . Vincent Gigante has been the victim of episodic mental illness and a deteriorating overall level of mental functioning, the defense wrote.

If in the past he feigned symptoms, he was able to do so not out of great psychological insight, but because he had to do no more than continue or copy those symptoms he could not help exhibiting during his episodes of acute illness.

Agent Charlie Beaudoin testified, too, recounting his nightly viewings from the yeshiva. When Slotnick challenged his eyesight, the FBI agent correctly identified—from fifty feet away—a driver's license.

Nickerson took a few weeks to review the testimony before issuing his opinion on May 15, 1996. The ruling was devastating to the defense, and provided prosecutors the first sign that the strategy hatched years earlier by O'Connell and Rose was now bearing fruit.

The evidence before the court clearly establishes that Gigante was a forceful and active leader of the Genovese family from at least 1970 on,

that he became the boss of the family . . . and exercised his prerogatives
until at least up to September 1991, that his actions and decisions were
wholly inconsistent with the behavior observed by doctors, Nickerson
wrote in his rebuke of years of psychiatric exams.

His motive for putting on a "crazy act" all those years was to avoid
apprehension by law enforcement.

Nickerson specifically cited the refusal of other Mafia families
to murder Savino over the Chin's objection, even though letting
him live could put them all in jail. The federal judge, in closing,
said he agreed with Gigante's Mob contemporaries that the
Chin was "not an incompetent." But, rather, Vincent Gigante
was an "active and potentially dangerous force with extensive
knowledge and understanding of their world."

After Nickerson ruled that the Chin was the sane and rational
head of the Genovese family, he asked the original Fab Four of
psychiatrists to reconsider their opinions in light of his decision.

"The psychiatrists will be asked to say to what extent, if any,
these findings alter their assessments of Gigante's competency
to stand trial," the judge ordered. The two prosecution doctors
quickly reversed field.

The new details "make me think that it is quite possible that
[Gigante] is competent to stand trial, and that much or all of his
mental illness has been malingered," Rappeport testified on
May 28. He was now convinced "to a medical degree of certainty"
that the Chin's insanity was a scam.

Schwartz concurred: testimony about Gigante's lethal rule
atop the Genoveses "convince me that he is fit to proceed."

Defense psychiatrist Portnow hedged his bets. Chin was competent to stand trial back when he first examined the Mob boss
in 1991, but he went around the legal bend in 1995 and was currently incompetent.

"His greatest enjoyment in life is to enjoy cartoons," Portnow
testified at an August hearing that finally wrapped up the long-
running sanity sessions. "He became as animated as I've ever seen

him when he talked about animals coming from the sky and Martians in the cartoons. [It was] the only time I ever saw a real smile come over Vincent's face."

Nickerson, in another scathing decision, questioned the validity of Portnow's new diagnosis.

It was unclear to the court just how someone incapable of functioning in any area of life, as Dr. Portnow and others had previously described Gigante's condition over the years, could have deteriorated still further, he wrote in an August 28 ruling.

The judge also noted that Chin's symptoms had never changed over the intervening three decades—contradicting defense claims that his condition was steadily worsening. Nickerson then lowered the boom on Gigante and shattered the crazy act for good.

Gigante deliberately feigned mental illness from the late 1960s until at least September of 1991, the federal judge wrote. *As he has presented no convincing reason for the court to conclude otherwise, the court finds that the symptoms that Gigante has demonstrated since that time are also the product of his malingering.*

Nickerson wasn't done. He took a direct shot at the defense shrinks, who now claimed the Chin's condition had gone further south in the years since his 1990 arrest in the Windows Case.

As Gigante has feigned illness for over twenty years, the reasonable inference from the appearance of any exaggerated symptoms . . . is not that his condition has deteriorated, but rather that the imminent threat of prosecution has increased his incentive to malinger, wrote Nickerson in a dagger to the defense.

And then he unloaded on the Chin's wife and mother as enablers who helped the Mob boss launch the crazy act back in the 1960s. The two created a new psychiatric and medical profile for Gigante once he sought "help" for his mental illness.

The examining psychiatrist [received] a revised account of his childhood and medical history, Nickerson wrote. *Gigante's wife and mother reported that as a child, he suffered from "severe temper tantrums, pho-*

bia for the dark, truancy at school, obesity and learning problems" and
that at 16 he was deferred from the Army for "psychiatric reasons."

*Accordingly, the court deems Gigante fit to stand trial and directs
that he appear for arraignment on the indictment,* he wrote. *So ordered.*

Chin was ordered to return on September 6, 1996, to face the
charges. For prosecutors it was the payoff for waging a long, difficult, endlessly challenging legal battle to unmask the Mob boss
who for so long covered himself in the cloak of mental illness.

"I remember the look of delight on Andrew's face after Judge
Nickerson's ruling," said coprosecutor Dan Dorsky. "It was all so
silly—walking around in a bathrobe and drooling on himself for
the public. And, otherwise, here's this fearsome and vicious
leader of a very large and lucrative gang."

The Chin's return to Brooklyn Federal Court, his first public
appearance in nearly six years, was a deranged tour de force. He
arrived in a blue windbreaker over a white T-shirt, sporting his
usual stubble. His eyes darted madly around the courtroom as
he entered, accompanied by his personal cardiologist.

As the judge and attorneys conferred, Gigante spoke to himself in an indecipherable internal monologue. His legs trembled,
and Gigante stroked his chin. The twelve-minute appearance was
so spellbinding that prosecutors apparently forgot their plans to
make a bail revocation motion.

The Chin's new attorney, the veteran James LaRossa, entered
a plea of not guilty more than a decade after his representation
of Castellano in the commission trial.

"Just getting Mr. Gigante here was an incredible task," he said.

Neither the disquieting courtroom appearance nor Nickerson's decision did little to change the opinions of those on either side of the debate.

"Boss? What boss?" his ever-loyal mother, Yolanda, asked a reporter for the *New York Post* that summer. "He's boss of the toilet.
My son is sick. Boss of shit. Six years he lives here with me. Every
day I care for him. I feed him. I wash him. I cry over him."

Lewis Schiliro, FBI special agent in charge of the criminal division in Manhattan, took the opposing stance: "The Chin is the number one show in the country, without question."

But Nickerson's was the only opinion that mattered—not that the defense was ready to wave a white flag just yet. The battle to delay the trial would soon stretch into a seventh and final year.

CHAPTER 18

NEIGHBORHOOD BULLY

*T*HE UNLIKELIEST GIGANTE TO APPEAR IN A CRIME STORY MADE headlines in the summer of 1996: Chin's mother, Yolanda. As her son fought to dodge prosecution, the elderly widow was mugged by a career criminal, who couldn't plead guilty fast enough once he was clued in about his thieving idiocy.

Willie King, a street thief with twenty-one arrests already on his résumé, headed to Greenwich Village for a little late-afternoon larceny on July 21, 1996. King, thirty-seven, spied what looked like the easiest pickings in the whole neighborhood: a frail, tiny, ninety-four-year-old woman with a cane—walking on the arm of an elderly priest.

Jackpot! Except the woman was the Chin's mother and the priest was her son, Father Louis.

King snatched Yolanda's wallet from her housecoat in broad daylight as she returned to her apartment at 2:55 P.M. after a trip to the grocery store. The purse snatcher outran the winded, nearly sixty-five-year-old priest; the aging hoopster gave up the chase after a block.

"I was yelling, 'Thief! Thief! Thief!'" the priest said. "I lost him. . . . I went home."

An in-line skater and a cabbie picked up the chase, flagging down an NYPD patrol car. Inside was Lieutenant Robert McKenna, a fitness devotee who ran six miles a day. He needed just four blocks to collar King. The arrest likely saved the mugger's life, since the petty thief's odds of survival on the street in a post-mugging-the-Chin's-mom world were poor, at best.

"The best part was in the car when I said to him, 'You are the world's worst mugger,' " the Sixth Precinct lieutenant recalled. "I said, 'Do you know who you mugged?' When I told him, he just slumped in the seat and rolled his eyes."

Yolanda Gigante nearly cried when McKenna returned the wallet holding $90 and a treasured old family photo. The elderly woman pulled out the picture and kissed it. Father G. bemoaned the changing neighborhood. "They're going after old women now," the Village native told McKenna.

A day after positively identifying King as the mugger, the priest told the press that King had no reason to fear retribution from the Genovese kingpin despite his obvious mistake. He made reference to the Chin's mental woes in declaring that King would remain safe and sound.

"This is stupidity," said Louis Gigante. "I know you like to talk about my brother. I just want to be left alone. My brother is sick. . . . He's home with Mama."

The priest said his brother was actually unaware of the crime or the arrest.

"He was sleeping," said Father G. "Should I wake him up and tell him? It'll make him so upset. He's depressed."

A laid-back and apparently unconcerned King appeared for his arraignment in Manhattan Criminal Court with a smile on his face. After King was charged with petty larceny and possession of stolen property, his lawyer said there would be no application to hold his client in protective custody.

"He does not seem to have any fear," said defense attorney Steven Warshaw. "Mrs. Gigante was not injured in any way. And other than the alleged reputation of the family, I don't think he has anything to worry about."

The arraignment was delayed for several hours when a criminal court judge, who once worked as a prosecutor in the Manhattan DA's office, recused himself, citing his role in a prior investigation of the Chin.

It took less than a month for King to reconsider his defense strategy. The thief entered a guilty plea on August 9 and offered a heartfelt apology to the Chin and his mother.

"He came to his senses and decided to come clean," explained Warshaw. "His motivation was to apologize to the Gigante family and Mrs. Gigante. In this way he is trying to put this behind him, and he also hopes the Gigante family puts this behind them."

King agreed to a sentence of 1½ to three years in prison, which sounded a whole lot better than whatever the Chin might consider appropriate for robbing his beloved mother. The defendant, in a strange sartorial choice, sported a shirt with the word BOSS on its front when he arrived for the August 19 sentencing. King whined that the sentence was too stiff for the crime.

"I guess you'll do the best you can," he finally told the judge.

Though none of the Gigantes were in court, Warshaw took the opportunity to deliver one final mea culpa.

"My client wishes to express great remorse," the lawyer said. "He does apologize to Miss Gigante and the Reverend Gigante. He's admitted his guilt at the earliest opportunity because he wants to put this incident behind him, and he hopes the Gigante family will, too."

Yolanda Gigante survived the mugging, but the beloved family matriarch was nearing the end of her long and complicated life. The mother of both a Mob boss and a priest died nine months later, more than seven decades after arriving in Greenwich Village from her native Naples. She was mourned by, among others, eight grandkids from Vincent's two families.

Yolanda passed away at St. Vincent's Hospital on May 8, 1997, shortly after complaining of stomach pains during dinner. Just hours earlier, Father Louis accompanied his mom to a Greenwich Village Laundromat. Her death came three years after another of her boys, reputed mobster Ralph, passed away. After decades of tending to her beloved Chenzino, Yolanda died without learning his legal fate.

In another strange twist dictated by the Chin's twisted family tree, his mother had spent time recently recovering from a broken vertebrae at the New Jersey home of her son's wife, Olympia 1. Gigante had appealed to the court to join his mother back in Old Tappan, apparently bereft by her absence. He also received the okay to visit with Olympia 2 three times a week.

The family initially decided to keep the devastating news of Yolanda's death a secret from Vincent, who did not attend his mother's wake or funeral—one of the more devastating consequences of his chosen career.

"He doesn't even know his mother passed away," said his latest defense attorney, Michael Marinaccio. "And I don't know that he is going to be told."

Bronx borough president Fernando Ferrer, a longtime friend and vocal supporter of Father G., was asked about the propriety of attending the wake of a mobster's mom.

"I didn't expect my attendance at a wake and praying for the dead to be an issue anywhere," he said. The other mourners, he noted, included Cardinal John O'Connor, who "is much bigger than I."

He dismissed talk about the Chin's relationship with Father G.

"I've never related to him on that level," he said. "The issue here is 'Did Father Gigante ever do anything wrong?' And the answer is 'No.' In fact, in my view, he did a great many things right."

The funeral was held just after Mother's Day, with six pallbearers in Armani suits carrying Yolanda's bronze-colored coffin into Our Lady of Pompeii Church. Father Gigante blessed the casket with holy water, and kissed his mother's coffin good-bye.

He also addressed the assembled media: "Vincent is not here. I know that's why you're here, and I'm sorry to disappoint you."

Yolanda Gigante left Greenwich Village for good in a silver hearse, followed by a procession of twenty-one cars, including three black stretch limousines and a flower car filled with pink roses, white azaleas and yellow lilies. She was laid to rest at St. John's Cemetery in Queens, among the many Mob bosses already buried there: Lucky Luciano, Joe Profaci, Joe Colombo—and even John Gotti eventually.

CHAPTER 19

TANGLED UP IN BROOKLYN

GIGANTE UNDERWENT A SECOND OPEN-HEART SURGERY IN EARLY 1997, and his Brooklyn trial was postponed until April 14 to allow a full recovery. A second continuance was granted on a defense motion citing his continued health worries.

A hard-and-fast June 23 date was set for opening arguments, with a warning from Judge Nickerson that no additional delays would be acceptable unless the defense came up with something new to stall the proceedings. And they quickly did.

The new claim abandoned the insanity defense to assert that Gigante was now incompetent for trial because the Genovese boss was afflicted with Alzheimer's disease on top of his assorted other physical woes.

Nickerson, whose spouse was legitimately battling the devastating disease, quickly recused himself. The case was assigned on May 13 to the no-nonsense dean of the Brooklyn Federal Courthouse, senior district judge Jack Weinstein.

The jurist was immediately greeted by a defense motion that claimed that pretrial publicity could prevent the selection of an impartial jury. Weinstein, one month into the case, shot it down— only to field another defense claim that Gigante was afflicted with potentially cancerous nodules on his thyroid. Oh, and blood in his urine. And there was a problem with his pacemaker. And also he had need for immediate dental care.

Weinstein didn't bite. On June 16 the judge informed both prosecution and defense that the case of *U.S.* v *Vincent Louis Gigante* would proceed to trial in one week, just as his judicial predecessor had ordered.

It was finally showtime, but Barry Slotnick was no longer a part of the courtroom drama. Disgusted by the government's relentless pursuit of the Chin, he walked away.

"Ultimately, I withdrew because I didn't feel it was appropriate for them to continue doing to Vincent what they were doing," he said recently. "It was wrong."

The long-awaited trial—dubbed the "Never Ending Soap Opera" by longtime Mob scribe Jerry Capeci—finally began not with the bang of Judge Weinstein's gavel, but with the gripe of a pissed-off prosecutor.

George Stamboulidis, standing in the well of the Brooklyn federal courtroom, turned to see Gigante arriving for opening statements in a wheelchair—with a cane across his lap. Father Louis pushed the Chin toward the defense table.

"I objected to the two props," recalled Stamboulidis. "I said, 'Your Honor, I don't mind one—but two props?' And Judge Weinstein said, 'I don't want it.' So I said to the defense that the judge said he didn't want it, get rid of one. And they did. They removed the cane from Chin's lap.

"Later someone pointed out that when the judge said he didn't want it, he might have meant he didn't want to hear my objection," the prosecutor said with a chuckle. "But everyone heard the judge, and I did quote him correctly to the defense."

So began the contentious court fight to put the sixty-nine-year-old Gigante behind bars for the first time in thirty-two years. It had taken seven years since the Windows Case indictment to get the Chin behind the defense table. The elusive Gigante, to prosecutors, had become Moby Dick in a ratty bathrobe—and the pressure was on to nail their wily adversary in what shaped up as their last and best shot.

If convicted, he faced a federal prison term of anywhere from ten years to life. At his age it seemed that even a decade loomed ominously like a death sentence.

The prosecution brought a literal murderer's row of witnesses to court: Gravano, D'Arco, Leonetti, Savino and Chiodo had confessed to a combined fifty killings. The trial promised high drama, contentious cross-examination, tales of Mob lore and unheard details of the Mafia's violent history.

Not that Gigante seemed to notice any of it. With his cardiologist sitting nearby, the Chin stared blankly into space as if in a trance. He appeared emotionless and detached, like the whole thing was happening to somebody else. But he saw no hallucinations, and he heard only the voices of the witnesses against him.

The life-and-death legal struggle was not without its lighter moments. Among the Chin's other purported health woes was a tremor in his left leg. One day in court Stamboulidis looked at the defense table to see Gigante's right leg twitching madly.

"So I mention to defense counsel, while looking right at Chin, that he's shaking the wrong leg," the prosecutor said. "Without missing a beat or looking at me, Chin repositions his legs and starts shaking the [correct] one."

Though Gigante's litany of mental and physical ailments was long enough to cover a half-dozen patients, the defendant never missed a single day of court. The demented don took his place each day at the defense table, from the first day of jury selection until the same panel—which was seated anonymously to guard against tampering—rendered their verdict.

Even before the trial started, Weinstein, who was six years older than the defendant, instructed the defense to insure that Gigante trade his unmade-bed look for more appropriate attire. The Chin should be neatly groomed and properly dressed; his son Salvatore eventually provided his father with a sport coat to replace his usual blue windbreaker. Weinstein was particularly irked by a dirty white T-shirt visible beneath Gigante's wrinkled polo shirt.

Marinaccio assured the judge his order would be followed to a point: "Mr. Gigante is who he is. I don't think a blue blazer, tan pants and deck shoes are in the offing here, Judge."

Weinstein did agree to let the Chin keep the wheelchair, and the judge okayed a defense request to keep a cardiac specialist on call in the courtroom. Dr. Wechsler regularly took Gigante's blood pressure during breaks.

There were some two hundred jurors called to fill out a forty-five-page questionnaire with some interesting queries:

Did they believe in the existence of the Mafia?

Had they ever seen The Godfather?

Had they read Underboss, *the best-selling biography written by author Peter Maas, with the cooperation of Gravano?*

Weinstein assured the candidates that neither the defense nor the prosecution would ever learn their identities. Forty of them immediately begged off, citing upcoming vacations or family weddings or work. It nevertheless took just two days to seat the panel for the last of the great Mob trials, with the last of the great Mob bosses as the lone defendant.

The jury of Chin's peers was more reflective of the city on the cusp on the twenty-first century than the Village of his youth: seven white jurors, four blacks, one Asian. Seven were women. They were described as a largely well-educated bunch, and Weinstein ruled they would not be sequestered.

Chin, in one of the oddball details to emerge during the case, estimated his monthly income at this time at about $900 a month from his pension. The money went directly to his wife.

Opening statements came on June 25, with the defendant's family offering their support both inside and outside the Brooklyn Federal Courthouse. The Gigante supporters filled about a quarter of the packed one-hundred-seat courtroom.

"To label him the boss of a conglomerate that extorts is ridiculous," said Father G. "He didn't run anything, because he couldn't run anything."

The priest doted on his brother throughout the trial, combing Vincent's hair and rolling the Chin's wheelchair into the courtroom. Outside, he provided a running rebuttal of the government's case—and he wasn't alone among the devoted Gigante clan. Daughter Yolanda, named for the Chin's mother, flatly described her father as a paranoid schizophrenic.

Defense attorney Marinaccio had assured one and all that his client would be front and center for opening arguments, virtually citing his courtroom presence as the most important defense exhibit.

"We want him to be there, so the public can see who the government is talking about, this shrewd Vincent Gigante, who's still running a crime family," Marinaccio declared. "In my view they're chasing a ghost."

The prosecution's opening statement was delivered by Stamboulidis, who offered his blunt take on the motivation behind the crazy act: "He didn't like prison, and he didn't want to go back."

The federal attorney provided a primer for the jury on Gigante's life and crimes before delivering a one-sentence summary of the prosecution: "This case is about a powerful crime family boss and the great lengths he would go to protect his position."

Marinaccio, in his opening, wasted little time in attacking the parade of murderous Mob turncoats lined up against Gigante as psychopaths covering their own asses.

The gangsters "have spent every waking minute of their lives either committing crimes or planning to commit crimes, who mastered the art of deception and deceit . . . [and] will tell you, in much the same way they told their victims before they murdered them, 'Trust me. Trust what I tell you.'"

Then he issued a challenge to the jury: "It's time to separate the man from the myth."

The Chin, his chair squeezed in between his two lawyers, showed no emotion as the dueling attorneys laid out their cases. He appeared in dire need of a shave and a shampoo.

NYPD detective Gaetano Bruno took the stand to testify about scores of surveillance photos snapped using a camera tucked inside an attaché case, with a button on the handle to snap the pictures. The cream of the Genovese crop, including Quiet Dom and Manna, were among the Mob cronies caught consorting with the Chin outside the Triangle by Bruno's candid camera.

FBI agent Beaudoin, taking the witness stand early in the trial, relished the chance to go toe-to-toe with the Chin. He recounted his reconnaissance missions on the Upper East Side, telling the jury that Gigante spoke in a "commanding way" to his visitors while unaware of the watching eyes in the adjoining yeshiva.

Gigante sat at the defense table, his lips moving as if in conversation with an imaginary friend. The FBI agent fixed his adversary with a hard stare.

"I looked at him all the time," he recounted later. "I looked at the sons. There was a break in the trial, and we were all standing in the hallway. One of the sons started giving me the stare-down. I stared right back. 'Don't you know who I am? Do you guys want to go to jail for life, too?'"

The mood was much lighter during another recess when, Beaudoin recalled, the Chin momentarily let his guard down.

"His son is pushing him through the courthouse hallway," the agent said. "And there's this hot-looking woman in a short dress. All the guys were looking. And then you turn around, and the Chin's looking, too."

Dorsky heard similar tales of Gigante's appreciation of the female form. "Some women said he would wink at them and make flattering comments," said Dorsky. The only other person the Chin was seen addressing was his brother Louis in whispered conversations.

All eyes were on the first of the Mob witnesses, Big Pete Chiodo. Chiodo was admittedly hard to miss, a hulking figure wheeled into the courtroom in a chair of his own. He was lucky to be alive, and ready to talk. Chiodo recounted driving one of his Lucchese betters to a commission meeting with Gigante.

"He apologized for dressing in his bathrobe," the big man testified.

Gigante, his wardrobe upgraded to a blue blazer and white polo shirt buttoned to the neck, offered nary a flicker of recognition or interest. For once, the godfather's stubble was absent as Chiodo testified.

The next time the two men met, Chiodo recalled, was as codefendants after their 1990 arrests in the Windows Case. It was a thin reed in the prosecution's case, as the typically blunt Weinstein noted.

"You are going to have a problem with a stale case," he warned Dorsky. "See if you can put a little excitement in it."

At what became an almost daily review of the trial, Father G. agreed: "It's obvious he doesn't know my brother."

Weinstein was perturbed at day's end when Chiodo's face appeared in the work of sketch artists. He ordered the group to "fuzz up the faces" when Big Pete returned to the stand—and when the other ex-mobsters followed. There was one exception to the edict: Gravano, whose face was well known thanks to a simultaneous media blitz for his just-released biography.

Marinaccio attacked Chiodo in the first of his fierce cross-examinations of the flipped Mafiosi, emphasizing the five murders admitted by the witness—including the execution of Windows co-conspirator John Morrissey. Chiodo had also acknowledged killing a man who date-raped the daughter of a Mob associate.

"Did you ever say, 'This is not the life for me?'" Marinaccio inquired at one point.

Chiodo's answer spoke for generations of made men: "It's the only life I knew."

The extra-large witness also confessed that while he had met John Gotti and Colombo boss Vic Orena, he never had a formal introduction to the Chin during his sessions with Mob higher-ups.

When Crazy Phil Leonetti took the stand, he looked the part of a Hollywood gangster: tanned and fit, his dark hair slicked back, dressed in a fashionable black blazer. His lip curled slightly in an Elvis Presley–meets–Lucky Luciano style as he recounted his story of the Chin's homicidal handling of the Philly Mob wars in a gripping yet almost nonchalant fashion.

As he was sworn in and began to answer questions, Leonetti noticed that Gigante appeared distant and disinterested—until the two shared a single moment of clarity.

"In the courtroom, for a brief second, he looked directly at me like he wanted to kill me," Crazy Phil recalled. "It was as if he was saying to me, 'I'm disappointed in you.' The whole rest of the time, he did the crazy act. But for that brief second I saw it in his eyes. Then he went back to being slumped over and he didn't even look at me. But in those few seconds I could see that he was normal."

Leonetti acknowledged his story was based on conversations with his uncle Scarfo, and he had never actually met Gigante. But he did drive Scarfo north to the meeting where Caponigro and Salerno received their death sentences, and he heard the whole tale almost immediately on the ride back to Atlantic City.

Gigante, in his wheelchair, sat stone-faced as Leonetti detailed Chin's role in the Philly bloodletting. After the Testa hit, "the Chin told my uncle to kill everybody involved," the witness said.

Under cross-examination defense attorney Phil Foglia, whose kids were baptized by Father G., confronted the gangster about charges that the Bronx priest was a made member of the Genovese crime family. The allegation was contained in an FBI interrogation report.

"No, I never said that," Leonetti insisted. The FBI agent who wrote up the report made a mistake.

The priest heard the testimony from his regular perch in the first row of the federal courtroom. And afterward, he provided more details about the FBI's claims.

The report charged "that I even committed murders and buried the people in my rectory, but someone else from another crime family told Leonetti, 'Don't believe it,'" said Father G. "[Foglia] didn't read that part."

Leonetti was also asked about his role in an ABC News interview piece titled "Walk with the Devil."

"And you were in the title role?" asked Foglia.

"Cosa Nostra was the Devil," the witness replied. "Not me."

Leonetti then offered his review of the show: "It was terrible."

The feds called an FBI agent to introduce photos and tapes
made at the late Fat Tony's club. One of the snapshots showed
Dr. Wechsler hanging out with Salerno in March 1984. This was
a revelation that seemed to make the good doctor's blood pressure spike. The well-tanned physician blushed deeply as the
photo was brought into evidence.

But Agent Peter Kelleher also acknowledged that Gigante was
never once spotted at the East Harlem club during the surveillance that ran from December 1983 through February 1985. Nor
was his voice ever heard on more than one thousand hours of
audio recordings.

"On any tape whatsoever, did you ever hear Mr. Gigante discuss a commission meeting?" asked Gigante's other defense attorney, James Culleton.

"No," replied the bookish, balding FBI agent.

The trial was interrupted by an appearance from attorney
Ronald Kuby, the ponytailed protégé of legendary radical lawyer
William Kunstler. Kuby hoped to land one of the coveted courtroom seats for Gravano's testimony, so he could serve the Mob
killer with papers in a civil suit brought by some of Sammy's
nineteen victims.

They were seeking to snare any of Gravano's profits from his
biography, but Weinstein steered Kuby to the state court for help.
The left-leaning lawyer was hardly the only interested party. Publisher HarperCollins asked Weinstein to declare details of Gravano's publishing contract off-limits during his testimony. The
judge refused.

And so the stage was set in a Brooklyn courtroom for the
trial's main event: Gravano versus Gigante, the Bull taking on the

Chin from the witness stand, the two business partners now working different sides of the Mob street. By the time it was finished, Gigante would be bloodied—and Gravano's value as a government witness would be zero.

The Gravano who put his hand on the Bible on July 10, 1997, was a different man—at least on the outside.

The mobster, no longer hiding as the anonymous "Jimmy Moran" in the Federal Witness Protection Program, was living openly in Arizona despite a reported $1 million Mafia bounty on his head. (Two years later, though, a Gambino family plot to blow Gravano up was thwarted when he was busted for running a multimillion-dollar ecstasy ring.)

The vain Sammy Gravano underwent plastic surgery to tighten up his face, and had recently sat for an interview with Diane Sawyer to promote his best-selling book. Life in the Southwest agreed with the old Brooklyn-born gangster, who arrived to testify under enormous surveillance that couldn't hide his burnished tan or fighter's trim.

There was a buzz in the courthouse hallways, where spectators arrived hours early for a seat. The in-house court reporters were guaranteed seats, but the rest of the media horde was left to fight for a coveted spot inside.

Before Gravano testified, George Stamboulidis placed a pitcher of water alongside the witness chair. The Bull's FBI handlers, Matty Tricorico and Frank Spero, watched carefully as they awaited Gravano's arrival. The prosecutor, with a grin, assured the agents that the ex-underboss was safe from poisoning if he decided to take a sip.

"It's our water," he mouthed to the pair.

Late on a Thursday afternoon the Bull arrived in a gray double-breasted suit. His hair was closely cropped and a pair of John Lennon–style glasses gave him a faint professorial look. The Gigante clan glared from the front row as Gravano swore to tell the truth, the whole truth and nothing but the truth.

They were not alone in fixing Sammy with the evil eye. The

family members of several Gravano murder victims turned out for a look at the man who had killed their loved ones. The prosecution complained that Laura Garofalo, whose father was murdered in 1990 on the family's front steps, was planted near the front to "rattle" the mobster.

Gravano—unlike the earlier Mob informants—had a business relationship with the Chin, and he once again recounted their get-togethers. The Bull noted that Gigante's standard business attire in their later face-to-face meetings was a bathrobe and pajamas.

His direct questioning by Weissmann managed to stir the Chin, who appeared more alert than at any prior time in the trial.

Gravano, who appeared nervous at the outset despite five years of working for the government, occasionally looked at the wheelchair-bound Gigante sitting across the courtroom. The Oddfather returned his gaze at times, intrigued by the traitor in the witness chair.

By the end of Weissmann's queries, Gravano appeared looser and more confident. His voice was permanently matter of fact, whether discussing cordial Mob summits or brutal Mob slayings. Occasionally, before answering the prosecutor's well-prepared queries, he slowly adjusted his glasses as if pondering the question.

But the real fun began once Marinaccio started his cross-examination. Many of the questions dealt with Gravano's publishing exploits, rather than his Mob doings. Money, as it turned out, was still at the root of Gravano's evil.

The underboss had parlayed his Gambino position into a multimillion-dollar income while on the streets, and he wasn't doing so badly in the Witness Protection Program. Yes, Gravano acknowledged, he had received a $250,000 advance for sitting down with author Peter Maas to recount his criminal exploits—including the nineteen murders.

Yes, he was expecting additional royalties as his riveting tale—including his decision to testify against his old boss, Gotti—catapulted up the best-seller list. There was even talk of a movie about Gravano, who once acknowledged that *The Godfather* was a major influence on his life of crime.

Maas, in turn, threw Sammy under the bus and said he was unaware of any financial agreement with the Mob killer—which would have violated the Son of Sam law preventing New York State felons from turning a profit on their crimes. Gravano disagreed: his deal was definitely with TJM Productions, author Maas's company.

BULL'S GOLDEN TALE, trumpeted the *New York Post* over a courtroom artist's sketch of the bespectacled Gravano.

Maas, in *Underboss,* weaved Gravano's words into a tale somewhat sympathetic to the Bull. But Gravano was on his own against the pugnacious Marinaccio as his testimony stretched into a second contentious day.

Gravano returned for the rematch looking more relaxed in a blue-gray suit, with a black golf shirt buttoned to the top. Not a hair was out of place; he looked ready for dinner at some suburban country club after eighteen holes of golf.

The defense lawyer, who hailed from the Bronx, began quoting liberally from the Maas-penned biography to illustrate Gravano's long history of treachery, mendacity and homicide. Gravano, under oath, did little to counter the image.

There was a recounting of Gravano's bloody decades in the Life, including his admission that it was "one double cross after another, one scheme after another, one betrayal after another."

"So facing a life sentence without parole, it took an epiphany to make you see that?" Marinaccio asked in mock disbelief. "You know what an 'epiphany' is?"

Gravano turned his palms upward and rolled his eyes in the same direction: "The way you said it, I get the idea."

Marinaccio asked about the 1986 murder of Gambino associate Robert "DB" DiBernardo, whose murder was ordered by Gotti based on a tip from Gravano that DB was running his mouth.

"DB was a good talker, a smart guy," Gravano explained when asked if secondhand info on the mobster was enough to justify his killing. "This is the way the Mob runs. It's not if [it's] good enough for me. It's not if it's good enough for you. You're a lawyer. It's good enough for the Mob."

The dead man's daughter, sitting in one of the coveted courtroom seats, gasped as tears welled in her eyes. She stared angrily at the witness before bolting for the hallway. Marinaccio, a copy of *Underboss* at the ready, inquired about the murder of John "Johnny Keys" Simone.

"On page one hundred twenty-six, you say, 'Deception is at the core of a clean mob hit,'" the defense lawyer read. "Deception—that's something you were very good at?"

"I guess," Gravano conceded.

"Deception all around?" the lawyer pressed.

"Yes," the Bull replied.

"And you were at the center of it?"

"I'm at the trigger end," Gravano fired back.

Marinaccio referred repeatedly to the Gravano book, its pages covered in brightly colored Post-its to mark the passages significant to Chin's defense. He asked how Simone was executed.

"I believe it was a single shot with a .357 Magnum to the back of the head," said Gravano, his voice as flat as if reading from a phone book. "I don't recall three shots."

The defense lawyer produced a 1993 FBI interview with Gravano where he never mentioned Gigante's name in connection with the Philly hit before honing in on the witness's cold-blooded approach to murder—asking about the 1981 killing of Frank Fiala. The Bull's unfortunate business partner agreed to pay Gravano $1 million for a Brooklyn nightclub; after Fiala handed over $750,000, Gravano settled the rest of the debt by murdering the man.

"That [money] rang your greed bell?" Marinaccio asked.

"That million seemed to ring it every time," said Gravano.

By this point of the questioning, Gravano was listening to the questions intently. He rested his head on his hand, or gently touched his right index finger to his lips. Asked a series of questions about Mob construction business meetings, he rubbed his chin—without irony or intent.

The cross-examination turned to the murder of Gambino soldier Louis DiBono, murdered after Gravano tipped the killers to a parking lot beneath the World Trade Center, where the victim left his car.

"I didn't accomplish nothing except to give John [Gotti] that information," said Gravano. "If you want to make that a major accomplishment . . ."

Gravano recounted how the Gambinos, gathered at Castellano's Staten Island estate, learned about Chin's 1981 hospital ascension to the top of the Genovese family.

"I was in Paul's house when word came," he recounted. "Tommy Bilotti brought it in. Tommy said that Fat Tony had a stroke and stepped down, and Chin was made the boss. . . . I had it at the table out of Tommy's mouth."

"We can't ask Tommy Bilotti," Marinaccio inquired, "because he's dead?"

"Yeah."

"We can't ask Paul Castellano because he's dead?" the defense lawyer pressed, exposing Gravano's treachery within his own family.

"Yeah."

"And you were involved in plots to kill both?" he asked.

"Yes."

Gravano even admitted a plan, conjured with murdered underboss DeCicco, to kill their pal Gotti. "John Gotti had the brains and the nerve to run the family," he said. "But he had some bad habits. Frankie told me, 'If it doesn't work out, we'll whack him out. I'll be the boss, and you'll be the underboss.'"

Gravano remained unfailingly polite as the questioning intensified. The man who seemed incapable of uttering a sentence without an F-bomb on government wiretaps apologized at one point for using the term "screwup." He acknowledged the Genovese plot to whack Vincent Gigante, but said he wasn't too good with times and dates of the payback plan. Occasionally the old street tough returned from beneath the cool exterior.

"Again, that's one of those slick lawyer moves," Gravano responded to one question. "He asks, 'Did I ever hear a rumor?' No, I didn't."

When Marinaccio read a lengthy book excerpt about the infamous 1988 commission meeting with Gotti and Gigante, Sammy asked to take a look.

"That's a mouthful," he said. "I'd like to see it, if possible, so I can understand your question."

When Marinaccio quoted from Gravano's direct testimony, he took a jab at the government's lawyer: "This is direct examination. The prosecutors. No slick lawyers here."

Sammy disagreed: "Why not? They're lawyers, too."

The defense lawyer, hell-bent on discrediting the star witness, quoted again from his earlier answers to the prosecution questions.

"Do you recall hearing those questions and giving those answers?" asked Marinaccio.

"Sounds like me," Sammy said brightly.

Gravano insisted his testimony was 100 percent legit, as required by his deal with the FBI. "There's no reason for me to bob and weave and not tell you the truth, when you know the government's not after you," he said.

He even maintained a sense of humor as the withering questions continued. Marinaccio read from a transcript of a December 12, 1989, conversation at Gotti's Ravenite Social Club, where Sammy's various business interests were discussed at length.

"Busy little guy, huh?" said Gravano, with laughter breaking the courtroom tension.

In the same conversation an angry Gotti talked about "busting him (Sammy) tomorrow."

"Tomorrow never came," Gravano responded with a touch of snark.

Gravano also insisted that Cindy DiBernardo and the other

mourning relatives would never see a penny of his book money. "I intend to fight that law," he said.

Marinaccio started another query with yet another reference to *Underboss*: "On page two hundred seventeen of your book—"

Gravano interrupted. "Don't quote me on my book," he replied curtly. "I'm talking to a person who wrote this book. This is not a book. This is a trial. I'm under oath."

The jury, which never heard a word about the Chin's extensive psychiatric history, was read a scathing excerpt, instead, from a March 1995 government psychological profile of the Bull when he was under consideration for the Witness Protection Program.

The candidate presents a good social façade that masks extremely shallow emotionality, high impulsivity, irresponsibility and unpredictability, a federal shrink concluded. *His outward presentation conceals a self-centered personality that is primarily, if not completely, driven by internal needs without regard for the needs of others.*

The evaluation made Gravano squirm before another uncomfortable moment: He acknowledged collecting another $20,000 off the book. Gravano was paid $10,000 for doing a commercial voice-over, and another ten grand for providing the publisher with personal photos. By the end, in his final turn as a government witness, the questions—even from the prosecution—were about Gravano's book and not Gigante.

"Are you here to publicize the book?" asked Assistant U.S. Attorney Weissmann in an effort at damage control.

"No," replied Gravano before departing.

The Gigante clan offered their harsh reviews of Gravano's testimony outside the courtroom.

"He's here, in our opinion, to promote the book," said the Chin's daughter Yolanda. "If you ask me, this is just a promotional stop. He's a pathological liar and a psychotic murderer."

Father Gigante said Gravano's appearance was enough to make him lose his faith . . . in the criminal justice system. "I'm more upset with the way the government is operating in collusion to prosecute a sick man," the priest declared.

After the Bull had put three dozen of his former crooked colleagues behind bars, Marinaccio's combative cross—with its incessant references to Gravano's literary effort—had ruined Sammy as one of the feds' most reliable voices. He would never again take the stand against his Mob cronies, his usefulness ruined by a best seller.

"It's not a good idea," said former U.S. Attorney Andrew Maloney of Brooklyn, "for a government witness to write a book."

Next up was Little Al D'Arco, the memory of his explosion at the sanity hearings still fresh in the minds of prosecutors and the press. But before he said a word, Judge Weinstein lobbed a verbal grenade at prosecutors. Was there, he asked, "any witness" at all who would directly tie Gigante to the crimes charges in the indictment?

"Yes, Your Honor," came the reply from the prosecution table.

"Then let's have those witnesses," he instructed the three-man government team.

The respected jurist offered a similar rebuke to defense attorney Foglia as he questioned Philadelphia mobster Eugene "Gino" Milano about the killings of Bruno and Testa.

"What sort of harm did he do to the defendant that you want to cross-examine him about whether he pistol-whipped somebody when he was eighteen or nineteen?" the exasperated judge asked.

"I think it goes to his credibility as a witness," said Foglia.

"How long is this cross-examination going to last?" Weinstein inquired. "Let's get to the merits of the case. It seems to me we're wasting a great deal of time. He didn't connect your defendant with the murders, did he? So, why are you wasting all this time cross-examining him and emphasizing it?"

Enter Little Al. He was the witness the federal judge was waiting to hear.

* * *

The diminutive D'Arco, now the highest-ranking Mafia member to ever flip to the feds, was cool and composed as he recounted the Chin's long-ago approval to run a gambling operation out of a luncheonette. He told of "getting messages from the Chin" about Mob operations in far-flung Kentucky. And he gave his version of the 1988 commission meeting, complete with the treachery of Amuso and Gigante to lull Gotti into a false sense of security. The turncoat testified that he learned of the Gotti murder plot from other mobsters, and he never doubted its veracity.

"You get killed for lying," he declared. Little Al was now facing the same penalty, albeit at a slower rate: lying would jeopardize his government deal, and he would likely die behind bars for his crimes.

He offered an insider's view of the Triangle, where the conversations were conducted in barely audible whispers and the walls warned of government bugs. D'Arco then detailed the Chin's bizarre embrace of Savino despite warnings from the other families that Black Pete was working for the other team.

He recounted Gigante's 1991 call to the Luccheses, trying to arrange the gabby Savino's murder. "Chin wants a favor from you," D'Arco quoted Genovese family leader Jimmy Ida telling him. The Genovese boss had a tip that Savino was living in Hawaii. D'Arco said he turned down the request after conferring with the Luccheses' two fugitive leaders, Casso and Amuso. It was a sign of how far the Chin's fortunes had fallen.

"Is there any doubt in your mind that Vincent Gigante was of sound mind up until 1991?" asked Stamboulidis.

"No doubt," replied the dapper D'Arco, who would celebrate his sixty-fifth birthday later that month in the gentle embrace of witness protection.

Marinaccio, on cross-examination, was hardly as tender. And the hotheaded D'Arco once again surfaced. On his third day as a witness, D'Arco was queried about FBI reports that contained no mention of Gigante during his debriefing.

"So you're saying the agents made a mistake?" Marinaccio asked pointedly, pacing in front of the witness stand.

"I don't know what they put in their reports," he shot back. "I'm telling you what I said. What they do is their business."

As the grilling continued, the murderous mobster turned to Weinstein for help. "Judge," he declared, "he's abusing me."

But D'Arco wasn't shaken from his main claim: the crazy act was indeed a performance and one that was known throughout Mafia circles, despite Gigante's secretive nature and wild public meanderings.

And Little Al remained unapologetic about turning on his old mob pal. "I was told that I should say every crime that I can remember," D'Arco declared. "And fortunately for some—and unfortunately for others—I have a good memory."

"The government told you that if you tell them all the crimes you committed, you would get a pass. Isn't that right?" asked Marinaccio.

"Absolutely not," D'Arco spat back. At another point, Little Al derisively referred to his inquisitor as "Mr. Mariachi."

The defense feared that D'Arco, with his Brooklyn accent, combative style and street smarts, had charmed the jurors during his long stay on the stand. In closing arguments Marinaccio would warn the panel deciding Chin's fate that Little Al was "not a Damon Runyon character, some benign mobster out of *Guys and Dolls*."

By the time the prosecution called Peter Savino to the stand, the onetime mobster was a dying man. He was gaunt, shaky and in obvious pain as he testified from a wheelchair via closed-circuit television from an empty courtroom in an undisclosed location.

The defense fought mightily to keep Savino from appearing at all. At a hearing outside the presence of the jury, Gigante's lawyers argued that allowing the devastating witness to appear via television violated their client's right to confront his accuser. In a ruling that noted the Chin's own health issues, Judge Weinstein overruled the defense motion. Savino would testify in the highly unusual arrangement, with the government providing transportation to the location where he would speak.

One attorney for the defense—it would be Phil Foglia—and one for the prosecution would join Savino, accompanied by a third party chosen by the judge. "None of them," the judge warned ominously, "will reveal this place to anyone."

The Brooklyn courtroom was packed as the onetime Mob bon vivant appeared like a ghost on the screen, using a white handkerchief to wipe the rivulets of perspiration rolling down his pale face. As he began to testify against his old boss, Savino was mortally ill, suffering from cancer of the lung, liver and pelvis.

The witness, when referring to Gigante, showed they were on a first-name basis; he referred to the Chin only as "Vincent."

His answers were measured, precise—and vitally important to the prosecution, although his dramatic appearance drew little of the media attention generated by Gravano or D'Arco. It was Savino who directly linked the Chin to the Windows Case and the murder of Gerry Pappa.

"Vincent told me Gerry Pappa was killed for shaking down the drug money," he testified.

Gigante, as noted by D'Arco and charged by the feds, had also plotted to whack Savino. Gigante, for his part, seemed disinterested in the appearance of his former underling. The Chin dozed off several times as Savino laid out their crooked history.

Savino detailed his face-to-face meetings with the Chin: "Twenty, thirty, maybe more." Some were business, others personal—he knew both Gigante's wife and mistress, along with Chin's children. More importantly, he was able to lay out the massive Windows Case scheme, from its infancy to the original indictment naming Gigante seven years earlier.

The dying witness's failing condition was evident even on the courtroom's TV monitors. He requested several recesses to gather his strength for another round of questioning. "I need to stop a minute now, guys," he declared at one point.

Savino later paused to request another break. The voice of an off-screen prosecutor sitting with the ex-mobster was clearly audible: "The witness is in a lot of pain." By the time he was finished testifying, so were Gigante and his lawyers. Savino emerged as the trial's true star witness—his testimony the last act of a dying man.

Even Weinstein was taken by Savino's bravura performance, although he expressed concerns about the witness's obvious poor health and whether he would even survive until cross-examination. "He's an important witness who has given extremely damaging testimony," the judge noted.

If Savino couldn't answer the defense questions, "we [would] have a problem and I'm anxious not to have a mistrial," said the judge.

Savino returned via the monitor, with the defense questioning his testimony about his initial meeting with Gigante and the rest of the Genovese hierarchy in the early 1980s. The get-together was not mentioned in his FBI debriefing reports, Chin's lawyers noted. Savino had no idea why it wasn't there, and remained resolute in his testimony before stepping down.

While Savino was initially slated as the last government witness, Stamboulidis had one last mobster in mind for a grand finale. And what a show it was.

Former Genovese underboss Venero Mangano arrived at the Brooklyn Federal Courthouse in a prison-issued blue jumpsuit. He did not apologize for his jailhouse outfit—or for anything else.

Prosecutors decided at the last minute to bring the longtime Gigante loyalist in from a Loretto, Pennsylvania, federal prison to testify against the Chin. Predictably, the hard-boiled Benny Eggs didn't crack.

Mangano was four years into a fifteen-year bid for his conviction in the Windows Case. One of the evidence photos in that prosecution included Benny Eggs chatting up Savino on a Greenwich Village street; a print of the shot still hangs in the office of ex-federal prosecutor O'Connell.

Prosecutors claimed their decision to call Mangano was the result of Weinstein's critique of their case. It was a bit of legal gamesmanship, too: even if he remained loyal to his oath of omerta, prosecutors argued his silence would deliver a strong message to the Gigante jury.

Calling Mangano as a witness is quite appropriate, given Gigante's claim that the government should have produced witnesses with first-hand knowledge, Stamboulidis wrote in a letter to the judge. *If Mangano refuses to testify it will also graphically illustrate why it is necessary to enter into agreements with people like the cooperating witnesses in this case.*

The late addition to the witness list, although more a legal roll of the dice than anything else, prompted howls of an ambush from the defense team. It took mere seconds for the crotchety Mangano to show that Chin's lawyers had nothing to fear.

Before Mangano even arrived in the city, his lawyer warned prosecutors that she had no idea whether Benny Eggs would accept an immunity offer from the feds to rat his boss out. But the expectation of Mangano flipping was, realistically, less than zero.

Mangano, delivered by federal marshals with the jury out of the courtroom, wasted no time in making his utter contempt for the prosecutors and unbending support of the Chin evident as the two old gangsters shared a courtroom before a rapt audience.

The Mob veteran was infuriated that prosecutors had publicly named him as a witness, suggesting to the world that he would turn his back on the very precepts and "family" that had defined most of his adult life.

Stamboulidis rose to question Mangano, a true tough guy who served as a tail gunner during thirty-three bombing runs over Europe during World War II, including a pair on D-Day. The sight of a government lawyer in a suit threatening him with contempt of court was little more than the buzzing of a well-dressed gnat to the ex-underboss.

Mangano refused to answer even the simplest of the prosecutor's queries.

"What do you want to do, shoot me?" he asked. "Shoot me, but I'm not going to answer any questions. You gave me fifteen years already, so do whatever you want."

"Did you have a nickname, Benny Eggs?" Stamboulidis asked.

"I refuse to answer under my Fifth Amendment rights," said Mangano.

"Were you the underboss of the Genovese family?" the prosecutor pressed.

"I refuse to answer under my Fifth Amendment rights," the mobster replied. "Anything else that you're going to ask me, I say the same thing. I don't feel good, and I'm looking to go back (to prison)."

"Mr. Mangano, would you refuse to answer all questions I ask?"

"All questions, anything you want to ask," sneered Benny Eggs. "I refuse to answer anything you ask. I don't appreciate you going to the press and saying that I was cooperating. If you could make innuendos, certainly I can, too."

Weinstein, at the prosecutor's prodding, declared Mangano in contempt of court. But Stamboulidis took one more shot at the stonewalling mobster.

"Mr. Mangano, are you a member of the Genovese family of La Cosa Nostra?"

"Stop wasting the court's time," snapped Mangano. "You're not making me a part of this charade here from a mental case and a physical case, like they done to me. So I'm not going to answer any questions whether you dance, whether you put me in prison—"

Weinstein interrupted: "All right. Stop."

But Benny Eggs wasn't done.

"So, do whatever ya want," he concluded, stand-up to the end. "Your Honor, I don't mean to be disrespectful to the court."

"I understand," said Weinstein.

"Do whatever youse want," Mangano declared, bringing an

end to his rant. "I don't wanna answer nothing no more. I don't want to be a part of this charade."

Weinstein showed the departing mobster some legal respect: he declined to impose any sanctions on Mangano for his refusal to testify, and declined to let the prosecution tell the jury that Gigante's underboss had appeared and obstinately refused to answer any questions.

Stamboulidis, years later, chuckled about his surreal show-down with the venerable Venero Mangano. "He had a lot of affection for me," the lawyer said with a laugh. "I didn't expect him to cooperate or be happy. He wasn't happy, and he definitely wasn't cooperative."

As the trial reached the finish line, an unlikely courthouse reunion drew far less attention than Benny Eggs. For a single court session all eight of Chin's kids—the five Gigantes and the three Espositos—sat as a group to watch the proceedings. It was the first time the Mob boss's progeny were ever together at once, and their dad took notice.

The Chin, rolling in his wheelchair toward the courtroom door, grabbed one of its wheels to stop his exit. He snapped out of his practiced stupor for a brief moment, turning to look at his children. And then he turned the wheel loose as his doctor pushed Gigante out of sight.

In the end the government produced eighteen witnesses and more than 250 exhibits, including a montage of surveillance shots capturing the Chin in action. The prosecution—after seven long years of pursuit, after the bruising battle to prove his sanity and endless psychiatric exams, after decades of failed investigations by their federal forebears—then rested their case.

"We thought we presented the case in its best light with the evidence we had," said George Stamboulidis. "You never know. After that, it's in the jury's hands."

The defense quickly followed suit without calling a single witness. Marinaccio and the rest of his team debated until about 2

A.M. on the day of the July 21 court session before opting not to bring in medical experts for testimony on Gigante's mental health. Prior to trial they decided not to call Fat Tony's old sidekick Fish Cafaro or the murderous Gaspipe Casso.

The volatile Casso, after violating his cooperation deal, had become a toxic witness that neither side seemed willing to risk under oath. (Casso, irate at missing his shot in the courtroom spotlight, later accused witnesses Gravano and D'Arco of lying during the trial.)

The defense decision sent the tacit message that they believed the government's case was too weak to sustain a conviction of their client. After resting, the Gigante team moved for a dismissal of all charges, a fairly pro forma maneuver. Although in this case they argued that the testimony of the prosecution witnesses was a tapestry of hearsay with no corroboration.

Weinstein disagreed, saying there was "ample evidence to support a verdict" on every count in the indictment.

The prosecution was somewhat surprised by the defense decision—the Chin's team had indicated they planned to call some witnesses. But they never, under any circumstances, expected Gigante to take the witness stand.

The jurors, at the defense request, were instead read a stipulation that Salerno was identified during the commission case as the head of the Genovese family at a time when prosecutors now claimed the Chin was running things. This was the fallout from the commission case, when the government argued Fat Tony was the boss right through 1985.

The panel also heard that the government had spent more than $2.5 million supporting the six ex-mobsters who took the witness stand before Weinstein sent the jurors home and the lawyers went to their respective corners to polish their summations.

When they returned a day later, Weissmann delivered the government's final argument that the incoherent man in a wheelchair at the defense table was actually the craftiest, cruelest and most cogent boss in the annals of La Cosa Nostra. The prosecutor, across five hours, neatly recapped the government's case.

"He couldn't stop people from talking about him," said Weissmann. "When there's a large organization to run, you cannot erase yourself from the minds and, more importantly, the tongues of your conspirators."

He mocked the idea that Gigante's lawyers would heap scorn on Gravano, D'Arco and the other prosecution witnesses.

"Who in the world is Vincent Gigante to say that people in organized crime are terrible?" he asked. "This isn't an ideal world. This is a world where organized crime exists, and it's necessary to have cooperating witnesses."

Marinaccio unleashed an acerbic rebuttal, a ninety-minute scorched-earth attack on the prosecution's reliance on "psychopaths and liars" to smear his client.

"The government's case amounts to little more than throwing mud at a wall and seeing what sticks," the defense attorney declared.

He also noted that barely a decade earlier, the feds had convicted Fat Tony as the head of the Genovese family in the commission case—a triumph that left prosecutors and FBI agents shouting about the most devastating takedown in the history of organized crime.

"Boy, is the government running away from that now," he said.

Stamboulidis delivered the final word in the government's rebuttal. The prosecutor, defending his most wanted witnesses, simply pointed at Gigante sitting a few feet away. "He's the reason we need a Witness Protection Program," he declared.

The jury began its deliberations on July 23 after two hours of legal instructions from Judge Weinstein. It took sixteen hours over three days for the panel to render its decision. Word of the verdict, declared in a note to Weinstein, spread quickly through the courthouse.

Lawyers hustled back to the courtroom, which was filled to capacity with spectators and tension. The Gigante clan, led by Father Louis, found their familiar seats in the front row. Their patriarch was wheeled to the defense table to await his fate.

It was a split decision: a conviction and a victory for the feds, but with a twist that would only become evident to prosecutors down the road.

Gigante sat in his wheelchair, his face a blank slate, as the jurors convicted him of racketeering and two murder conspiracies—including the failed plot to eliminate Gotti. He was cleared in the Philadelphia Mob war murders, and acquitted in the Gerry Pappa killing.

One courtroom observer saw the Chin's eyes briefly widen as the verdict was read aloud. He then slipped quietly back into befuddled character, mum and semicoherent as reality sank in. His thoughts were his own.

The Gigantes sobbed in unison as the mobster was convicted as godfather of the Genovese family a full sixteen years after taking the seat. Almost four decades after beating the rap in the Costello hit, more than three decades after walking out of Lewisburg Federal Prison, Vincent Gigante was a convicted felon headed back to jail.

The announcement hit Father Louis hardest. For once, the priest had nothing to say. He rushed to Vincent's side at the defense table to wheel his brother out of the courtroom. But even as the faint echo of the foreperson's announcement hung in the courtroom, some could not acknowledge the dramatic end to an extraordinary era.

"He doesn't know what's going on," insisted Dr. Wechsler. "People are crying all around him, and he doesn't know what's happening."

The racketeering conviction alone carried a jail term of up to twenty years. The acquittal on the seven murder counts spared Gigante a life sentence, although he still faced a possible twenty-seven years after the jury found him guilty of thirty-three of the forty-one counts in the racketeering charge.

Weinstein was right: Peter Savino's testimony about the Windows Case was indeed devastating to his bathrobe-wearing pal. Much of the racketeering case focused on the long-running scam.

"It was a good feeling when they polled the jurors: 'So say you all?' And they affirmed the verdict," said Stamboulidis.

The defense, shaken but unwilling to surrender, announced plans for an appeal and quickly moved to keep Gigante free on bail pending his sentencing—a move challenged by prosecutors. "His criminal charade is over," said Stamboulidis, asking Weinstein to revoke Gigante's $1 million bail. The prosecutor argued that the Chin—his wheelchair aside—was now a "tremendous flight risk."

Weinstein ordered Gigante to surrender within twenty-four hours. Any other ruling, the judge said, would be "unnecessarily cruel." The man who for decades only left the Greenwich Village streets to further his deception was headed to a federal prison in Butner, North Carolina, where he would be evaluated in their special medical facility.

Gigante would enjoy one final last night of freedom before starting his sentence—however long it turned out to be. Pumped-up prosecutors cheered their long-awaited victory against their elusive adversary.

"His obstruction of justice is over. . . . Gigante has engaged in a charade his entire life," said Stamboulidis, using the same word that Benny Eggs used to describe the trial. "When you've committed the kind of crimes he has, it is appropriate for that person to die in jail."

Marinaccio vowed the Chin's legal battle was far from finished.

"We will continue to fight what we believe to be a gross injustice," he said. "We were hampered by the fact that Mr. Gigante has been and remains mentally ill and unable to assist in his defense."

After blasting the feds, the defense attorney turned his attention to the twelve people who just convicted the Oddfather.

"The jurors weren't able to put aside their preconceived no-tions about organized crime in general and Vincent Gigante in particular, because the evidence just wasn't there," he said.

Stamboulidis, Weissmann and Dorsky left the courthouse for a celebratory lunch at an Italian restaurant near the Brooklyn Bridge. "A couple of slices," Dorsky recalled of the low-key event. Stamboulidis called his wife to firm up plans finally for a long-delayed vacation. Dorsky had an even more pressing issue: his parked car had received a number of tickets for an inspection sticker that expired as he logged endless hours on the case.

He would end up back in court to resolve the issue—but like the Chin, he couldn't beat the rap.

"I finally went before a judge and explained what happened," he said. "I think he cut my fines in half."

Years after the trial was over, a top Justice Department official confided that one of his in-laws had saved the Chin's life during one of Gigante's tune-ups in suburban Westchester. When the Mob boss started choking on a piece of food, the relative—an employee at St. Vincent's—applied the Heimlich maneuver and popped the food free as a grateful Chin resumed breathing.

The relative was later offered a pricey trip in return for the impromptu rescue, which became a bit of a running joke within the family. "I used to tell her, 'Imagine how much money you could have saved the government if you didn't save him,'" the official recounted with a grin.

CHAPTER 20

DESOLATION ROW

*T*HE CHIN SHIPPED OUT TO THE FEDERAL CORRECTIONAL INSTI-
tution (FCI)–Butner in North Carolina, arriving one day after
the verdict. He was accompanied on the flight south by federal
marshals—as well as some mysterious friends, who began appearing in his cell in the wee hours of the morning.

There were dancers and violinists, children and a large black
cat. There was even the biggest boss of them all, a fairly regular
guest: God Himself.

With Gigante's racketeering conviction on appeal, there was
still a chance of beating the case; and the defense, after losing
the trial, resurrected his mental-health dodge as a reason to
spare the Chin from sentencing.

Sure, he was ruled competent to stand trial. And yes, the government's argument of his sanity while running the family during the 1980s had carried the day and convinced a jury. But
Chin's lawyers now insisted he was too mentally feeble to serve
any prison time.

The defendant's contribution to the cause quickly became
evident: the catatonic Chin of the Cadman Plaza courtroom disappeared, replaced by the openly deranged Gigante of the Sullivan Street sidewalks.

Given the crucial tug-of-war with the government, the FCI
staff kept meticulous records of the Mob chieftain's stay. Within
weeks the Chin was fully immersed in his old role—De Niro in a

prison jumpsuit, performing for a very select audience—and his bizarre presentencing stay in Butner was off and running.

His admission interview was fairly tame: Gigante insisted he didn't know the date, the time or even where he was. He couldn't identify Bill Clinton as the president. A staff psychologist described the Chin as "alert, but not oriented in all spheres." Within a week Gigante upped the ante.

A mumbling Chin informed the staff on August 3 that "he was hearing bad voices." These voices, he stated, were "telling him things too bad to reveal. Then God tells him good things."

Six days later a "calm and cooperative" Gigante reported a brand-new black car parked outside his cell in the morning. The next day brought a detailed report of a festive 2 A.M. gathering in the prison hallway.

A doctor's report read: *He saw 30 people . . . outside his cell door in costumes. They were dancing to violin music and speaking in English. The men wore suits and hats (brown, black, dark colors) and women wore long dresses. He insisted they were real, not his imagination. He laid down for a while, and the people disappeared.*

The Chin paused at this point in his nocturnal narrative. "I'm not crazy, Doctor," he announced. And then he began moving his lips without saying a word.

The treating physician was not impressed: *May represent fabrications or symptoms of med adjustments—I suspect the former.* Despite the plan Gigante's show still went on.

The Chin refused offers of a shave or a haircut. He recounted visions of a prison unit sinking slowly into the earth, and a car driving into the building. A group of kids arrived to stage a musical production outside his cell. Gigante stated "it was enjoyable," prison records showed.

An August 26 sit-down with his chief prison psychiatrist produced Chin's observation that "the media is on my side." He also dodged questions about his conviction and prospects for appeal.

The report concluded: *Patient answers were generally cogent and thoughtful. [Gigante] at time seemed to deliberately be avoiding answer-*

*ing questions about legal issues and later indicated a good understand-
ing of his legal situation if not his charges.*

The next day, though, Gigante refuted the suggestion that he
had any lawyers working on his appeal. He also complained
about loud singing outside his cell keeping him awake the night
before. A nurse's report stated the Chin was sleeping like a baby
when checked.

The big black cat appeared on consecutive nights in September. Gigante asked for some Tylenol to help him sleep.

"I'm not sick now," he declared on September 7. "I talked to
God, and He told me about everything."

But his complaints continued: inmates dancing in the hallways all night or bombs going off in the darkness. According to
the Chin, his most peaceful prison times came during his art
therapy sessions, where he once drew a picture of the New York
skyline.

With his sentencing date approaching, Gigante confessed
that life at Butner was actually pretty good and he hoped to stick
around. "I hate to leave this place," he told a staffer before a trip
to Brooklyn for a court hearing.

But he clammed up quickly: *Today, Mr. Gigante stated God told
him not to talk to anybody,* read a September 30 evaluation.

The defense filed a motion for Chin's release prior to sentencing, asking on behalf of Gigante's family for his release in
their custody pending his sentencing. U.S. Attorney Zachary
Carter, in an August 27 letter to Weinstein, said the government
would handle the travel arrangements from North Carolina to
New York City in a "humane fashion," which was apparently
more than he believed the Chin warranted.

*We have taken these measures even though we are aware that Gigante
has overstated the gravity of his physical ailments since he was arrested
on May 10, 1990,* read Carter's pointed two-page missive. *For instance, although Gigante presented testimony of doctors that he would
die if required to go to jail on the charges against him, this medical pre-
diction was erroneous.*

Indeed, in spite of the opinion of his doctors before the trial, Gigante elected to attend the court proceedings every day. Further, there is no reason for Gigante to be given preferential treatment because of his prominence as a criminal and the leader of the largest organized crime family in the nation.

It's worth noting that Carter's reference to Chin's position atop the Genovese family was written in the present tense.

After almost two months of scrutiny, the medical staff at Butner delivered its decision: Gigante should not go into the general federal-prison population, but instead should do his time in a federal medical center for additional treatment.

It is our opinion that Mr. Gigante is suffering from a mental disease or defect of which he is in need of custody for care and treatment, Warden Harley Lappin wrote in a September 16 letter to Weinstein. *He currently has significant medical conditions that also require close monitoring. For these reasons, if incarcerated, we recommend placement in a [facility] that can manage both his psychiatric and medical needs.*

The report also concluded that there was evidence of "malingering" as a get-out-of-jail-free card. The defense, however, hailed the findings as proof of their assertions.

"The doctors say he is suffering from dementia, which is what we've said all along," said Phil Foglia. "Here's a man with memory lapses so severe he couldn't communicate with his own lawyers. The bottom line is that he is incompetent and shouldn't go to prison."

It was déjà vu all over again—including Weinstein's subsequent opinion. The judge shot down the Gigante family's bid to have the Chin returned to the Village.

"I don't want him shackled, but I'm not sending him home," the judge declared at a September 24 hearing attended by several members of the clan. He rejected a defense motion to throw out the verdict because of Gigante's mental woes, ruling the Butner evaluation provided no "new evidence" in the case.

"Contrary to the defendant's assertions, the report does not undermine the prior findings of competency by this court," Weinstein ruled in yet another victory for prosecutors. "Rather, the suggested partial diagnosis of 'malingering' supports . . . [a] determination that the defendant Gigante feigned mental illness over many years in order to avoid his day of reckoning."

The venerable jurist unleashed a few shots at Chin's old doctors, suggesting they produced "dubious" diagnoses based on "speculative scientific theories" guaranteed to produce prodefense findings. He also noted Gigante's posttrial change in persona upon arriving at Butner.

While appearing "catatonic" at the defense table, Gigante had "responded to the questions posed to him by Butner's staff, participated meaningfully in the evaluation procedures and communicated effectively with his evaluators," the judge said. He specifically noted Chin's "emotional warmth and sense of humor."

And while he dismissed Chin's conviction in the 1987 Gotti murder plot, due to statute of limitations, Weinstein also lobbed a bomb at the defense appeal. "As far as I'm concerned, all the information we have, plus the Butner information, supports the court's contention that the trial was a valid trial," he said.

Prosecutors were prepared for the mixed conclusion of the Butner doctors; they had discovered the Chin was a lot more unfiltered when speaking with prison staff instead of the psychiatrists. With just seven words to a federal corrections officer, Gigante undercut weeks of mental-health misdirection.

CO Christopher Dale Sexton oversaw a special observation section where Gigante was an inmate. His workstation abutted the Chin's cell, and they soon established a fairly friendly rapport, given the circumstances. During one of their conversations Sexton inquired if the Mob boss was catching grief from his fellow inmates or fielding any annoying requests for favors.

"Nobody bothers me," Gigante replied, waving his right hand for emphasis. "Nobody fucks with me."

Sexton went on to note an assortment of interactions with the lucid Chin so long obscured by the Oddfather routine. Gigante showered himself, dressed himself and preferred to eat alone. He quietly made his bed every morning. The old fighter occasionally shadowboxed alone in his cell. His manners were impeccable. Sexton found himself with a soft spot for the ruthless Mob boss, who liked to present himself as a hardworking everyman rather than a cold-blooded killer.

"That's the way he was trying to make me feel," Sexton testified at a Brooklyn presentencing hearing. "I understood that, you know, [he meant] that government is pretty much making up a bunch of bull here. And I understood. I mean, I'm on the bottom poles, so I understood. And even if I didn't, I generally nodded just to [get] along."

Sexton wasn't going to fuck with the Chin, either.

Gigante recounted how an annoying inmate once approached him in the visiting room to strike up a conversation. The Chin fixed the man with a stare and uttered a *"ssshhh."* When the prisoner pressed the issue, Gigante flat out told the man to leave him alone.

End of conversation.

At another point Gigante was looking for the associate warden responsible for the mental-health units. He spotted a woman in a white uniform and asked Sexton if that was the right person.

"I thought he wanted another nurse or something," Sexton recounted. "And he said, 'No, no.' He kind of stuttered for a second. He said, 'No, the fucking broad that runs this joint.'"

Sexton, his Southern sensibilities a bit strained, recalled his one-word reply: "Whoa!" Sexton added that it was clear Gigante was treated with deference by the other prisoners and viewed as a leader as soon as he arrived in North Carolina.

"He was very charismatic," Sexton explained. "Because he made you feel like he was, you know, he knew you. He got along with you . . . the way he carried himself and the way he did speak. He was soft-spoken. He was respectful. He just kind of commanded respect."

The Chin even provided Sexton with his Manhattan address and urged the officer to stop by the big and beautiful home—presumably Olympia 2's town house. Gigante, like any proud family patriarch, talked about his kids and grandkids back in New York. And he offered a little insight into his life on Sullivan Street.

"I wasn't a saint in the past," he acknowledged. "[But] you gotta do what you gotta do to take care of your family."

The Chin explained that he avoided phones, although his reason for steering clear of calls had changed over the years. "All my friends are in jail now," said the famously uncommunicative Gigante, "so I don't use phones."

Gigante never discussed his old Mob contemporaries other than a mention of his old mentor, Vito Genovese, and a verbal broadside at his old Gambino nemesis Sammy Gravano. "He said [Gravano] was a fucking rat," Sexton recalled. "He was just a worthless piece of shit."

Stamboulidis called Sexton to a November presentencing hearing where the prosecution was once again challenged to prove the Chin's sanity. The feds also called Sharon Brown, a registered nurse working at Butner.

Brown testified that Gigante was coherent in dozens of conversations—when he was discussing his medications, his diet and his family visits.

"He would say (son) Salvatore is coming back and my brother will probably come back or my wife will come back," she recounted. When dealing with the staff, he was fairly normal. With the doctors he "tried to isolate himself," she said. "He'd sit on the bed more."

Brown recounted one day when she was escorting the Chin through the prison to his cell. One inmate was raising a ruckus, yelling and screaming at the COs for hours to bring him some items banned from the prison. The crazed man finally flagged down Gigante to introduce himself.

"He said, 'My name is George Roseberry,' " she recalled. "And Mr. Gigante looked at him and said, 'You need to shut up. You are getting on my nerves.' And the inmate said, 'Huh?' "

The Chin evenly repeated his statement before moving on.

"How did Roseberry respond to that?" a prosecutor asked.

"He called out for the officers one more time," the nurse said. "And then (Gigante) goes, '*Shhh*. Never mind.' And we haven't had any problems with him since."

The Chin later explained to Brown exactly why he had landed in Butner. "He would say, 'They're testing my mental status to find out if I can go back to trial,'" she recalled.

Brown summed up her experiences with Gigante in a single damning sentence: "Other than having a memory loss, he's just like you and I."

One other incriminating bit of news came from the prison: Gigante was regularly given prescription drugs to treat his purported mental-health woes. Yet, a urinalysis showed no trace of any drugs in his system—reminiscent of his pill-spitting days inside St. Vincent's.

The defense made one final stand before sentencing. With the Chin relocated to a prison medical facility in Westchester County, psychiatrist Dr. William Reid appeared before Weinstein to argue against the judge's competency ruling.

"He is not malingering," Reid said at a hearing, again attended by Father Louis and other family members. "He had lucid moments, but there were no times that I was there that I believed he was normal or near normal."

Under questioning by defense attorney Michael Marinaccio, the bow-tied Reid recounted the six hours that he spent with Gigante in the northern suburb.

"He knows the jury didn't find him innocent . . . [and] he understands that he may go to prison," Reid conceded. "He knows something bad is going on and may happen or not. He understands that he is the star of the proceedings, but that's the extent of his understanding."

Reid acknowledged Gigante, unlike his appearances during the trial, was warm and engaging—right down to kissing him on the cheek when the sit-down was done.

"That might be something very familiar to those in New York's

Italian-American community, but not to me," said the non-plussed shrink, "I'm an old Texan."

Judge Weinstein—yet again—was unmoved. In harsh language he flatly dismissed the seemingly endless defense reliance on psychiatric evaluations that supported their incessant contention of mental illness.

"Defendant has been consistently feigning insanity for many years and is still doing so in a shrewd attempt to avoid punishment for his crimes," Weinstein said. Sentencing was set, in stone, for December 18, and the players returned to Weinstein's court for the promised day of reckoning—one that many on both sides believed might never come.

The Chin eschewed his wheelchair this time, arriving with a halting walk to sit alongside his attorneys. He initially wore a pair of sweatpants, but the court provided a pair of gray slacks kept on hand by the judge for underdressed defendants. Gigante, who also sported a blue blazer, paused at one point for a long look at the assemblage of relatives in the courtroom, including all but one of his eight children.

The Gigante clan had collected twenty-four thousand signatures in eight loose-leaf notebooks supporting their call for leniency, harkening back to the Village's outpouring of support for Gigante before his long-ago drug conviction. Many in the courtroom crowd were stunned when the Chin actually spoke.

"Good morning, Your Honor," he said as Weinstein took the bench. Gigante fell mute for the rest of the hour-long hearing, although he seemed to listen intently as the sentencing proceeded with one final pitch from the defense to keep Gigante out of jail.

This time the lawyers offered sympathy instead of sanity as the grounds for their application to let Gigante do his time living under house arrest with family members—the same arrangement generously granted during the trial.

"My client may not have long to live," said Marinaccio. "I urge the court to allow him to live out what time he has left close to his family."

Weinstein, unsurprisingly, ignored the lawyer's appeal. Gigante was sentenced to twelve years in prison as his children and other relatives once again wept. He was also fined $1.25 million—quite a sum for a deranged, bathrobe-wearing defendant to cover.

Weissmann earlier spoke for the prosecution, urging the maximum term of twenty-seven years for an "inveterate gangster who committed his life to crime—and committed his life to not being caught. He spent years dodging bullets before he was brought into this courtroom."

The judge asked if Gigante wanted to say anything before sentencing was imposed. Marinaccio replied that the Chin had nothing to offer. However, Marinaccio told reporters that the Chin delivered a short statement as he was led away by federal marshals: "What's going on? I don't understand anything."

The prosecution was irked by Weinstein's decision to hand down the more lenient prison term. The judge said he believed the Chin had a "fifty-fifty chance" of serving out the full jail term, which could drop to ten years with good behavior. If Gigante was indeed diagnosed as terminally ill, he could appeal for early release with prison authorities, the judge noted.

He is a shadow of his former self—an old man finally brought to bay in his declining years after decades of vicious criminal tyranny, Weinstein wrote in a twenty-one-page opinion issued after the hearing. The judge then quoted no less an authority on the slings and arrows of outrageous fortune than Shakespeare himself: *"And one man in his time plays many parts . . . Last scene of all, that ends this strange eventful history, is second childishness and mere oblivion."*

A disgusted Father Gigante was more eloquent than his imprisoned brother—if not the judge—and hardly appeased by Weinstein's lesser sentence.

"He should never have been brought to trial," barked the priest, singing his familiar song. "He's incompetent. What's a downward departure? Ten years? He could be dead in about three?"

Before leaving, Marinaccio said the defense appeal would continue. Weinstein dispatched Gigante back to Butner. It seemed the last chapter in Gigante's decades-long war with FBI agents and federal prosecutors had finally come to an end. His lawyers would contest the conviction. The Chin would do his time. And so on, and so on.

Dorsky and others in law enforcement didn't see things that way. As it turned out, they were unsatisfied with jailing the Chin, who was proven sane; they would now go after his crazy alter ego—along with the family members and physicians who aided in the scam.

The Chin wasn't the only Gigante to land behind bars in 1997. His oft-arrested older brother Mario, and Gigante's nephew Salvatore, found themselves convicted in a decades-old arrangement to funnel millions of dollars in extortion payments to the Genovese coffers through their dominance of the garbage business in suburban Westchester County.

Prosecutors said the operation, which dated to 1960, imposed a Mob tax on local residents, who paid more to get their trash hauled. Mario picked up the cash, and admitted squirreling away "significant amounts" of money generated by the power play.

How much? He owed the Internal Revenue Service $1 million in unpaid taxes. The Genovese capo said he was now retired. When asked in court what he did for a living before that, he replied, "Mostly gambling."

There was a bizarre moment when Mario entered his plea. Manhattan federal judge Jed Rakoff asked Gigante if he was seeing a psychiatrist.

"No, sir," he replied emphatically.

The Chin returned to Butner to start his first jail term in thirty-three years, settling into the routine of prison life as his lawyers battled on. Even before the December sentencing occurred, the defense team received a ghoulish bit of good news:

Peter Savino had passed away on September 30 at the age of fifty-five. The Genovese turncoat survived for barely two months after testifying against the Chin.

Word of Savino's death at an undisclosed location came via a court filing by federal prosecutors. The ultimate Gigante informant died before he could face sentencing for the six murders in which he admitted playing a role.

"Bobby [Ferenga] always said, 'Pete will never do a day in jail,'" O'Connell recalled. "And he was right."

O'Connell thought back on Savino's immaculately buffed white sneakers. "I always thought there was a Lady Macbeth thing going on," he reflected.

The Gigante defense team, rather than looking back, was looking at a suddenly brighter future. If they could somehow get the verdict tossed, a retrial—without Savino's damning first-person accounts of life with the Chin—was likely to end with a far different result.

Gigante was transferred to the U.S. Medical Center for prisoners just before the turn of the year, and he spent the next 402 days in the Springfield, Missouri, facility. He signed the transfer documents with an X. A 1991 test showed the Chin with an IQ of 71, a drop of thirty points across thirty years; a subsequent test after his incarceration put the number at 68.

O'Connell dismissed the plunging numbers as part of the overall psychiatric scam: "I think the Chin is a pretty good guy. He just didn't test well."

With the case still on appeal, and a glimmer of hope remaining, Gigante slipped back into his oddball character with the staff. After his chatty behavior in Butner bit him in the backside, he was far less communicative with the prison employees.

Patient is confused and disoriented, read a New Year's Eve, 1997, admission report. *He is not able to give a history. Patient responded slow and followed simple commands on admission. He is not physically violent at this time.*

One week later, Vincent Gigante sat down with the Springfield psychiatrist for an evaluation.

He denied depression, but said he was sad on occasion when he thought about his mother, with whom he said he had lived for the past 10 years, the doctor wrote. *He stated that he occasionally hears voices of "bad people" and frequently hears God's voice. He said his most enjoyable activity is praying and talking to God.*

Reports noted that the Greenwich Village godfather was greeted warmly by his fellow inmates, letting down his guard among the prison population. He was spotted chatting amiably in the hallway, and visited another inmate in the man's cell. He spent time in the prison's common room, watching television with his imprisoned peers, and was observed reading on the bed in his cell.

Daily reports repeatedly described the Chin as cooperative, cheerful, taking his medication and popular with the other prisoners. Three months after he had arrived, the ailing old man approached the prison physical therapist for some help in getting healthy.

Patient asked for advice concerning a gradual conditioning program and he was advised to initiate a gradually progressing walking program, wrote prison worker Matt Taylor. *The patient voiced understanding of conditioning program.*

There were occasional reports of hearing voices, both good and evil, and one staffer observed that Gigante couldn't remember people, places or times. The Chin, while struggling with insomnia, invoked the Almighty in a visit with one doctor.

"I need another sleeping pill," Gigante said. "God told me I could have one."

The treating doctor ignored the Higher Power's recommendation and sent him back to bed.

His loyal family members made the long trip west once a week for visits with Gigante, whose physical condition indeed improved. Now sporting a beard on his famous chin, Gigante was moved out of the treatment facility for a two-week pit stop in Greenville, North Carolina, before landing at the remote Federal Medical Center in Rochester, Minnesota. The staff in the

Land of Ten Thousand Lakes was ready to take a dip in the Chin's psyche for a full evaluation after his arrival in March 1999.

The Chin, having sworn off smoking and coffee, made just a single request before checking in: he wanted to take Communion. Gigante also told a staffer that he was "praying for the other inmates." Gigante said he had been "Catholic since he was born, and he is deeply religious."

Gigante's legal fight had suffered a major setback just two months earlier. His defense team was challenging the verdict by arguing—once more, for old time's sake—that the trial was a sham because their client was crazy.

On January 22, 1999, the Second U.S. Circuit Court of Appeals agreed with Weinstein's assessment of the Chin's mental health and upheld his racketeering conviction. The Gigante lawyers pressed on, taking their case to the Supreme Court. The federal government, determined to keep the crazy Chin from overturning their hard-won conviction, hailed the decision and braced for the next round.

"It took seven years to bring him to trial, after all sorts of delaying tactics," prosecutor Weissmann said of the ruling. "It's nine years later, and it's very gratifying, to put it mildly."

In his first meeting with a Rochester prison psychiatrist, Gigante seemed worn down by his long-running ruse. The doctor, unsure of what to expect, visited the Chin in his cell in the Special Housing Unit.

"No disrespect, I love you people (psychiatrists) dearly, but I don't want to talk to you," Gigante said after the doctor introduced himself. "How will it help to do another evaluation? I still have to do my time."

Gigante finally sat down for the once-over by a prison doctor in early April, appearing with a grin that the psychiatrist interpreted as the Chin (who was a three-decade veteran of such sessions) "simply humoring me." The Q&A went on from there, taking a few odd turns along the way.

"I've hurt no one in my life," Gigante said by way of introduction. "I've got nothing to fear from anyone."

Gigante informed the doctor that he had no history of symptoms consistent with any kind of mania or obsessive-compulsive disorder.

Mr. Gigante emphasized that his psychiatric problems were a thing of the past, and at the time of his arrival at FMC Rochester, he did not believe he was suffering from any mental condition except "problems with memory," wrote the doctor. *Mr. Gigante said he enjoyed playing cards, watching TV and talking with his friends from the old neighborhood.*

Gigante was succinct about his legal history: "Whatever it was, I'm innocent." The inmate again appeared tired of perpetuating the crazy act. He held up one hand several times to stop the questioning, and addressed his inquisitor directly.

"I mean no disrespect, Doctor," Gigante said. "But I can't see why this is important to you."

The staff psychiatrist summarized their session by describing the Mob boss as "smooth and charming." Gigante seemed to be "polite, cooperative and seemingly honest"—with a single caveat.

Mr. Gigante manifested a dramatic style of speech and an air of superiority, including demands for special attention during the interview, which suggests to me that he harbors both histrionic and narcissistic personality traits, the doctor wrote.

Little Al D'Arco couldn't have said it better himself.

In mid-July a nurse returning from a two-week vacation was surprised when she ran into Gigante in a prison hallway. "Hi, Marsha," he greeted her pleasantly. "How have you been?"

That same month the Chin politely opted not to take his medicine when approached by another staffer: "I promise I will take it later. Thank you for being so nice. God bless you."

Gigante, on a third occasion, apparently caught himself being a bit too pleasant with the staff. "Thank you for being so nice to me," he said before reversing field. "Why are you torturing me? I'm innocent."

He also began demanding sit-downs with the warden on a daily basis.

"Perhaps," one psychiatrist mused, "Mr. Gigante has simply never given up his 'crazy act.'"

On July 12, a case conference was held with fifteen participants—doctors, nurses and a representative from the warden's office—for a full review of Gigante's mental health. After four months in Minnesota there was general agreement that the Chin was not quite ready to swear off the Oddfather routine.

Mr. Gigante really manifests very little clinical evidence of dementia, their report concluded. *Mr. Gigante's malingering had never before been subject to such close scrutiny as it had been here and that is a more likely explanation for the fact that his malingering has seemed more "transparent" than previously. . . . The [diagnosis] of malingering seems to be well-substantiated.*

In a prison summary of Gigante's history, one doctor—almost as if channeling the Judge Eugene Nickerson ruling—noted the patient had late in life "developed a new history of childhood tantrums, truancy and learning problems" in an effort to create a psychological profile to support his strange behavior.

Whereas I initially found it difficult to believe that Mr. Gigante could have been hospitalized for psychiatric reasons repeatedly over many years without having a major mental illness, the findings of the court now lead me to believe that a crime figure as powerful as Mr. Gigante could have indeed manipulated the mental-health system to further his goal of feigning mental illness, the doctor observed. *[His family] may well have been perpetuating Mr. Gigante's "illusion" of mental illness.*

Meanwhile, back in Brooklyn, federal prosecutor Dorsky and FBI agent Mike Campi found themselves thinking the same thing.

CHAPTER 21

EVERYTHING IS BROKEN

ONCE THE 1997 SENTENCING WAS DONE, FEDERAL OFFICIALS SOON learned from an informant that Gigante had hired someone to learn the identities of the anonymous federal jurors in a bid to fix the case. There was another revelation, too, this one regarding the length of the Chin's jail term.

"The informant told us if the judge had given Chin the full twenty-five years, it would have essentially shelved Gigante," said Dorsky. "It would have taken away his full force. But with the shorter sentence, he was allowed to run things from prison."

The postconviction Genovese family, instead, answered to a ruling commission, with the Chin calling the shots. Except now, the typically vigilant Gigante—who so memorably chastised John Gotti for bringing his son into the Life—opted to use his own son Andrew as a go-between to relay his directives.

It was incredible, unlikely and almost unbelievable, given Gigante's history. But the pursuit of a lucid Gigante, calling the shots from a distant jail cell, was suddenly on. The government was now working with a new Genovese insider, one without the name recognition of the witnesses from the first trial. More important, this one didn't flip while in custody: Michael "Cookie" D'Urso was still on the street.

"A tremendous witness," recalled Dorsky. "With respect to the Chin, he was essential."

The obscure Genovese soldier, like Savino before him, became the unlikely lynchpin of the prosecution case against the suddenly vulnerable Gigante. Much of the boss's old street insulation was, like him, locked up: Mangano, Manna and Canterino were no longer around to cover the Chin's back.

D'Urso was two things: one of the youngest Mob informants ever used by the government—and incredibly lucky to be alive. He was just twenty-three and already running with the Genovese family when he stopped by a Brooklyn Mob hangout for a November 1994 card game. The nascent mobster survived a bullet to the back of his head during a robbery inside the San Giuseppe Social Club in Williamsburg.

Another player cashed in his chips: D'Urso's cousin Sabatino Lombardi, a Genovese family loan shark, was killed by the gunmen who just minutes earlier were sitting at the table with the doomed mobster. One of the killers later described the nervous seconds before the shooting started.

"I'm combing my hair in the [club's] mirror and I just said to myself, 'Screw it,' " recalled gunman Anthony Bruno. "I turned around and pulled my gun out and shot Mike in the back of the head. I pulled the trigger and I saw Mike's hair split as the bullet went in."

The murder attempt didn't sour young D'Urso, even though his slain cousin was his mentor. "I pretty much idolized him," D'Urso later acknowledged.

His criminal career included robbery, fraud, extortion and loan-sharking. D'Urso, after his narrow escape, even served as the getaway driver in another Mafia hit. His approach to handling Mob business was direct: when a Brooklyn bakery shop owner showed D'Urso even the slightest bit of disrespect, the young thug would pay him a visit.

"I would give him a beating, to be honest with you," he acknowledged.

His introduction to the ranks of Mafia informants came under similar circumstances. A pair of screwups by a clerk at a mobbed-up betting operation left D'Urso holding the bag when two bettors won $50,000 in 1997. The mobster laid a beating on the clerk without a second thought. A short time later his pager started beeping. When D'Urso called back, the enraged voice at the other end launched into an angry diatribe.

"A guy just screaming at the top of his lungs," D'Urso later recalled. "He says, 'You can't hit my clerk!' I says, 'Oh, no? I'm the one who got screwed here.' I says, 'I'll go hit your clerk right now.' I didn't know at the time who [the caller] was."

D'Urso quickly discovered that he'd delivered a dressing-down to Frank "Farby" Serpico, then serving as the acting Genovese boss in Gigante's absence. Serpico—no relation to the corruption-busting NYPD detective of the same name—wasted little time putting out a murder contract on the mouthy kid for his violation of Mob protocol.

That was enough of the Genovese family for D'Urso, who immediately decided to start a second life devoid of organized crime.

"I was disappointed," he said. "You know, getting screwed for the money, getting shot in the head once before, and my life being on the line again. I decided to reach out to the federal government."

The FBI welcomed D'Urso with open arms and a new Rolex, which was fitted with a tiny listening device. The beef with Serpico was resolved, and the clock immediately began ticking on Gigante—once D'Urso returned to the fold with his new timepiece.

The tapes, recorded secretly, contained the details of how Gigante, now in a Texas penitentiary, remained the power behind the Mob family. D'Urso's taped conversations exposed Andrew's new gig as his father's Genovese go-between.

"Whatever the kid (Andrew) says, it comes from him," Bronx soldier Pasquale "Patty" Falcetti said during a March 30, 2001, conversation in his home. Falcetti then touched his chin: "Who's going to challenge that?"

Family member Paul "Slick" Geraci made the same gesture during an October 2000 meeting with D'Urso. The Genovese soldier acknowledged Serpico, like Salerno before him, was sitting on the throne truly occupied by Gigante.

"[Serpico's] still there, but he ain't the guy," said Geraci, touching his chin. "This guy is the guy. Don't say nothing."

Acting family capo Salvatore "Sammy Meatballs" Aparo echoed his associates during a January 22, 2000, meet with D'Urso. Aparo said Gigante was continuing with the crazy act while imprisoned, while still directing the family from deep in the heart of Texas. Aparo explained that Gigante "gets visits," and the orders were then brought back to New York.

"I mean, the guy still sends messages," said Aparo. "He gets them, [too]. How he gets them and how he sends them, I don't know."

He suggested that Chin's longtime cardiologist, Dr. Wechsler, was perhaps the mule for the back-and-forth.

"The doctor that always goes and sees him and everything," Aparo said. "He's a good guy, the doctor. So I don't know if he gives him a message. He's got this doctor for years and years and years. So actually he can trust him."

Just four days earlier, Gigante's last hope at beating his racketeering rap had disappeared. The Supreme Court, without comment, rejected the Chin's last-ditch appeal at overturning his 1997 conviction. Yet, according to another capo, the family's influence was expanding under Gigante's absentee leadership.

"Don't let anyone tell you we're dead," announced Alan "Baldie" Longo during an October 18, 2000, meeting with D'Urso at an Upper East Side café. "We're not. Because Vito (Genovese) ain't here no more. Vincent is. We're here."

The duped Longo, in the same chat, told the undercover mobster that the family might need him to murder his colleagues as the Genoveses tried to keep the organization free of informants.

"If there's a problem, the guys . . . we're going to pull together—you'll be one of them," Longo promised. "If we ever step out and do something, we go to the guys we can trust and

do it. We ain't going to put guys on the line who are going to become rats a day later."

D'Urso captured Savino's old capo Joe Zito reminiscing about
the days when Gigante was on the street. A Colombo capo named
Joe Beck had violated some bit of Mafia etiquette, and a sit-down
was called between the family hierarchy and the Genovese leadership.

A proposal was made by another Colombo capo to "punish
Joe Beck by breaking him." That meant suspending his Mob
privileges, Zito recalled.

"We don't break our capos," Gigante had declared evenly.
"We kill them."

The damning D'Urso tapes started the wheels spinning back
in the Brooklyn prosecutor's office. What if Gigante was using
the phones at his Texas prison for Mob business?

"We immediately thought he had to be," said Dorsky. "And
superstar Mike Campi went down to Texas and came back with
six months of tapes. In all of them the Chin was talking in the
same way: sane and lucid."

The FBI agent had previously worked cases involving labor
racketeering and the Colombo family. But as their power waned,
he wound up working with the team chasing the Chin. The tapes
only confirmed what he'd believed all along: a rational Gigante
was still running the nation's most powerful family in the new millennium.

"It was like, 'What a surprise,' " he deadpanned. "One of the
things you find is when you get in prison, it's a different life.
There's a complacency. I didn't know if it would ever get to the
point of a major indictment, but I did expect what I heard."

Vincent Gigante, like any other federal inmate, was well aware
that all prison calls were taped by authorities. And while it seems
shocking that Chin would speak so freely—a repudiation of the
very mandate that spared him from decades of wiretaps—
Dorsky wasn't surprised, either.

"Two things—first, he wasn't thinking that we would think

like this, that we would still think about showing that he wasn't crazy—that he was obstructing," said Dorsky. "And the other half was that if you were in prison, and couldn't talk to your family and friends, you would actually go crazy."

But there was nothing loony about the prison conversations, where Gigante casually discussed his legal situation and his medical woes. One of the calls came after D'Urso's role was exposed in April 2001 by a massive Mob sweep that used his information to net forty-five mobsters and associates—most from the Genovese family. While the Chin was not charged, prosecutors revealed in court papers that they had new evidence indicating Gigante was still running the family from his cell.

Gigante dialed his wife, Olympia, to discuss the latest development. "They say I'm indicted on something," said Gigante, adding that a fellow inmate heard his name mentioned on the television news.

"All I know is they said some men were arrested," she replied. "They said you were with a family, and you were running it from Texas."

"I'm running it?" Gigante replied. "I'm running around the park."

There was a brief pause.

"Call everyone," the Chin declared before hanging up.

On Christmas Day, 2000, Gigante called Olympia 2 for a Yuletide chat.

"Merry Christmas," he greeted her before the talk turned to one of their daughters battling a sore throat.

"She can't talk," Gigante said. "There's something—she says she's lost her voice."

The Chin then poked fun at his loopy alter ego: "I says you, you got like me." This was followed by a mumbling impersonation of his days wandering Sullivan Street. "She's . . . she's all right."

A third call to his wife a few weeks later captured a long, coherent conversation about Gigante's assorted health woes.

"I went to the doctor today," Gigante began.

"You did?" she responded. "What did he say?"

Gigante, in great detail, recounted a hernia examination—complete with directions to turn his head and cough—before switching to his heart problems. The prison doctor offered his endorsement of the facility's cardiologist to an unimpressed Chin.

"Then he told me that the heart doctor is a fine doctor," said Gigante. "I says, 'I didn't say he ain't.'"

The Mob boss then delivered a detailed recounting of their conversation, complete with medical jargon.

"He says, 'You know, your ejections through your groin on the echocardiogram, your ejection fraction is down to thirty-five. Normal is sixty,'" Gigante said. "I says, 'Then I'm in trouble.' 'Oh, no,' he says. He says, 'You'll be all right.' I says, 'But the pains in the chest don't mean nothing, Doc?' [He says,] 'Take your Nitrol.' I says, 'I do, but it gives me headaches.' Uh, things like that, hon. He . . . he was nice. I ain't saying he wasn't there. He does the best he could."

The most stunning of the tapes, never admitted as evidence or publicly released, came on September 11, 2001. As the World Trade Centers were burning after terrorists crashed two planes into the Twin Towers, word of the attacks, just two miles south of Sullivan Street, burned through the prison.

Gigante immediately grabbed a phone and dialed his son Vincent Esposito—the call came so quickly that the voice on the other end remained unaware of the horrors in Lower Manhattan.

"They didn't even know what's happened, and he's telling the son that they're under attack," Dorsky recounted. "He's letting him know, 'Hey, kid, this is happening.'"

Gigante's last words before hanging up the phone were those of a protective, if imprisoned, patriarch: "Make sure everybody is safe."

The recordings were instantly seen in Brooklyn as the ultimate repudiation of Gigante's "mental illness" scam—and in his own voice. Campi went to work alongside the prosecutor, listening in amazement to hours and hours of heavy New York and New Jersey accents.

"I personally transcribed months and months of coherent, cogent conversations," Dorsky recalled. "Six months of this. He had to remember all the numbers. He had to remember who he was talking to—this is a guy with two families. He picked up on subtle things—in one [call] he was asking his daughter why she was yawning."

The tedious task wore on Campi, who later joked about the playbacks. "I was just praying that I wouldn't hear those voices in my sleep," he wisecracked. "I was laughing . . . those voices."

Campi even procured a prison videotape that illustrated the government's case even better than the audiotapes. The three-minute clip captured the Chin with sons Andrew and Salvatore, accompanied by his cardiologist. The quartet engaged in animated conversation, with the elder Gigante even combing his famously unkempt hair.

"I'd see people, when they looked at that video, looked at how he treated people, and they knew, 'This is *not* a crazy guy,'" said the FBI agent.

As he heard the voices on the tapes, Dorsky thought back to the first Gigante prosecution: "I wish those psychiatrists had been there to see how they reacted when we played all these tapes."

He was also reminded of a 1998 *60 Minutes* piece that included an interview with Father Gigante, along with a video provided by the Gigante family. The clip featured a confused and clearly uncomfortable Vincent during a psychiatric evaluation from two years earlier.

"I done nothing wrong," the Chin declared. "I ain't done wrong at all. God is the judge. God will judge everything."

The piece stuck in Dorsky's craw for years.

There was another sign of continued prosecutorial interest that happened in the same year as the news magazine piece. In February 1998 federal officials raided the Newark, New Jersey, offices of a shipping container repair company linked to Andrew Gigante, the Mob boss's oldest son. Documents and records were seized in what authorities described as a new probe into the waterfront, which was long dominated by the Genovese family.

The New Millennium

There's a legitimate reason longtime Genovese waterfront boss George Barone looked like he was pulled directly from central casting: the gangster was once a member of the Jets, one of the two gangs immortalized in the 1957 Broadway production of *West Side Story*.

But Barone didn't dance. And he wouldn't sing . . . until Vincent Gigante ordered his murder.

The veteran mobster's defection to the feds was the final nail in the Mob boss's coffin. The move was as unexpected as productive for prosecutors: Barone had spent decades inside the Genovese family, doing the Mob's bidding on the waterfront in New York and Miami.

He was a contemporary and onetime friend of family founder Vito Genovese. He was a killer and an earner and among the family's truest believers. He did time in the 1980s without ever uttering a word about Mob business. Once he finally opened his mouth, what spilled out was a tale as riveting as any Hollywood screenplay.

Barone came to organized crime as a World War II hero, a participant in five Allied invasions—including bloody Iwo Jima—after enlisting in the Navy. His assorted military honors and ribbons included a Good Conduct Medal. His behavior changed quickly, once he joined the International Longshoremen's Association in the late 1940s, working for a company owned by Albert Anastasia.

Violence became his stock in trade. In 1954 he was arrested—shades of *On The Waterfront*—for beating a longshoreman who griped about getting ignored for a work crew. There was little cinematic about the assault; Barone and two thugs dragged the man to a Ninth Avenue meat market and beat him unconscious.

The last words the battered man heard were from Barone, who swung an eighteen-inch metal bar during the savage attack: "What are you, looking for trouble?"

Barone, who was bounced from his job for the beating, found work as a straight-up gangster. He found a kindred spirit in Johnny Earle, another kid from the neighborhood, and together they founded the Jets. Their "rumbles" with other West Side gangs inspired Leonard Bernstein's most beloved score, but these Jets wielded more than just switchblades.

The duo's biggest score came when they targeted a Long Island bank robber named Ninny Cribbens, recent beneficiary of a $650,000 score. The two slipped into a suburban cottage, where the cash was hidden, and waited for Cribbens to return. When he came through the door, Barone shoved him into a chair and shot Cribbens to death.

He eventually became closer to Genovese as the crime family took note of the Jets, and was even privy to the details of Gigante's botched 1957 hit on Costello. There was a falling-out with Don Vito after the June 19, 1958, murder of Earle, who had become a protégé of Genovese.

Earle, shot three times while eating inside the Fifty-Seventh Street Cafeteria, died at Roosevelt Hospital "without giving any information to the police," according to an FBI document. Though Barone denied any part in the hit against Earle, Genovese cut him off after the killing—and the aspiring Mafioso landed with Tony Salerno's East Village crew.

Once installed there, Barone became a Mob killer and eventually Fat Tony's representative for waterfront business. The killing part came first: Barone traveled to Kentucky to murder a man messing with the Genovese gambling operations in the state. The victim was an African-American man, and Barone never even learned his name—not that he cared.

"Black, green, yellow, whatever," said the equal-opportunity hit man. He estimated killing somewhere between twelve and twenty victims. Pressed later for an exact number, Barone snarled his answer: "I didn't keep a scorecard."

He stayed local to whack a gangster known as Tommy the Greek for some ill-advised talk about Anthony Scotto, the Gambinos' waterfront rep. When a problem arose within Salerno's crew, Barone took care of him, too. Why? "Because Fat Tony told me to," he explained decades later. "I did whatever he asked me to. He is my boss."

Barone took the Mob's policy of omerta seriously, too—even before he became a made man. He refused to answer questions when summoned in 1960 by the Waterfront Commission. Barone, who had half-Italian heritage, on his father's side, was finally inducted at a ceremony in the early 1970s. It was a big day for the gangster, who dropped a malapropism in explaining its importance.

"I believed . . . that I would have loyalty to the family until death that departs," he said. The East Harlem crew, numbering fifty men, then welcomed the new initiates with a big breakfast.

George Barone became vice president of ILA Local 1804-1, a notorious Genovese-controlled operation based in North Bergen, New Jersey. The money was good: he earned $50,000 a year in salary, and another $100,000 annually in crooked cash.

An ILA official testified to Barone's continued hands-on approach, even as his job prospects improved. Harold Daggett said Barone surprised him inside an East Harlem grocery store when Daggett attempted to relocate the union's office from Lower Manhattan to New Jersey. Barone put a gun to Daggett's temple, cocked the trigger and delivered a simple message: "I'll blow your brains all over the room."

The terrified Daggett wet his pants before canceling the move.

The wild times on the docks ended in 1983, with Barone's conviction for racketeering. He did seven years in prison, giving him plenty of time to reflect on where things went wrong. His mind kept returning to one thought: Andrew Gigante, the Chin's son, was getting rich while he was sitting behind bars. He was just as angry with Burt Guido, a business owner with reputed Genovese ties.

Andrew Gigante was on Guido's payroll, collecting a healthy $350,000 a year. Barone later said they made millions while he was locked away.

"Bitter," Barone reflected years later. "Very bitter. I went to jail, and that was the end of everything."

When Barone was sprung from prison, two old Genovese pals reached out to bring him back into the family fold: Barney Bellomo and Tommy Cafaro, son of the Fish. Around the turn of the new century, there was even a reunion with Andrew Gigante.

The Chin's son was looking for Barone's help in landing a contract for a new steamship line coming into the Port of Miami. Barone, still nursing his grudge, said he was willing to help if Andrew Gigante was willing to assist him in settling an old financial score.

"I asked him to prevail upon his partner, Burt Guido, to pay me monies that he owed me for a period of some twenty years before," Barone recalled. "This had nothing to do with the waterfront. It had nothing to with anything illegal."

Barone was still angry about getting stiffed on his slice of an expensive real estate deal. He told Andrew Gigante that he was owed $90,000, and he wanted Guido to pay up. While Barone had respect for the Chin, he had little for the Mob boss's eldest progeny.

"A drunk, a junkie," Barone later declared. "He'd go in the bathroom and come out flying like a kite, for chrissakes. You know, a known addict, between the vodka and the junk—who knows what?"

Around the same time Barone threatened to organize an army of two thousand Cubans and go to war with the Genovese family if he didn't get the cash. According to the cantankerous Barone, he was visited by Guido with a $3,000 peace offering, which was quickly rejected. The aging gangster told Guido to bring young Gigante a message: "Stick it up his ass." During one

angry confrontation the old man even bumped the Mob scion—
a potentially fatal faux pas.

Genovese soldier Falcetti, in one of his conversations with
D'Urso, blasted Barone as a "senile old fucking man." The family hierarchy also delivered word via Falcetti and Salerno's East
Harlem replacement Ernie Muscarella that Barone was no
longer affiliated with the Genovese family.

"It was a hairy thing," Falcetti recounted. Even hairier was
Chin Gigante's admonition—relayed by Andrew—to keep the
ancient gangster "'close' to the family, and make him feel 'comfortable,' so that he could be [murdered] when the time was
right," prosecutors later alleged.

Barone eventually received $45,000 on February 6, 2001, at a
north Miami restaurant ominously named Shooters. Vincent Gigante signed off on the deal, and Falcetti delivered the cash. In
a subsequent phone call that same month, Barone was told the
other half was waiting for him in New York. But the caller was an
old ILA pal, and his invitation came with a warning: any trip to
the city would be Barone's last.

Barone never went, and the FBI banged on the window of his
Miami Beach home two months later. The aging gangster came
to a hard-to-swallow realization: the feds were his last port in this
storm.

The mobster flipped in April 2001, joining the limited ranks
of Genovese defectors: Joe Valachi, Fish Cafaro, Black Pete
Savino and Cookie D'Urso.

Barone took the stand against Peter Gotti in January 2003
and explained his motivation for testifying. "I wanted to get
even," he declared. "I wanted to survive. I didn't want to get
killed by them. I wanted the truth to come out about this whole
sordid thing."

"Was it an easy decision for you to cooperate?" the prosecutor
asked.

"Of course not," replied Barone, whose hearing was now so
bad that he was at times reduced to lipreading. "Because it is a

very, very difficult thing to be a witness against anyone, particularly in matters such as this. I am seventy-nine years of age. I lived all of my life without being an informer. Now I am. That is a difficult thing."

His appearance served as a preview for Vincent Gigante's defense team, with Barone clearly emerging as a damaging witness who could recite the crooked past of the mobbed-up waterfront as if reading from a history book.

All of this was old news to Dorsky, Campi and the rest of the team bent on nailing the Chin for a second time. Mike Campi, himself the son of an Italian father and Irish mom, quickly found common ground with George Barone as they spoke during debriefing sessions.

"I knew he was angry with them," said Campi. "He was bitter about some monetary deal that was minimal. He was one of the most loyal guys, and he wouldn't have cooperated except for the stupidity of how they were treating him."

The Barone information also gave the feds a road map in deciphering some of the Chin's jailhouse calls from Texas.

"Utilizing his knowledge, it became so easy to just go in and listen to the Chin's conversations in prison," Campi recalled. "The thing I found interesting about him was he would correct other agents. His statements were consistent. He would ask, 'Did they read my reports?'"

With George Barone in their corner, prosecutors were ready to unveil the fruits of the latest, and ultimately last, federal prosecution of Vincent Gigante.

CHAPTER 22

I SHALL NOT BE RELEASED

GIGANTE WAS STILL INSIDE THE FEDERAL CORRECTIONAL INSTITU-tion in Fort Worth, Texas, when the January 23, 2002, indictment was made public. While the case against his Genovese codefendants focused on the usual—waterfront corruption, extortion and rip-offs of union benefit funds—the court papers clearly detailed how the Chin and his crazy act were square in the federal crosshairs.

Counts six and seven dealt directly with his long-running subterfuge. During the seven-year 1990s prosecution, *[Gigante] knowingly and intentionally engaged in misleading conduct toward other persons, to wit: doctors evaluating his mental competence, with intent to influence the testimony of such doctors,* read Count Six.

Count Seven raised the stakes. The indictment suggested the Chin's long and successful crazy act was no one-man show. It specifically cited the same time period: *[Gigante], together with others, knowingly, intentionally and corruptly obstructed and impeded and endeavored to obstruct and impede the due administration of justice, to wit: by feigning diminished capacity during the prosecution.*

It appeared the feds were targeting Gigante's relatives, most likely Father G. and Chin's long-suffering wife, although a source indicated no family members were ever threatened with charges. They were unquestionably going after Andrew alone, identified as a Genovese family associate and accused of extortion. The charges against his father carried stiff penalties: ten years in prison on each count.

Vincent Gigante "is not a figurehead," said Assistant Director Barry Mawn of the FBI. "He is a hands-on leader who remains actively involved in the running of the organization."

While the elder Gigante was used to the legal routine, it was a first-time experience for his forty-five-year-old son. Andrew Gigante had worked on the docks since he was eighteen years old, generally keeping his head down and his nose clean. His lawyer suggested the son was guilty of nothing more than sharing a surname with the Chin.

"I hope this isn't an unfortunate situation of the son being punished for the sins of the father," said Andrew's lawyer, Peter Driscoll. Friends of the son later came to his defense, insisting Gigante was a beloved figure on the New Jersey docks and a philanthropist whose charitable endeavors included raising money for orphanages, an annual Christmas party for cancer-stricken children and stints in a soup kitchen with his uncle Lou.

There was no denying that Andrew was in the company of some big-league gangsters named as codefendants. The group included a pair identified as acting bosses during Chin's incarceration: Bellomo and Muscarella, along with Genovese capo Charles "Chuckie" Tuzzo and family soldiers Falcetti and Michael "Mickey" Ragusa.

Last but hardly least was Tommy Cafaro, the son of the turncoat Fish and the best man at Andrew Gigante's wedding. The younger Cafaro, reportedly, had offered to murder his own father over his Mob betrayal, although the family hierarchy never pressed the issue, prosecutors said.

Andrew was freed on $2.5 million bail after two nights in jail, with a federal judge ordering house arrest at his pricey Norwood, New Jersey, home. When Driscoll asked if Andrew could be cleared to show up at work, the U.S. magistrate Steven Gold—noting the defendant also owned a $1.7 million property in exclusive Alpine, New Jersey—said that wouldn't happen unless Gigante could prove that he needed a paycheck.

Andrew, while free to go home, was barred from any type of contact with his father. Any violation would mean immediate incarceration and the forfeiture of the three homes that he used to secure his seven-figure bail. He later won a pair of concessions: the court cleared Andrew to attend Mass every Sunday with his wife and children, and to take the kids to their parochial school every morning.

"This is all trumped-up charges," his brother, Salvatore, said as they left court. "Leave us alone."

The elder Gigante returned to Brooklyn for a February 7, 2002, arraignment, where it was clear the Chin was still clinging to his now-exposed ruse. He sat slumped in a chair during the hearing, staring at the floor or straight into space, during his first court appearance in more than four years.

"I don't understand," he declared when asked if he had discussed the charges with his lawyer.

Defense attorney Gary Greenwald asserted his client was "not in any position to enter a plea because of his state of mind," and Federal Judge I. Leo Glasser entered a plea of not guilty on Gigante's behalf. The judge added that he was considering a competency hearing before setting a trial date—a suggestion that no longer sent shudders through prosecutors.

"All we had to do was hit play on the tapes," said Dorsky.

In court papers the prosecutors noted that past psychiatric reports had asserted Gigante was incapable of speaking a single complete sentence—a claim refuted by the new batch of prison recordings. "In the face of such evidence, Gigante cannot credibly maintain that he is now mentally incompetent and no longer a malingerer," prosecutors argued.

For once, the defense agreed and would not raise an insanity claim. The "crazy" man in the bathrobe and pajamas was legally laid to rest, a move approved by new Gigante attorney Benjamin Brafman. Brafman was a well-regarded defense lawyer, who had helped Sean "P. Diddy" Combs beat a weapons charge in a Manhattan nightclub shooting one year earlier.

Glasser concurred, and Gigante was—for the third and final time—declared legally sane by a federal judge. Court papers also indicated that some of the Chin's old doctors were receiving grand jury subpoenas, and that Gigante family members could be next.

Pulitzer Prize–winning columnist Jimmy Breslin's latest book, *I Don't Want to Go to Jail*, appeared in paperback that summer. It told the tale of fictional Mob boss Fausti "the Fist" Dellacava. The title character was an ex-boxer who had become a philandering Mafioso working out of Greenwich Village. The inspiration was obvious.

The world of the real-life boss was considerably more turbulent. With the devastating impact of the D'Urso tapes and the threat of witness George Barone, Vincent Gigante was clearly in serious trouble—again. The government was hell-bent on squeezing an admission from Chin about the long-running scam. In the end the wizened Mob boss, worn down by decades of battle, decided the easiest thing to do was cop a plea.

The frail Chin sat with Brafman in Brooklyn's Metropolitan Detention Center, where the Mob boss personally informed the lawyer of his decision to go quietly—ending the psychiatric ploy launched thirty-seven years earlier in a New Jersey doctor's office.

Gigante, quite rationally, couldn't see the point in another contentious trial. While his relatively short ten-year sentence had convinced the Genovese family to keep him as their boss, Vincent now believed he would die before doing his time. Family members completely supported his stance.

"He clearly understood the proceedings and intelligently waived his right to a trial," Brafman recalled. "My impression of Mr. Gigante was that he was a very complicated man, who was just too old, too tired and too physically ill to continue to fight the government."

Word soon leaked to the media, with reports that Gigante's last stand was imminent. It was all over except for one final appearance where the Chin would play a character unseen by the general public: Vincent Gigante, the quite rational head of the Genovese crime family.

The day of the oddest court proceeding in federal history arrived with appropriately bizarre weather: a spring blizzard that forced the New York Yankees to cancel Opening Day in the Bronx. It was a perfect storm for federal prosecutors, ready to take their final swing at Vincent Gigante just down the East River in Brooklyn.

Thick flakes pelted pedestrians in the park opposite the front door of the U.S. Courthouse, and the wind whipped remorselessly down Cadman Plaza. Among the early arrivals on the nasty morning was Andrew Gigante, who passed through a metal detector; his father was already inside.

The promise of Vincent Gigante finally coming clean about his "crazy act" guaranteed a packed courtroom for the April 7, 2003, hearing. Columnists from *Newsday,* the *New York Times* and the *New York Post* turned out. A pair of sketch artists perched in the jury box to capture the Chin one last time.

Father Louis chatted amiably in the fourth-floor hallway with Breslin. For the last act of his brother's long legal fight, he arrived in street clothes, and he declined to speak with the rest of the assembled media. Brafman, standing nearby, killed time by sipping from a bottle of water. He and Gigante had earlier stopped by the judge's chambers to finalize the day's details. Now he walked through the courtroom's double doors and headed inside to wait at the defense table for his client.

As always, a contingent from the Gigante clan filled the front row of the courtroom, with the South Bronx priest joined by Chin's children Vincent, Carmella and Lucia Esposito and Salvatore Gigante. Five FBI agents who had pursued Gigante for years filled some of the other seats, which were divided like a wedding: friends of the defendant on one side of the aisle, guests of the government on the other.

Prosecutor Dorsky and his team took their spots in the front. Judge Glasser finally took the bench as the audience rose to their feet. The judge quickly gestured for all to take their seats.

And then, with the courtroom hushed in anticipation, Gigante finally entered—stage right.

The Genovese boss appeared promptly at 9:30 A.M., coming through a side door and wandering inside as if he'd just made a wrong turn. White stubble covered his chin, and his hair stretched toward the ceiling. He wore a seriously outsized blue smock that hung limply from his thin shoulders, an ill-fitting outfit that was somehow perfectly fitting. His pants were khaki, and his sneakers were slip-ons. Stamboulidis, the prosecutor from his first Brooklyn trial and now in private practice, would have noted the defendant required neither a wheelchair nor a cane.

Vincent Gigante looked around the room carefully before walking toward Brafman, his gait slow and unsteady. In one hand he clutched a plastic prescription bottle—his heart medication. He was frail and hard of hearing, a shadow of the once-feared head of the nation's most powerful organized crime family.

There was no fight left in the old man, his days as a boxer and a hit man reduced to nothing more than a yellowing clip in some ancient newspaper file. Gigante made his way to the front of the bench, where he signed a court document with an X. Then he nodded at Brafman, and the remarkable hearing began.

The judge moved to put Gigante under oath, asking the Chin to raise his right hand. The defendant instead slowly lifted his left, and Dorsky wondered for a half second if everything was about to fall apart at the moment of truth.

"I remember thinking he was trying to walk a tightrope between his silly act and allocuting to the judge," Dorsky recalled. "I wasn't sure if he could carry through with it all, based on his stake in the entire act." It was, the prosecutor agreed with a laugh, somewhat like Al Pacino rising to return his Oscar.

The Chin corrected himself, raised the correct hand, then swore to tell the truth that would wipe away nearly four decades of living a lie. Gigante stood with his head tilted, listening intently as Glasser began to speak. The Chin had sat in the same courtroom, one year earlier, staring aimlessly into space. This time he was all business as the judge addressed him first: "Vincent Gigante, how old are you?"

"Seventy-five," the Chin replied, his voice raspy and hard to make out in the large, crowded room.

"Do you understand why you're here?"

"Yes," replied Gigante as the courtroom filled with a silent, palpable buzz.

Had the Mob boss taken any prescriptions drugs that could affect his ability to participate?

"No, Your Honor," Gigante replied, firmly shaking his head from side to side.

Glasser delivered the money question: "Mr. Gigante, did you knowingly, intentionally mislead doctors evaluating your mental health? Is that true?"

"Yes, Your Honor," the defendant said softly while nodding in agreement.

On seventeen occasions the judge asked Gigante, "Do you understand that?"

Gigante confirmed each time that he did.

Gigante occasionally turned to Brafman, who translated any legalese or simply repeated some of the questions to his client. The Chin reacted just once—that was when Glasser mentioned the maximum penalty for obstruction of justice was ten years.

The plea deal was for three. Gigante, after conferring with Brafman, seemed appeased before Glasser handed down the preapproved term: "Thirty-six months."

The sentence would run consecutively with his 1997 jail term, meaning Gigante's earlier chance at freedom would come in 2010. It was a term he was unlikely to survive.

"Yes, Your Honor," Gigante said. And just like that, the charade was over. Glasser asked if Gigante wanted to address the court, to offer some explanation or deliver some parting words.

"No, thank you," he politely declined.

*   *   *

With Vincent Gigante's fate now sealed, the most astounding part of the hearing was about to commence. The newly unburdened Chin revealed something long tucked somewhere in the darkness: his personality. Brafman noted Andrew Gigante's presence in the courtroom; the two had not seen each other in more than a year under the son's bail terms.

The Chin noticeably brightened when Glasser approved the lawyer's request for the codefendants to share some time together before the old man was taken back to prison. Reporters and federal agents craned their necks as Andrew came forward and took a seat at the defense table. Gone now was the prescription drug-addled don of dementia, replaced by a father greeting his son after a long absence. The two chatted amiably for about ten minutes, their conversation unheard despite the best efforts of the assembled media, their necks craned toward the front of the courtroom.

Gigante smiled frequently as they spoke. His brown eyes seemed to sparkle, and some in the courtroom believed he shared a few secret jokes with his oldest child. With the mantle of his old life lifted, the Mob boss appeared both relieved and relaxed. The Chin sipped from a cup of water, shook hands with the defense team and turned to blow kisses to his kids in their front-row seats. Two kisses were directed at the departing Andrew as he walked back to his seat.

"It played a lot like a ten-minute silent movie," observed Mob chronicler Jerry Capeci.

Lights. Camera. Sanity.

Before he departed, the Chin offered a final, memorable coda. Gigante offered the sentencing judge a broad wave as he headed for the exit. "God bless you," the Oddfather said cheerily before disappearing through the side door, where Mob pal Bellomo was arriving for his own sentencing. The Bronx boss winked at Gigante as they passed.

Brafman, after the hearing, compared Gigante with John Forbes Nash—the brilliant and troubled Princeton mathematician whose battle with schizophrenia framed the cinematic smash *A Beautiful Mind.*

"I think anybody who has seen [the movie] will tell you that the person could be seriously mentally ill and have some degree of rational thought," the defense lawyer contended.

A decade later, Brafman recalled his emotions as Gigante stood in the courtroom spotlight before Glasser. "I remember the plea well," said the renowned defense attorney. "It was clearly an important plea for the government, as they had been chasing Gigante for years. I personally, however, remember feeling sad watching him plead. Despite what the government claimed he was, I saw an elderly, frail man near the end of his life taking one more hit that was perhaps unnecessary given the 'life' sentence he was already serving."

U.S. Attorney Roslynn Mauskopf spoke for an assortment of prosecutors, police officers and federal agents who had chased the Chin into the new millennium. "Our position is that for decades, he had fooled mental-health experts. With his guilty plea there is no further debate of the issue," the Brooklyn federal prosecutor said.

Andrew Gigante entered his own plea to extortion in the same courtroom one hour after his father's dramatic departure. He was sentenced to two years behind bars, and ordered to forfeit $2 million. The son left the courthouse clutching an umbrella against the still-falling snow, with reporters asking about his defense table farewell with his father.

"How would it be for you guys?" he asked rhetorically.

Dan Dorsky and fellow prosecutor Paul Weinstein stared straight ahead, their faces betraying no emotion throughout the short hearing. But Dorsky, after twice prosecuting Gigante, said there was little doubt that forcing the Chin's admission was a long-awaited triumph.

"It was a real vindication . . . the end of this long absurdity," he said years later. "It was a good feeling, not to sound corny, to get truth and justice to prevail. It was a great feeling to get a really bad guy."

Dorsky, still nursing his grudge against *60 Minutes,* actually called a producer after the plea and asked for a piece to correct the impression made in their 1998 report.

"They thought about it, and rejected the idea," he recalled, now more bemused than irate. "But you think about the idea that this guy was incoherent, and you'd have to laugh your head off."

Vincent Gigante, at his request, was shipped back to FCI-Fort Worth to serve what prosecutors also figured was a life sentence, given his age and health. Andrew, drawn into his father's world, was set for his own jail term imposed three months after his father's memorable farewell.

Though he faced up to twenty years in prison, the plea bargain assured that Andrew would face only two. There was much speculation that the lighter sentence was facilitated by his father's decision to surrender rather than fight.

"It's a complicated decision and a lot of factors entered into the plea," Brafman said after the Chin's sentencing.

Dorsky was somewhat more noncommittal: "I mean, I heard that. I don't know that definitely. But Chin didn't have much of a chance at trial."

The younger Gigante returned to the federal courthouse on July 25, 2003, where he was officially sent away and barred for the rest of his life from any further work on the waterfront. *[The last concession] was demanded by the government in an effort to permanently remove organized crime elements from the New Jersey and South Florida piers,* wrote prosecutor Weinstein in court papers.

Andrew arrived in court armed with letters from the police chief and mayor of his New Jersey community, reminiscent of the campaigns waged for his father in the past.

[Gigante is] a friend who I feel has been an outstanding member of our community and church, offered Police Chief Frank D'Ercole.

Norwood Council member Delores Senatore, after the sentencing, took it a step further: *He's innocent. I really do believe that. I think he just decided to cut a deal rather than take a chance on a jury trial.*

Prosecutors made it clear that while the younger Gigante insisted he never resorted to violence in his labor racketeering work, his familial ties took care of that.

There was "an implicit threat of harm," said AUSA Weinstein. "That if monies were not paid to the Genovese family, and that included associate Andrew Gigante, it would lead to violence."

Despite the menacing description Andrew was later given a pass to take his family to Disney World before beginning his jail term on September 23.

With the weight of the crazy act now gone, Vincent Gigante seemed happy and upbeat despite the near-certainty of his death behind bars. The returning Chin told the Fort Worth staff that he felt "'a lot better than in a long time,'" read a prison report written one month after his plea. But the mobster's health was clearly failing, and prison officials arranged for the Chin's transfer to a facility better equipped to take care of him.

Gigante arrived at the U.S. Medical Center for Federal Prisoners in Springfield, Missouri, on August 1, 2003. The Chin was now seventy-seven, far from home and in failing health: a bum ticker, bad kidneys, insomnia. The list of his fifteen medications filled a full page and a half.

And Springfield was the place where old Mob bosses went to die: Old pal Vito Genovese passed away in Missouri on Valentine's Day, 1969; while old nemesis John Gotti died in the medical center from complications of cancer in 2002. Fat Tony Salerno drew his last breath behind bars in Springfield.

His family was worried about the Chin's increasingly troubled health: Carmella Esposito called the prison on August 5, and was given a full update on her father's health issues. A prison official answered some of her more specific questions about the Chin. But there was no good news as the old fighter's body continued to fail him.

In September a baseball-sized hernia was found after Gigante's cellmate called for a doctor when the Chin began "moaning from the pain." By November the once-mighty Mob boss was reduced to asking for an appointment to get his toenails trimmed. The request, as usual, was written by another inmate. The Chin always closed with a cheery sign-off: *Thank you for your kind assistance.*

As he settled into life at the jailhouse/medical facility, Gigante went through good days and bad days. By now, the Chin was in some ways just another inmate in the massive federal system: one prison report regarding his problems with chest congestion actually misspelled his last name as Giganti.

The Chin had periods where his body showed some resilience and his mood brightened, when his mood was upbeat despite the circumstances.

"I was sick, [but] now I'm all right," he told doctors on May 12, 2004. "God helped me. I used to go to St. Vincent's. They gave me a lot of medicine."

A prison doctor stopped by Gigante's cell the next month to chat with the Chin, who was complaining of anxiety, restlessness and trouble sleeping. Gigante, very specifically, had asked for Ativan to help him sleep. The doctor found a relaxed Gigante lying in his bed, calm and cooperative.

His voice was soft, and he spoke slowly, read the doctor's report. *No signs of restlessness or agitation were observed. From a clinical standpoint, there is no evidence currently that Mr. Gigante requires treatment for anxiety with medications.*

His appetite stayed healthy: over the Fourth of July weekend the Chin told doctors that he knocked back a dozen hot dogs and enough watermelon to give him indigestion.

In mid-October, Gigante was locked in a private room for his own protection after a pair of bizarre incidents where he told prison officials that he wanted to go home to "Mommy and his kids." On another occasion he appeared "very confused, talking to 'ghosts.' " The Chin was "shaking and shouting at roommates." He was "urinating in [a] trash can in [his] room."

Gigante still submitted to regular psych evaluations. But as the end of 2005 approached, there was little left of the sidewalk song and dance that kept the authorities at bay and the Chin on the streets for decades.

Dr. Thomas Hare paid the Chin an October 31, 2005, visit after Gigante, in failing health, was transferred to the prison's intensive nursing care unit—known as No. 1. It was a purely social call, with staff doctor Hare arriving to check on Gigante's adjustment and chat a bit. There was nothing remotely scary about the Halloween drop-in.

Mr. Gigante greeted me as usual, smiled, asked how I was and shook my hand, Hare recounted. *He asked me how long he would be required to live on No. 1. I explained to him because his physical condition had deteriorated somewhat and that more intensive nursing care was required, [that] was the reason he was transferred.*

He seemed to understand and nodded his affirmation. During my interaction with Mr. Gigante, he was alert, smiled, asked appropriate questions, provided appropriate answers and was alert to his surroundings. He asked me about my family, and appeared to understand why he was living in a different housing situation.

A day later, when Dr. Robert Denney arrived for a neuropsychology consult, the Chin slipped back into his old ways. Denney was a nemesis from the past—he had interviewed Gigante in the early 1990s and found the Chin was faking his mental illness. The two men sat in Gigante's room, where Chin—disheveled, unshaven, in clean clothes—appeared "alert and affable." To a point.

He behaved in a manner suggestive that he recognized me, but said he could not remember my name or who I was, Denney wrote. *His speech was normal in rate, comment and form.*

But Gigante volunteered that he didn't know the day, the date, the month or the year. The Chin allowed that he believed it was almost winter, but he declined to name the season. And then he stopped answering questions. Denney tried another approach, asking the Chin to fold a piece of paper and place it on the floor.

"What?" asked Gigante, holding the piece of paper in his hand. "I am not gonna throw no piece of paper on the floor."

Denney, like so many before him, departed with a degree of admiration for Gigante's efforts.

Mr. Gigante is exaggerating gross neurocognitive dysfunction, he wrote. *The sophistication of his malingering attempt suggests to me that he likely has the level of cognitive skill necessary to be considered competent to make basic legal or medical decisions for himself.*

If the brain was still working, Chin's body was increasingly failing. At the request of his family and his lawyer, the Chin was taken to St. John's Medical Center in Springfield later that month, suffering from heart and kidney problems. A guard stood watch at his hospital room, where Gigante—despite his worsening condition—had his ankles shackled to the bed. Oddly enough, one of the attending physicians was Edward W. Gotti, M.D.

Gigante's return to the prison after his November 23 discharge came with twin diagnoses: congestive heart failure and acute renal failure. The Chin, faced with his own mortality, made a decision. Over the objections of his doctors, the old man did not want to go on dialysis.

According to prison records: *He expressed that he understood the nature of the problem. He agreed that he did not want to be maintained on a dialysis machine.*

The former teenage lightweight was throwing in the towel. When placed on an IV for his kidney woes at one point, Gigante pulled the needle from his arm and tossed the bag in the trash. He refused to wear a heart monitor on another occasion.

"I believe in God," he told a nurse. "He will assist me."

Gigante became increasingly thin and frail—so weak that a note in his medical file said his "condition overall" would "limit the amount of tests which should occur."

On December 18, Gigante was alert and cooperative before lights out. Hours later, at 2 A.M., prison staff was called to his room after the old Mob boss had trouble breathing. They arrived to find Gigante's oxygen tubing was disconnected. It was quickly reattached, with the staff offering some words of comfort before putting Gigante back to bed a half continent away from the familiar streets of Greenwich Village, from his wife, his mistress and his eight kids.

Prison medical staff would check on the ailing inmate throughout the rest of their overnight shift.

At 3:05 A.M., the room was quiet and Gigante asleep. Ditto at 4:20 A.M. But when they returned for the morning inmate count at five minutes after five, it was immediately clear that something was wrong.

Prison records provided a cold, clinical account of what happened next: *Entered room with officer . . . to find inmate laying across bed with 02 (oxygen tube) off in floor, inmate warm to touch, nonresponsive to verbal stimuli, no respirations noted. Code called by officer while crash cart obtained, chest compressions initiated.*

As a nurse started CPR, a "Code Blue" emergency call immediately went out. But there was nothing that could be done. At the end Gigante faced no blizzard of bullets, felt no soft kiss of betrayal, sensed no impending twist of criminal fate. At 5:15 A.M., in a small room with the nurse and EMTs, Vincent Gigante was quietly pronounced dead.

The night shift workers summoned the prison chaplain. The jail's duty officer was told, and calls went out to the next of kin— his wife, Olympia, as specified on Gigante's prison paperwork. She was notified at the Old Tappan, New Jersey, home where she had lived without her husband for decades.

Word spread quickly to New York, where the Chin had ruled for so long. First notice for many came via an obituary by Richard Pyle of the Associated Press: *Vincent "The Chin" Gigante, the powerful New York mob boss who avoided prison for decades by wandering Greenwich Village's streets in a ratty bathrobe and slippers as part of an elaborate feigned mental illness, died Monday in prison, federal officials said. He was 77.*

Stamboulidis recalled his phone ringing early that morning with word of Gigante's demise. A short while later, it rang again— this time with a reporter on the other end looking for comment.

"Are we off the record?" the lawman asked.

Assured the conversation would stay between them, Stamboulidis paused before delivering his deadpan reply: "He's faking."

The cause of death was officially listed as cardiac dysrhythmia, and the Chin had apparently passed about fifteen minutes before his body was found. The autopsy notes indicated he was clean-shaven, his once de rigueur stubble gone. The death certificate noted Gigante was a salesman, peddling "haberdashery"—a throwback to his long-ago days in the women's hat business.

The Chin's passing set off a war between the families: the Gigantes of New Jersey and the Espositos of the Upper East Side. Olympia Esposito and daughter Carmella both wanted Gigante's personal effects and property from prison sent to them; Olympia Gigante held the final word as her husband's designated next of kin.

There was another bone of contention: Both families wanted to handle transportation of the body and the funeral arrangements. Prison attorney Dennis Bitz urged the two sides to work things out before word of their dispute went public. *In this way,* he wrote diplomatically, *we can avoid the media circus that might occur.*

Olympia Gigante also notified prison officials that she wanted an independent pathologist present for the autopsy—the renowned Michael Baden, a former New York City medical examiner. Prison officials initially blanched, but they caved in when they were notified five minutes before the procedure was set to start that relatives were set to file for an injunction blocking the autopsy.

In the end a deal was cut and the uneasy peace between the two clans restored. Olympia 1 faxed a handwritten letter to prison officials with the specifics, where she ceded some ground to the Espositos, while letting one and all know that she remained the Chin's one and only spouse: *I, Olympia Gigante, would like to have Vincent Esposito handle the arrangements concerning my husband Vincent ID #26071-037. Thank you! Sincerely, Mrs. Olympia Gigante*

Family lawyer Flora Edwards was dispatched to Springfield to take possession of the body. She first insured that all samples taken during the autopsy were cremated and "not [commingled] with any other remains."

Once the details were settled, Vincent Gigante was finally headed home, back to his old haunts on Sullivan Street, just down the block from the Triangle and the apartments that he had shared with his mom, Yolanda. In death, as in life, Gigante would show himself one last time as the antithesis of the showboating Gotti.

There were two separate funerals, one for each faction of the Chin's family. Olympia 1, joined by her children and an intimate group of family and friends, gathered at a small Garden State church for a funeral Mass three days before Christmas. The Chin's body was not present as they bid farewell to the late patriarch.

One day later, Olympia 2 and her three children held their own funeral at St. Anthony of Padua Church in the Village. Father Louis Gigante presided over a larger but still understated service that featured none of the trappings of old-school Mob boss funerals—no line of limos, no ostentatious floral arrangements, nothing like the glitzy 2002 Queens send-off for Gotti.

The church was about three-quarters full, with few—if any—of Chin's old Mob cronies in attendance. His brother Mario was among those in attendance as Father G. spoke about their lost sibling.

"In the eight years Vincent was in prison, I visited him nineteen times," the priest said. "There wasn't a day he didn't suffer. He did his time like a man. He was going to come home. He was dying to come home. But he couldn't. They allowed him to die."

Father G., standing in the pulpit of a church that survived the neighborhood's massive gentrification, flashed back to the days when his older brother was the local padrone.

"The world had a different view of him through the media," he said. "But we, his family, his friends, the people of Greenwich Village, me, his brothers, his mother and his father, we all knew him as a gentle man. A man of God. Vincent never traveled. He was always on Sullivan Street, walking and helping others, neglecting himself."

The white-gloved pallbearers carried the coffin, covered in red-and-white poinsettias befitting the holiday season, from the church. Gigante's remains were finally cremated at the historic Green-Wood Cemetery in Brooklyn, the final resting place of Mob contemporaries Albert Anastasia and Crazy Joe Gallo.

An agreement between the Gigante and Esposito families allowed each to keep a portion of the Chin's ashes. Son Salvatore Gigante brought their half of the ashes across the George Washington Bridge to Gigante's wife, ensuring the Chin would rest in pieces—half in New Jersey, half in his hometown.

EPILOGUE

IF NOT FOR YOU

*F*ATHER G. IS ALMOST DONE WITH HIS BREAKFAST IN BRUNO'S. HE'S told some old stories, and held a few more back. His fondest memories of Vincent are kept in a 550-page memoir cowritten in the mid-1970s with a trusted newspaper reporter and friend. There are just a few copies, printed and bound, all in the hands of family members. And that, he says firmly, is where they will remain.

"I made it, with a few pictures and everything," he explains. "I asked him, I said, 'I'd like to write my life, because I may lose my brain and I'll forget.' In my book I've got everything about Vincent."

The conversation winds down as the waitress clears the table and the street traffic outside picks up.

"My brother was a good man," he declares, speaking quite deliberately. "My brother was part of the very essence of New York at the time, in this neighborhood. . . . He's gone quite a few years now. That's why I'd even talk to you about him."

Very little in the now-upscale neighborhood outside remains the same. At 208 Sullivan Street, once home to the Chin and his Triangle card games, the Sullivan Street Tea & Spice Co. now serves the city's "finest and most extensive selection of organic teas."

Across the street, apartments once populated entirely by im-

migrants are morphing into luxury homes for the 1 percent—
the wealthiest of the wealthy. At 215 Sullivan a large sign prom-
ises the imminent arrival of four luxury town houses, seventeen
lofts and four penthouses. Construction workers and equip-
ment fill the street where Vincent Gigante once strolled in a
robe instead of a hard hat.

The entrance to 225 Sullivan, where Gigante and his mother
shared an apartment, remains unchanged—the buzzers to ring
residents upstairs in the building remain affixed to the right of
the front entrance.

Hit-making Tommy James finally wrote a book about his time
working for the Mob, but not until after the Chin and the other
Genovese bosses were dead. His effort may turn into a Broadway
musical.

Sammy Gravano is behind bars, where he will take his last
breath after leaving the Witness Protection Program to resume
his life of crime. Bobby Manna and Benny Eggs Mangano, silent
to this day, face the same fate. Phil Leonetti is out of the Witness
Protection family, enjoying his second life after finishing his government testimony. He wrote a book, too: *Mafia Prince.* Unlike
with his ABC News appearance, he shared a voice in choosing
the title.

George Barone continued to testify against his former Mob
compatriots until he died at age eighty-six in December 2010.
The feisty gangster went down swinging. In July 2009, Barone
swore to tell the whole truth one last time before blasting old pal
Harold Daggett: "The bastard. No fucking good, never will be."

One of Father G.'s nieces, Chin's daughter Rita, came out as a
lesbian and even wrote a book of her own, *The Godfather's Daughter.* The priest did not approve. She is now happily married to
her longtime partner.

But other things endure. The Genovese family lumbers on, its
ranks depleted and its subsequent bosses unable to rule in the

Chin's imperious style. Law enforcement attention and the steady parade of informants eroded the family as surely as the conviction of their longtime leader. There was now a reluctance to become the boss, a position that came with more problems than perks.

SEBCO remains a force in the South Bronx, run now by Chin's son Salvatore. Father G., who stepped down in 2007, still stops in about three times a week. The agency created six thousand new or rehabilitated homes in some 450 buildings throughout the South Bronx, and employs more than three hundred people.

The priest spends his weekends at the upstate getaway purchased from Morris Levy.

In the ports of New Jersey, Chin's son-in-law and his nephew Ralph were two of eleven relatives making a combined $2 million a year, according to a 2010 investigation by the Waterfront Commission of New York and New Jersey.

"So the port has been pretty good to the extended Gigante family, hasn't it?" inquired commission lawyer Eric Fields at a 2010 hearing.

"Unions are always good for family," replied Ralph Gigante, son of Chin's brother Ralph.

In Las Vegas, there's now an attraction devoted to the history of organized crime: the Mob Museum. Among the exhibits is a photo of Gigante, in his bathrobe, walking along Sullivan Street.

Father G. reflects back on Vincent one last time.

"You know why my brother went to jail?" the priest finally asks. "Because all of the underworld couldn't keep their mouths shut. If they all just kept their mouths shut . . . you don't rat on your own people."

Gigante holds his glasses in his right hand and reaches across to squeeze a guest's wrist.

"If he didn't go to jail, he would have been alive today," the priest declares before very pleasantly deciding that he's said enough. "I hope I threw out a few things to you. I gotta really think about this, 'cause he is really sacred to me and I don't see a purpose to this."

A few minutes after this remark, Father Gigante gets up to leave. Before the check arrives, he takes care of one last bit of business: it's his treat.